Praise for
Rabbit Heart

A *New York Times Book Review* Editors' Choice

Named Best Book by *The New York Times*,
The New Yorker, *People*, and *Oprah Daily*

Named a Most Anticipated Book by *The Washington Post*,
Elle, *PureWow*, *Bookshop*, and *Kirkus Reviews*

"[A] poetic, moving memoir."   —*People*

"This graceful . . . memoir wrestles with failures of justice; the nuances of gendered violence; and the difficulty of making do when we are not whole."
                                        —Lauren Puckett-Pope, *Elle*

"A devastating account from the other side of murder, outlining in stark detail the trauma we fail to recognize when we consume tragedy as entertainment . . . Melding true crime with memoir, Ervin reminds us of what happens when we conflate people with the transgressions committed against them—the collateral damage we inflict when we turn human beings into moral allegory. She asks, too, what it means to live in a world where even death does not spare women's bodies from the indignity of surveillance . . . *Rabbit Heart* is a powerful treatise on love and loss, on mothers and daughters, but it is also a warning to all of us who consume true crime."   —Alissa Bennett, *The New York Times Book Review*

"[Ervin] follows the case with devastating rigor, shingling its developments with her memories of growing up without a mother."
                                                —*The New Yorker*

"A heartfelt memoir . . . This daughter's tribute will stand as a passionate, powerful memorial."   —Kate Tuttle, *The Boston Globe*

"Ervin's courage is breathtaking, her truth-telling a gift to women everywhere, and her story ends by landing a jaw-dropping cosmic punch that you will never see coming." —Marion Winik, *Oprah Daily*

"It's part true crime, examining the original corrupt trial as well as DNA evidence that emerged decades later, and part memoir—in poetic, heartbreaking prose, Ervin pieces together an image of her mother and revisits her younger self with the empathy and understanding she needed so desperately at the time. To say it's a difficult read would be putting it mildly, but it's even more so empowering, revelatory, and abundant with love." —Arianna Rebolini, *Bustle*

"With an unwavering gaze and in sharp, poetic prose, Ervin asks readers to bear witness to the violences her mother experienced and examines how patriarchal systems incite further violence through language, through silence, through the story of our bodies, through absence, and through generations. *Rabbit Heart* is a story about the ache of an everlasting grief, about growing up under the shadow of an impossible loss, and about how language can become a form of light in the dark, but only if we are ready to face the truth of a life in all of its complexity." —Jacqueline Alnes, *Electric Literature*

"Stunning . . . Ervin achingly portrays not just the unmoored girlhood she experienced, but the lifelong processing of trauma that comes from personal and early knowledge of the violence against women lurking around every corner . . . Ervin is a poet, and her language here is lyrical. Her depictions of unimaginable cruelty cut so close to the bone that they feel almost tangibly interior. Rhapsodic and startling, *Rabbit Heart* moves inside of you and explores the places of rage and grief that are often left unmonitored, revealing both the power and danger of womanhood in a violent world." —Anna Spydell, *BookPage* (starred review)

"The author's investigations of the concept of victimhood are insightful and urgent . . . Ervin laces the poetic text with unforgettable moments of startling, shattering honesty, many of which feel impossible to witness. This is the genius of the author's prose and what makes this book remarkable: Ervin's unflinchingly brutal gaze, combined with her insistence on facing the worst parts of her past, make it equally impossible for us to look away." —*Kirkus Reviews* (starred review)

"[A] lyrical, genre-defying memoir . . . Her observations around gender are particularly sharp and at times heart-wrenching. No matter how hard the material, and it's all either hard or bittersweet, Ervin approaches her story with unflinching vulnerability . . . This may be the best way true crime should be written, with nuance and unfettered compassion and with the words of the living victims or their families at the center."
—*Booklist* (starred review)

"The memoir in general rejects simple statements and always finds a way to root itself in complexity . . . Ervin's poetic and nuanced writing style is immersive and deeply rewarding." —Caitlin Thomson, *The Rumpus*

"Written in fearless, often poetic prose, *Rabbit Heart* weaves together themes of power, gender, and justice into a manifesto of grief and reclamation." —Dorothy Rice, *Hippocampus Magazine*

"A beautifully written, immersive read. . . This inaugural book from poet and essayist Ervin feels like such a punch to the gut. As you read through her gracefully composed pages on her unmoored girlhood and growth past the age her own mother was when she was taken, we realize that her story is the story of every family from all those anthology episodes we turn on while we knit or fold laundry or run."
—Eve Batey, *Reality Blurred*

"Poet and essayist Ervin grapples in her moving debut memoir with the emotional damage caused by a parent's violent death . . . In lucid prose, Ervin unflinchingly documents her grief and untangles how her mother's murder impacted myriad aspects of her life. This will haunt readers long after they've turned the last page." —*Publishers Weekly*

Rabbit Heart

Rabbit Heart

A MOTHER'S MURDER,
A DAUGHTER'S STORY

Kristine S. Ervin

COUNTERPOINT ◆ CALIFORNIA

First Counterpoint edition: 2024
First paperback edition: 2025

Portions of this book first appeared, in different form, as essays in *Fourth Genre*, *CrimeReads*, *Passages North*, *Crab Orchard Review*, and *Silk Road*.

Here I Am (Just When I Thought I Was Over You)
Words and music by Norman Sallitt. © 1981 Emi Al Gallico Catalog Inc. (BMI) and Embassy Music Corp. (BMI). Exclusive print rights for Emi Al Gallico Catalog Inc. administered by Alfred Music. All Rights Reserved. Used by permission of Alfred Music.

All Out Of Love
Words and music by Graham Russell and Clive Davis. Copyright © 1980 by Nottsongs and DJDMP Harry. All rights for Nottsongs administered by Universal Music - Careers. All rights for DJDMP Harry administered by Songs Of Kobalt Music Publishing. International Copyright Secured. All Rights Reserved. Reprinted by permission of Hal Leonard LLC.

The One That You Love
Words and music by Graham Russell. Copyright © 1981 by Nottsongs. All rights administered by Universal Music - Careers. International Copyright Secured. All Rights Reserved. Reprinted by permission of Hal Leonard LLC.

When The Time Is Right
Words and music by Gerald Milne. Copyright © 1984 Stamford Bridge Publishing. All rights administered by Songs Of Mojo One. All Rights Reserved. Used by permission. Reprinted by permission of Hal Leonard LLC.

The Library of Congress has cataloged the hardcover edition as follows:
Names: Ervin, Kristine S., author.
Title: Rabbit heart : a mother's murder, a daughter's story / Kristine S. Ervin.
Description: First Counterpoint edition. | Berkeley, California : Counterpoint, [2024] | Includes bibliographical references.
Identifiers: LCCN 2023041428 | ISBN 9781640096370 (hardcover) | ISBN 9781640096387 (ebook)
Subjects: LCSH: Ervin, Kristine S. | Murder—Oklahoma—Case studies. | Murder victims' families—Oklahoma. | Children of murder victims—Oklahoma.
Classification: LCC HV6533.O6 E78 2024 | DDC 364.152/309766—dc23/eng/20231006
LC record available at https://lccn.loc.gov/2023041428

Paperback ISBN: 978-1-64009-695-0

Cover design by Nicole Caputo
Cover photograph © Amy Weiss / Trevillion Images
Book design by Laura Berry

COUNTERPOINT
Los Angeles and San Francisco, CA
www.counterpointpress.com

Printed in the United States of America
10 9 8 7 6 5 4 3 2 1

For my eight-year-old self and the ones who go searching

When perhaps all along what I have really wanted most is the friendship, the love of women.

—Carole Maso, *AVA*

Contents

✦

Woman Gone Missing 3

Cleaving To, Part I 7

The Teenage Girl's Body Book 19

Cleaving To, Part II 40

The Distance to You 43

Cleaving To, Part III 62

Truly Innocent Victim 70

Cleaving To, Part IV 123

The One That You Love 131

Cleaving To, Part V 135

Motherline 146

Cleaving To, Part VI 179

The Sound of Punishment 206

Cleaving To, Part VII 267

The Sleeping Place 277

Acknowledgments 279

Notes 283

Sources 285

Rabbit
Heart

Woman Gone Missing

◆

AFTER THE POLICE FOUND AND GUTTED MY MOTHER'S CAR,
a 1981 yellow Dodge Colt, my father, not wanting us to lose something
else we loved, asked me and my brother, Rolland, if we wanted it back. I
was eight then, Rolland thirteen, and for years we'd want to know what
had happened inside, even while wondering if it was best not to.

If we had said, "Yes, Dad, bring the car back home and put it back
in the driveway," Dad knew what could happen—every time he walked
to or from the car, his muscles might tense, fists close, ready to punch
whatever was behind him, for no other reason than he could. If he sat
in the driver's seat, he would be in the murderer's position, hands on
the wheel, rearview mirror tilted down. If he turned to the back seat,
he might see her body, bruised and shaking, curled in sweat and rapid
breaths. Instead of the radio, he might hear her screams.

When I looked up at him and answered no, I didn't realize the burden he had offered to take.

I didn't know love meant the willingness to suffer.

My decision had been a practical one—the police said they wouldn't
put the car back together and how can you drive without seats.

Maybe someone revived it, installing new seats, new ashtrays, dis-
infecting its windows and glove box, and maybe it sat in a used car lot,
until a young woman said, "This is perfect for my needs, and I can't believe it is *this* cheap." Or maybe it went to a scrapyard, had many men's
hands on its engine and frame, and, if it still exists at all, only a skeleton
remains.

But twenty-five years later, prosecutors will try to track it down, to put all the evidence back in it, the computer paper, the Goody hairbrush, her sweater, her skirt, her bra, so a jury can peer inside and get closer to the truth. It's her death they'll want to reconstruct, without thought to how memory and the imagination keep it whole, intact, fingerprintless, bloodless, clean. The steering wheel's still wrapped in yellow vinyl and punctured with holes, Mom has one hand on the wheel, the taut sleeve of her brown leather blazer reaching for her wrist, her other hand holding a Salem cigarette, its filter stained pink with the semicircles of her lips. We're driving back to the wallpaper store to look for her sunglasses, even though they're really on the floorboard, under her seat. Through the untinted window, I'm staring straight at the sun, a lavender-and-green disc oscillating in a cloudless sky, as we sing the lyrics to Air Supply: *I'm all out of love, I'm so lost without you.*

It seems we're always searching to recover something—her keys, our bodies, the words to say, and the voice to say them.

My niece, Kenzie, and I lay in my father's bed, off-white comforter covering our toes, her on the left where my mother once slept, me on the right, my father's side. We were watching *Bambi*, her first time, though she knew a few lines from the commercial for the newly released DVD, lines like "Hurry, the new prince is born" and "Man was in the forest." She curled her body, small at four years old, beside me, placing her arm across my stomach, her head to my chest. I wondered if my mother and I had been like this, if she had placed her hand on the top of my head, as the doe keeps twitching her ears, sensing what's in the distance.

I was twenty-seven when Kenzie and I watched this, me living in Houston with my husband, Jerry, and working on my PhD. Kenzie kept asking why I wouldn't stay in Oklahoma, where every day could be a day for movies and making chocolate chip cookies, eating spoonfuls of dough as they baked. "You can't go back to Houston," she said. "There are lions and tigers at your house!"

I didn't know how to explain that after living in New York and then in Houston, I could never return to Oklahoma, even as much as I missed her and Dad and thunderstorms. I didn't know how to say there are tigers in Oklahoma too, some of them living next door.

The objects in my father's room—a cedar chest, a macramé planter that hung from the ceiling and held nothing, a crystal box in the shape of a shell—were mostly the same as when Mom was alive, though Dad didn't keep up with the house the way she would have. Strips of olive-green wallpaper, its adhesive deteriorating, were falling, little by little, so that they looked like the peels of half-eaten bananas. I kept thinking, *How can Dad sleep like this, where above your head wallpaper seeks to smother you, micromillimeters at a time?*

When Bambi and his mother walk in the meadow, desolate in winter except for the single patch of April grass, I said to Kenzie, "There's a sad part coming up," and she, hearing the music grow more ominous, held on to me more tightly.

Rolland had felt uneasy about our watching the movie, worrying about the mother's death. "But you let her watch *Lion King*," I said, "where a lion murders his brother, and *Snow White*, where a man tries to stab Snow White and the witch tries to poison her, and then there's *Finding Nemo*, where the mother dies in the first minute of the movie."

"Yeah, but there's something about *Bambi* that's worse."

Kenzie pressed her body even closer, the mother sensing danger and frantically scanning the empty field. We were watching and listening to her panic, her yelling for Bambi not to look back as they ran. I didn't hear my mother then. But then Bambi's in the thicket, snow descending thick and heavy, he's calling out "Mother," calling out "Where are you," calling out "Mother" again, he's running through the forest, ears flat and back. I know that desperation and know he'll forever be looking.

Kenzie, her body so small next to mine, asked, "Is she dead? Did the mommy die?"

"Yes, Goose, the mommy died," I answered, looking over at the chest, my mother's picture lying face down, dust thick like fur. Years ago, the glass cracked, and Dad had planned to replace it. Had it been upright, Kenzie would have seen her grandmother, wearing pearls and a cream sweater with shoulder pads, her hair nearly black and to her shoulders, her eyes looking to her right. It's the photograph the police used and displayed on the afternoon and evening news, back when they were searching still.

"But what happened?"

"She was shot by man," I said.

Bambi's staring up at his father, so tall, so stoic in the snow. I hear my own father say, *Your mother cannot be with you anymore.* I see my own head go down.

"Is the daddy going to take care of him?"

"Yes, the daddy will take care of him." I kissed Kenzie's forehead.

But I didn't say, as perhaps I should have, *The forest is all around you, the meadow isn't a meadow but a parking lot, a closet, a bed.*

Or the front yard, where your neighbor watches you lay out in the sun, ice in your lemonade melting.

I didn't tell her that sometimes you seek the meadow precisely because man is there, though you aren't sure why. Maybe it's because you've been taught he has exactly what you need, that he's the one who planted the spring grass when you're hungry and thin. Or maybe it's because the meadow is where your mother has been and you'll do anything it takes to feel close to her again.

Cleaving To

PART I

+

I DON'T WANT TO REMEMBER IT THIS WAY.

Images and fragments, like yellow gingham curtains tied back.

A pear-shaped crystal—a memento from when we went digging for diamonds in the dry dirt of Arkansas—dangling in the window, sprinkling small round rainbows around my bedroom.

The sun so bright through the window. A late-morning sun.

My stuffed animal monkey named Toad on a wicker chest.

An intercom, plugged into the wall, with three buttons: Call, Talk, Hold.

The silence of that intercom.

That sun, too bright for my usual wake-up time.

Thinking, *Don't I have school today?*

A drawing of a kangaroo with keys. For my *K*, for her *K*.

Toad with my yellow visor on his head.

Waking, then sleeping. Waking, then sleeping. Thinking, *She'll call on the intercom to tell me to get up.*

Like she always does.

A flower made from purple and pink tissue paper, pinned to a corkboard.

The sun growing brighter and brighter in my room.

Thinking, *I'll still ask for five more minutes. Like I always do.*

A knock on my closed door.

Dad and Rolland walking in.

I see the golden shag carpet as spotless now, though they would have stepped over my Barbie in her glow-in-the-dark gown and her red Ferrari and the little ponies in their skating outfits and my Trapper Keeper with papers falling out.

I don't know why memory wants to clean my room.

Dad and Rolland sitting on my bed.

On my thin-as-a-sheet yellow gingham bedspread.

Dad starting to cry. Not sobbing, not blubbering, not wailing. Just a few restrained tears.

I'm terrified.

Because daddies aren't supposed to cry.

Memory won't clear that terror, the rupture between what's supposed to be and what is.

Dad would have said she stopped by Shepherd Mall.

Then he said the words *your mother.* He said the word *kidnapped.*

Or maybe he said *your mom.* Or maybe just *Mom.*

Maybe he said *two men kidnapped your . . .*

But no option sounds right.

Maybe there's no way to tell your children that does sound right.

I can't remember what happened then, if we held each other, if I stayed tucked in.

They left my room so I could get dressed and go downstairs. I imagine the house was buzzing with people, neighbors mostly, because almost all our family lived out of state.

Rolland remembers we refused to eat breakfast.

He says neighbors offered us cereal, offered Pop-Tarts, offered to make us eggs. They offered to bring us McDonald's. We might have said no because McDonald's was for special mornings with Mom, when we'd go and eat the cinnamon Danishes and the pancake meal. I can still hear the scraping of a plastic knife against the Styrofoam.

I don't remember not wanting to eat; something tells me I looked to my big brother, heard him say he wasn't hungry, and thought, I shouldn't be hungry either.

But then the father of Rolland's friend, the only person we knew who had a microwave, brought Rolland a bag of steaming popcorn and a cherry Coke.

Rolland, over thirty years later, chokes up when he tells this story.

Because the father didn't even ask what he needed.

He just knew that sugar and salt and the crunch of a half-popped kernel could comfort and nourish a boy in pain.

I wish I could fill the blankness of that morning with a moment like this, holding, as Rolland does, on to a gift, but this memory isn't mine.

What I remember is Rolland and Dad left my room so I could get dressed. I stood in the center of my room and felt sad, a deep, in-the-gut sad.

Then I pulled my nightgown up over my head, pulled my underwear off, and stood naked in front of my dresser, picking out clothes for the day, perhaps the first time I had chosen clothes without her.

Women, neighbors and friends of my mom, walked in and clutched me and sobbed.

I'm sure they thought they were helping, being there for the girl whose mother was taken, never considering how she was naked, embarrassed, and cold, and far too young to know what to do as they wept.

I remember feeling like I was supposed to perform for them, like they were needing something from me, though I didn't understand what.

I still don't know, really.

But I know I want that moment back, where instead of remembering how I kept quiet for them, not saying what I really wanted to, *I just want you to leave my room*, I could remember being alone in front of my dresser, staring in the mirror, at the body that was there, the body that was gone.

Memory kept her teddy bear on my dresser, my alphabet wallpaper with the orange *K*s.

But I want to remember hurting.

I owe her some pain.

She was, as far as I knew then, trapped in her car with two strangers, and she deserved to be loved, more than the objects in my room.

I remember Mom's face on the news, her eyes looking to her right. A zoomed-in photograph I did not know, with her hair shoulder-length and black, her mouth partially open, as if she's about to speak.

I remember the news people out on our front lawn, how my father wouldn't let me go out and talk to them. How I wanted to be famous on TV.

I would have given the news people the picture from when I was three or four. We're at the Oklahoma City Zoo, Mom, Rolland, a couple of my cousins, and Mom's twin, Barb. I'm sitting in a stroller and wearing a blue hooded sweatshirt and jeans, one of my long blond braids peeking out of my hood. I have a cheesy grin, my head tilting to the left: a look-at-me pose. We're all eating popcorn out of red-and-white-striped cereal-type boxes that say "Fresh Pop Corn" on the front and sides. I don't remember being at the zoo, but I know the popcorn was stale and had the texture of moistened cardboard between my teeth.

The photo shows a cloudy day, every tree bare except for a few wisps on a willow. It must have been early spring. Mom has tucked her hair, a chestnut brown, behind her ears, but a few strands are still blown horizontal by the wind. She's wearing her large dark sunglasses, you can't see her eyes, and she smiles *her* smile, one I can't accurately describe— something between a smile and a smirk.

It's a photo of the mother I know.

She gave me this picture to stop me from crying on the school bus, those first weeks of kindergarten, when separation felt sharp, like a pang.

When I no longer needed it, understanding she'd be waiting for me when I got home, I kept it in an old school box, the cardboard type we'd have to buy each year to hold the required glue stick, the ruler, the scissors, the pencil, the rectangular pink eraser with its sloped ends. It's where I kept my half-used crayons. I don't know why I stored it there. Maybe the size was perfect, or maybe I wanted the box to hold the things I loved.

While she was missing, I excavated it from under the crayons and held it as I lay on the floor of my bedroom, listening to Air Supply's *Greatest Hits*, our favorite album. The singers' voices were high-pitched like a girl's, which made it easier to hear them as my voice, as Mom's voice. Air Supply knew the pain I was in. Their songs said what I didn't yet have my own words for, as I lay crying and staring at the photo, at Mom, at the brown leather blazer she always wore, at her fingers poised to reach into the popcorn box to grab another stale bite.

> *Just when I thought I was over you*
> *And just when I thought I could stand on my own*
> *Oh [Mommy], those memories come crashing through*
> *And I just can't go on without you*

I turned the photo over, its back streaked with crayons from all the times I went searching for the ones I loved most, blue violet, red violet. Why couldn't I keep her voice, but I kept midnight blue? I remember sobbing, my stomach heaving against the carpeted floor, as I imagined Mom, curled in the back seat of her car, and the men driving, always driving, never resting or sitting in the back seat with her. I wrote on the back of the photograph the only words of my own I had:

Save

mommy

Save mommy

I remember not sleeping at night.

I remember holding on to Toad, the monkey that, as my mother told me, jumped from a shelf into the aisle of a store and demanded that she take him home to me.

I lay in bed, imagining. Not a winged unicorn, not flying on it to school. That couldn't be my dream anymore.

I would write her a note on the 3½" × 5" notepaper she gave me, with a blue border, rounded corners, and hearts of red, blue, yellow, and green in the lower right-hand corner. I'd practice the cursive I'd learned that year, trying to write pretty for her, as if to say, See, Mommy, how much better my *r* is looking? Then I'd stand in front of my bedroom window, struggle to slide the metal lock with my thumb, and push the window up and open, its screen conveniently gone. Holding the note outside, I would listen to it flap in the wind, the strong Oklahoma wind, then turn it loose, watch it float like a robin and drift away.

I saw the Colt going down a highway, its driver's side window open. In the back seat, Mom lying comfortably on her back, knees slightly bent in the air, her head behind the driver's seat, her hair loose around her face and shoulders. Two men in the front seats, eyes on the road. They'd be listening to the sound of the wind or to Billy Joel's "Uptown Girl" playing through the speakers. That's the song we danced to in the mornings before she dressed me for school.

My note would fly fast through the window, land in her hands, she'd read it and cry a happy cry. I would make her laugh, even with everything happening around her. I knew the man in the passenger seat was mean, that he'd rip it from her fingers. But then he'd read the note aloud, and my words would make him sorry. They'd turn the car around, bring her home, let us hug her and have her. They'd apologize.

I remember going to my father in the morning and asking him if I could write Mom a note, if I could let it go in the wind.

I remember he said, "You can try, if you think it will help."

I wish I could forget the hours before my teachers visited my house.

My friend had called and tipped me off that they were coming. I changed into a favorite outfit to impress them—yellow shirt and matching pants, with decorative mesh on them—and rode my bike up the street, in the cul-de-sac, so I could watch them arrive from a distance and then make a grand entrance. I'd draw my hands to my chest, I'd gasp in surprise, I'd blush at all the attention.

But I grew bored riding in circles by myself, so I went back home and waited.

I don't remember how well I performed shock, but I know the card was made from purple construction paper, *Thinking of You* in my teacher's pretty cursive handwriting on the front, each of my classmates' signatures on the inside. I know the African violet had six purple blooms, the banana pudding Nilla wafers on top. It came in Tupperware, and I lied to my teacher and said, "I like banana pudding."

The details so vivid and close, the Nilla wafers half-crunchy, half-soggy, how disappointed I was to answer the door for my teachers, rather than keeping them waiting for my return.

A couple days after the men abducted her, the police found her car abandoned at a truck stop in Tucumcari, New Mexico. Then they were at our house. We stood at the kitchen table, Rolland, his best friend, and I, the table piled high with tackle boxes and plastic bags and gloves, while detectives pulled strands of our hair from our scalps, right behind our ears. A detective told us that's where the hair, from inside your body, reaches all the way down to your feet and that's why it hurts so much when it's pulled out.

I think now of those hairs in tiny Ziploc bags, Rolland's short, straight brown locks, his friend's little curls, my long blond strands, of how I didn't yet know the ways evidence would bind us together, how it would reemerge decades later.

Another detective rolled my fingers in ink and then again on a white card, each finger pressed into a rectangular box. I thought it was fun seeing my fingerprints held up to the light over the kitchen table, like they do on TV.

"Will you take my toeprints too?" I asked.

The detective didn't look at me when he said no.

"But I rubbed my bare feet all over the car windows."

It was a lie.

And he didn't believe me.

"Here," he said, as he rolled my fingers in ink again and then on another card. "You can keep this one, just for you."

I looked at the squares and thought about how cool I was going to be at the next show-and-tell. I imagined it would be even better than when Mom brought our cocker spaniel puppy to class.

Part of me wishes I had saved that card, stored it with the photo in the crayon box. Maybe then, years later, I could see the tiny arcs of my fingers, the cresting wave of my left pointer, with all the white space around each print, and I could make myself understand that I was eight, that there's no reason I should feel ashamed.

I can't remember how Dad broke the news to us, a week later, that her body had been found in an oil field in Sayre, Oklahoma. I have no memory beyond the words *oil field*, the word *Sayre*.

I remember feeling like something beyond Mom had been taken from me. I knew we came from an oil family, my great-grandfathers, my grandfather, my father, all with a history of working in oil fields, on pipelines, on pump pumps. I loved the Sinclair dinosaur and now, with Mom's body in a field, it felt tainted.

I remember Toad was a good hugger, his body made to hold on to my waist.

How the grass outside the church was wet with dew, spotted with dark and sunken footsteps. Dad wouldn't let me run in it. He spoke to people leaving the service and held my hand so tightly I couldn't slip away.

I remember the shooting stars, how they smelled like grape bubblegum. I picked them in a field in Iowa, a day before she was buried.

I wore a lavender dress to the graveside service. And white tights. And white shoes.

I think now of that girl in purple, surrounded by everyone in black, her hair uncurled without her mother to fix it. I think of her father, shucking off decorum because purple might be the only thing to soothe what is broken.

Dad sat between me and Rolland, and in memory no one else was with us in the front row, as if it were just the three of us, framed by nothing but open space.

I know the casket was silver and so large it blocked the horizon in front of me.

I remember asking to open it.

"I want to see her," I said.

My father told me I couldn't do it. He said, "She just looks like she's sleeping."

I remember her naps on the living room couch, her head opposite a window, her face forward, toward the front door, hands curled up under her chin. How her hair cradled her face. Many times, I'd seen her sleep like this, cheek pressed against a round pillow, sunlight streaming through the opened blinds. I'd run in through the front door from school or from playing, and I'd immediately halt, then tiptoe through the house so as not to wake her.

Though the casket was smaller than the couch, I believed she had plenty of room to bend her knees, to rest on her side, cushioned by layers and layers of white satin; I imagined the sun penetrating the casket, shining on her face.

But of the moment Dad told us she was dead, I have nothing.

Maybe the forgetting made it easier to believe the story I wanted. I know not opening the casket did.

I listened to Air Supply and heard Mom singing

> *When the time is right*
> *I will come back for you*
> *With arms to hold you tight*
> *Just like I always do*

and told myself the police lied about her body; she was really in witness protection. She was hiding out from her boss. She never liked him anyway. Or she had her memory wiped and was wandering from small town to small town trying to figure out who she was and why the name Kristine sounded familiar. Or she walked a giant city somewhere, waiting for some danger to pass. One day I'd find her, pass her on a street, or I'd get off the school bus, walk up our steep driveway, and see her waiting for me on the step of our porch, her arms open, sun gleaming off her brown leather blazer.

I wanted the men kept in a dungeon, their wrists chained to a slimy rock wall, black in places, black like oil. Their skin from the shackles bloody and raw. I wanted them shivering in the cold, damp dark. I wanted rats and spiders and centipedes crawling all around their bare feet.

I wanted them to be made to stand in front of me.

With their bodies slumped and still, they'd know there's no use in fighting anymore.

I wanted to walk toward one of them, my shoulders stiff, my head level with his ribs, to look up at him, so tall in front of me, and smile. Then with all the weight of my eight-year-old body, I would stomp on his toes, stomp hard, stomp repeatedly. I wanted him to yelp, I wanted to hear his pain.

I asked Dad if the police would let me stomp on their toes when they were caught.

"We could always ask," he said.

I wanted to stare hard into their eyes, black like the wall.

To kick them between the legs.

To watch them double over.

To watch them cry.

I wanted to walk away, never looking back at the broken bodies on the floor.

Maybe if I had actually written a note and flown it from my window, if I had acted rather than leaving the story in my head, I could have brought her back to us.

I told her sisters, as they cleaned out her things, I wanted Mom's purple dress, her purple sweater vest, her purple shirt, the black cocktail dress and suede high-heeled shoes. I wanted her nightgown and the purse with a tassel on it. What I should have said: I want Mom's red robe. She'd wear it in the mornings, as she read the paper on the kitchen floor, the air warm from the vent beside her. I didn't know then that the mother in the robe would be the one I'd remember.

My heart it's not mending.

Weeks after she died, I snuggled beside Dad on the family room couch, placing my head on his chest and hearing the crinkle of his soft pack of Marlboro Lights in his shirt pocket. I loved the smell of tobacco and burning paper right after he lit a cigarette, before the exhale, before the air filled with smoke.

I asked him exactly how she died.

"The police don't know," he said, unwilling to lie.

I asked him why.

"Because her body was exposed to elements and had begun to decompose."

Years later I'd learn it was oil field workers who found her body, that they smelled it before they ever saw her.

I held my hand on Dad's stomach, watching it rise and fall with each breath.

I didn't fully understand the word *decomposed*.

But I knew a body would eventually become bones.

"How did the police know it was her then?"

"Through her dental records," he said.

I didn't consider what that could mean, that her teeth may have been the only thing left. I thought it was weird and cool that you could be identified by your fillings.

But I still needed an answer to my question. It didn't feel fair not to know. To keep wondering and wondering.

"How do *you* think she died?" I asked him.

He pressed his cheek to the top of my head.

He said, "I hope she died like a bunny rabbit would."

Then he explained how bunny rabbits can get so scared their hearts stop pumping, long before anything happens to them.

I saw a bunny crouched in the grass, Mom curled on the back seat of her car. I saw their bodies trembling. A dog approaching, a hand approaching. The bunny's heart and my mother's heart beating so fiercely they clench.

I was a child then and so have the memories of a child, the details fragmented, haphazard, insignificant now. I don't care about the Barbie's metallic swimsuit, the circle design of a raft we floated on at the lake. I want instead a memory of Mom's cesarean scar, the texture of it, my fingertips grazing her body while she tells me the story of my birth.

But more than this I want to have preserved this gift from my father, the softness of it. To go back to a time when I believed in a merciful death, before I resented it, became consumed by the impossibility of it, before I destroyed the bunny to know my mother in a way a child never could.

I want to tell the girl I was then not to go searching for a death that's truer than this.

I want to embrace her with my body, wrap my arms around her, to somehow protect her and the bunny she holds from the evidence and the violence she'll come to know.

I want her to still believe in a heart's quick seizing, to hear a breath, a long exhale, a silence.

To see Mom's body as a fist unfurling.

The Teenage Girl's Body Book

✦

SHE WALKED INTO OUR KITCHEN AND STOOD BESIDE OUR table, this woman my father had begun dating, nearly a year after my mom's death. Her hair was brown, shoulder-length, curled perfectly under with an iron, her cheekbones high and prominent.

I sat on the floor with my cocker spaniel, Sally, and showed this woman how Sally loved to have her belly rubbed.

"She holds her like a baby," she said to my father.

Brenda stood in our kitchen, her fingers long, bony, and shiny from lotion or oil. Her fingernails were long too, painted a rose pink, the opposite of Mom's chewed nails. I would later learn they were fake, just like her eyelashes, which she carefully glued on. Dad would say, "She definitely needed those eyelashes."

She stood in our home, and she must have surveyed its rooms, noting the needlepoints on the walls, the plants with sparse and limp leaves in the corner of the family room, the high chair that was my mom's when she was a child. What must it have been like, staring down at the daughter of a murdered woman, as she told the story of how she and her mother bought Sally at Shepherd Mall?

Weeks later, I would be sitting at the top of the stairs with Rolland, in the spot where we once conspired to steal M&M's while Mom was in the other room, and he would explain that it wasn't that he hated Brenda but hated what she represented—the woman after Mom—and I would nod as if I understood what he meant.

But on that night, I stood up from the floor, the kitchen walls covered in the wallpaper Mom spent hours searching for, flipping through tome after tome of samples, and I wrapped my arms around Brenda. Because she was a woman. There, in the house. And then against my body. Where I needed a mother to be.

On the kitchen table, cleared of Dad's usual newspapers so he wouldn't appear messy, was a bag of twisting balloons, the ones clowns use to make animals and flowers and swords and hats. Unable to blow up the balloons with my breath, I used a bicycle pump. I never made any animals though, finding out early on that I can't stand the sound of latex rubbing against itself; there is no word for that horrific scratching, that grating sound. But I kept buying the balloons, stuffing them into my backpack each day, because the kids on the school bus liked them. I'd pump up a balloon and tie it off, and the girl in my third-grade class would shape it into a heart. Or the boy in the back would stretch it at the edges of the opening, making it sing. Each day my classmates would hold out their hands, waiting for a balloon to play with.

By nine, I had already learned I was loved when I had something to give.

I unlocked my arms around Brenda and said, "Let me blow up a balloon for you." I held a lavender one on the nozzle and with my other hand pushed and pushed, the balloon stretching out like a dachshund's torso or the arm of a trombone, Brenda right beside me, in her long dress and perfume, with her lipstick perfectly in place, with her hand on my shoulder, trying, perhaps, to picture a future as a mother of an open-armed nine-year-old girl, and then, just then, the balloon burst.

In one terrific, boisterous pop.

Like one of my brother's M-60s.

She jumped and shrieked, and I felt her wanting to pull away, but instead she let out a forced laugh.

It might have been that I was looking at Dad, smiling at him for bringing this woman into our house, when I should have been paying attention to how full the balloon was. It might have been my thumbnail, grown long and fierce to play Mercy with the boys. Or perhaps a part of me knew she wasn't the one I wanted, so I popped the balloon on purpose.

A few years later, I was talking to Brenda in the bedroom of her duplex. I whispered that I got my first pubic hair, and she, excited as though it were her own, as though it were an announcement for all womankind, asked to see it.

I wonder now who does this, if mothers ever want to see. Maybe the impulse is a good one, as if to say, *Let us not turn away from our bodies,* but I still can't imagine ever asking my niece, Kenzie, the only young girl I've really been around, to sit with spread legs on a toilet for me, not unless something was wrong and she needed my help.

In Brenda's bathroom, lights bright above her mirror, I pulled down my pants and underwear, sat down, and stretched the skin to show her.

She bent down, squinted, stepped back, her nose cinched in disgust, her eyes perplexed.

She said, "It's really long . . . Mine never get that long."

She handed me some scissors.

I want to go back to that bathroom and hide those scissors. I want to tell the girl on the toilet, *Everything looks as it should, and you'll soon get more hair here and here and here.*

From Brenda's bedroom to the living room where Dad lounged, I walked slowly and with small steps, delaying what was at the end of the hallway. She nudged me from behind, her hands on my shoulders. If I kept heading straight, I'd hit the back door and could run away, but she guided me to the right, to a seat on the fireplace, its gray bricks cold against my legs. Dad sat facing me, from across the room.

"Kristine has something to tell you," Brenda said, her mouth now pursed in something like pride, and I, head down, wanting nothing but to be invisible, mumbled, "I am no longer a girl."

I was eleven or twelve years old, and I thought, *I am a woman now.* But a wrong kind of woman.

This was before commercials for the Schick Quattro Trimmer aired on television and showed women walking by a pool, by a building, by a house, with bushes becoming smaller as they passed, because metaphor is still needed for our bodies. All I had then was *The New Teenage Body Book*, given to me by my aunt Alice. I went home and studied the diagrams about pubic hair growth, which look like a child's drawing, a six for the belly button, the pubic hair like the fifty-cent toy Wooly Willy, where you use a magnet to drag slivers of metal to give Willy hair, a mustache, a beard. I searched the text. Nowhere did it say what length was normal. Nowhere did it mention a need to trim. It said *coarse*; it said *coverage*; it said that in stage 3 the hair looks like an adult's, but I did not know what a woman's hair looked like. I only knew my body needed shearing.

Late at night, desk light on, towel tucked around the crack at the bottom of my door, I laid toilet paper on my chair and snipped the hairs with scissors I stole from my father's dopp kit, the ones with rounded tips that seemed safer than the Fiskars in the house. I guessed at the proper length, eighth of an inch. Headlights gliding across my ceiling, my dog rolling over, the heater kicking on, each caused me to freeze, to listen for a sign of being caught. Only after seconds of silence would I lift tufts and snip again, pinching and rolling and stretching my skin. There was the occasional slip, the nip of skin between blades, a thin line of blood surfacing. When every hair had been reduced to stubble, I folded the toilet paper like an envelope, then wadded up the tissue, then wadded a sheet of notebook paper around it, to pass off shame as a homework mistake, and stuffed it in the bottom of my trash can.

One morning, I told Dad my stomach hurt.

"What's it feel like?" he asked, as he pulled the razor through the shaving cream on his cheek.

"I don't know," I said. I stood behind him at the edge of his bathroom, wearing the fraternity shirt and Bugs Bunny flannel boxers Rolland had given me as a Christmas gift.

"Well, is it high? Low?"

"Low."

"Kind of achy?"

"Yeah."

He stretched the skin along his neck for a clean swipe.

"When was the last time you had a bowel movement?"

"I don't know. Maybe a few days ago," I said.

"Well, it sounds to me like you're constipated, so you should take a laxative and . . ."

"A what?"

"A laxative. It will help get things moving in your system, there's a package in the medicine cabinet downstairs, and you can stay home from school today so it can run its course."

All day I watched MTV and ate Kudos granola bars and strawberry Fruit Roll-Ups, and the laxative did its job. A friend called to ask why I wasn't at school. "It's kind of embarrassing, but I was constipated," I said, unaware of the egg shifting in my body.

I'd eventually fake cramps whenever I didn't feel like going to school, even when I wasn't on or close to my period. Dad would say, "Well, since I can't know what that's like, I have to trust you."

I never once felt guilty for these lies. In fact, I saw it as retribution for the Dulcolax.

I was paused at the top of the stairs and petting Sally, asking her to show me everything was going to be okay, while I made designs in the shag carpet with my toes. I walked a few more stairs down, then a few more, pausing again by the banister rung I had split while sledding down the stairs in a sleeping bag.

I wanted to wind up the small brass rocking horse that sat in the entryway window, to listen to its happy tune of "Toyland, toyland, little girl and boy land" as it turned and rocked.

Instead, I turned the corner to the kitchen. Dad sat at the table, reading the newspaper and watching golf on TV. I sat down across from him, saying nothing. The chair creaked under me. I studied the yellow oval placemat, small decorative holes punched in a smaller oval on the inside of its edge. I ran my fingers along those holes. The pulse on my neck pounded, as if trying to burst through.

"Hey, Dad, can we go to the grocery store?" I asked, my voice cracking. I counted the holes in the placemat until my vision stumbled over them.

"Sure," he said.

I had been wearing the pads Brenda had given me months before, before she and Dad broke up. I had wrapped the box of inch-thick Kotexes in a blanket and hid it far under my bed, but the stash had run out.

"Do you know why?"

He kept his eyes on the paper. "Well, since you didn't say, I can probably guess."

He said it as if it were nothing, as if this were not the moment he had prepared for.

Or maybe he hadn't prepared at all.

Either way, he said it the way I wanted it to be said: flat and without looking at me.

At the store, I stood in the aisle and was faced with too many possibilities. Cardboard. Plastic. Thick. Thin. Scented. Unscented. Wings or without. Brenda's brand lay on the bottom shelf, a sign it was the wrong kind to buy. I wonder now where Dad was, if he wandered the aisles and pretended to shop, as I studied the fronts of boxes and peered around, afraid I'd see someone I knew. I think he stayed in the car, after handing me neatly folded twenties, enough to ensure I wouldn't have to return and ask for more. I finally picked out Always with Wings, so much thinner than the pads Brenda had given me and in a prettier box, and a box of tampons.

Back at the house, I waited until Rolland and Dad left to go somewhere and then stood in the bathroom. The diagram in the tampon instructions shows a profile of a woman's lower body, as if we see ourselves from that angle, as if we can translate the profile when we are looking down, bending over, upside down, trying to determine how to aim at the small of our backs while spreading the lips with one hand and trying to push a soft syringe with the other. And nothing about her two-dimensional body looks tense.

I propped my right leg on the toilet, then on the bathtub ledge. I tried squatting in front of the mirror or raising my leg to the counter, but the mirror was too high and I could see nothing below my waist. I spread, I pushed, I struggled. The diagram didn't say anything about resistance, nothing about pressure, nothing about pain. The instructions said Playtex tampons do not hurt, that they are easy to insert, use, and remove. Just follow the six simple steps in the guide, but I couldn't get it to go in. I thought it must be defective. I threw it away. I opened another. It would not work. My thighs shook. I crumpled the diagrams in my hands. I smoothed them out and tried again. *I must not have an opening, or at least one big enough.* I screamed from the gut, no one home to hear, launching tampons at the bathroom door, wanting them to break like glass. I had blood drying on my fingertips, under my nails. Bending over the sink, I held my hands in my hair, saying over and over, "What's wrong with you? Why can't you do this?"

A few months later, a boy taught me how to insert a tampon, when he slid his fingers inside me and I felt, for the first time, the interior side.

Sometimes my father and I would talk about sex, but it focused mostly on anatomy. It always seemed to happen in the car, on the way home from somewhere. We'd pull into the driveway, Yanni playing through the speakers. Dad would press the button for the garage, but we'd stay parked in the driveway, car running, headlights reflecting off the back wall of the garage. I wonder if we stayed there because the house was too intimate, as if the objects within it—my boots left by the stairs, his stained coffeepot—would be too much of a reminder that we were father and daughter in a strange new relation.

He'd explain the science of the body, like how and why the testicles descend or why I had hernias when I was a toddler—"the muscles hadn't come together properly when, in the womb, your body decided to be a girl."

I intentionally asked questions that'd mislead him, like when he explained how "the function of the prostate is to produce pre-ejaculation fluid," and I asked what pre-ejaculation fluid was, making certain to get the pitch correct, as if I had not felt it on my hands, sticky and warm.

But I never asked the questions I really wanted to know, like was my body normal, was it sexy, did the lips hang down too low, does it taste bad when you go down on a girl, how do you give a blow job without your jaw cramping, why does the room have a distinct smell after sex, or how do you keep it from hurting?

When I wanted to be on the pill, I complained to him my periods were irregular (they weren't) and said the pill would help, something I must have learned from a magazine. For years, Dad called it the "menstrual cycle regulation pill" rather than birth control.

I laughed at the lengths he'd go to in order to deny the daughter in front of him; I couldn't see the ways I pushed her away too.

I chose a female GP at our regular clinic because I didn't want Dr. Walcott, a grown man who had delivered me, who had delivered Rolland, to see me between my legs. Not when he always brought up kissing whenever I visited his office. I don't know why my father didn't find me an ob-gyn; after all, my mother would have had one.

In the GP's office, I placed my feet in stirrups and didn't want to separate my knees. I counted marks on the ceiling tiles while she reached for what I thought of as a metal duck's bill.

In the middle of the exam, I asked some question about female anatomy.

The doctor said, "Go ask your mother."

I sat up, legs still in the stirrups, and glared over the paper sheet. "My mother was murdered when I was eight."

"Oh, uh, well," she stuttered through some response, giving me an answer that I can't remember now.

But I do remember I intentionally used the word *murdered* to make her feel worse. I don't think I would have done this had the doctor been a man. I would have blushed, turning my head toward the wall, cinder-blocked like a school's, feeling like I was wrong to ask about my body. And while the dismissal would be fucked-up either way, it felt like a betrayal coming from this woman, in her glasses and white coat and clear annoyance for having to crank open my teenage body, because I believed all women should be my mother, swaddling me in answers when I finally found the courage to ask a question.

I was in my early teens when I told Dad that Dr. Walcott was making me uncomfortable.

"He keeps asking me if I like kissing boys," I said.

"He's just teasing you. You know he likes to joke around."

I remembered the newspaper headline—"Iowa State Beats OU"— that Mom had worn pinned to her shirt once, when we visited Dr. Walcott's office. She bantered with him, teased him, and he laughed back. He kept the headline tucked into my medical records, even years after she died. I supposed my father was right.

But then I was sixteen years old, speeding home in my car and shaking with rage.

That night, after Dad came home from work and sat down, sighing as he leaned back into the cushions of the couch, he asked me what the doc had to say.

I had waited hours to tell him, and when I started, the words broke like a fast-moving wave. "I was sitting up on the table with my legs tucked under me and playing with that water-ring game. I had taken my temperature and then set the thermometer on the table in front of my knees and he came in and said, 'Is that an in-between-the-legs thermometer?' and then he read the temperature and said, 'You're pretty warm down there,' and then I laughed, I can't believe I laughed. I just wanted to get out of there, I didn't even realize I was angry until I got in the car."

My body began to shake again as I sat on the couch, Dad on one end, me on the other.

"Isn't there always a nurse in the room with you?"

"Never," I said.

"That's why I'd assumed he was always just joking with you."

I remember Dad didn't say anything after this, though I was expecting him to. Shouldn't there be a reworking of what you know and feel and then a new articulation, something like "a doctor should *never* make comments like that"? Instead, a silence occupied the space between us on the couch. Beside me on the wall hung a small wreath my mom had made, each acorn in its cupule meticulously hot glued into place, and next to it a framed mirror, reflecting a room that felt cavernous. Thinking of Dr. Walcott towering above me, the thermometer held between the tips of his fingers, I wanted to slam the side of my fist into that mirror.

But I just placed my chin on my knees, my arms around my legs, and asked my father, "What am I supposed to do?"

"You can ask that a nurse be with you, or you could change to another doctor in the office," he said.

I didn't want to ask the nurse to stay in the room because Dr. Walcott would know something was wrong and then I would have to tell him or make up an excuse, and I didn't want to change doctors because he might see me in the waiting room and ask why he wasn't my doctor anymore. I didn't want to have to face him and say, "You are making me uncomfortable," and then to hear how I had misinterpreted him and then to have to say, "I'm sorry. I must have misunderstood."

I didn't tell my father this. I didn't know how to explain the fear I was feeling, not when no one had taught me that when I said *uncomfortable*, I really meant *unsafe*.

If Dad had had a woman in his life, a woman in her fifties like my mother would have been, she could have explained how terrifying it is to be made to second-guess what you know. How he's wrong to assume a man would never harass a girl with another woman in the room. Or how vulnerable a girl is, how when a male doctor makes comments about sex or her body, it makes her feel like she's an object for kissing and for men.

I wish it weren't the truth that he stayed our family doctor, that I continued to see him when I felt really sick, even into college, but I always took a boyfriend with me, a boyfriend who would stand broad-shouldered when Dr. Walcott walked into the room and who would shake his hand like a vise. I wish that many years later, Dad didn't tell me how he had called up Walcott, who was, by then, the director of an Oklahoma City hospital, to ask for medical advice. "You know how I've always trusted and respected him," Dad said.

When I winced and Dad asked why, I said it upset me how he still reveres Walcott, given that he harassed me.

He said, "That makes sense, I guess."

I thought back to the teenager on the couch, how she should have shattered that mirror, bloodied the side of her fist so her father could see the effects of Walcott's words, so she and I might not be so inconsequential. I told myself the next time, and I knew there would be a next time, I'd bloody my hand by saying, "*Never* utter that name to me again."

But the next time Dad expressed a longing for a doctor like him, all I could hear was an old man, desperate for answers about his aging and changing body. I couldn't bring myself to smash anything, not when I recognized fear and vulnerability in his voice, so I offered what he couldn't give: "I know it's scary and unfair, and I'm sorry you're having to go through this."

There were others.

There always are.

Mr. Breytenbach, the teacher who hugged me when I told him that I'd had a nightmare about my mother. We were putting up microscopes in the classroom closet during his free period. I rested my head on his shoulder because I was hurting and wanted to be held. But his grip became tighter, his chest pressed so hard against mine. The next day, he told me, "I really wanted to kiss you, but it's probably best that I didn't."

When I told my father what had happened, he suggested, "You could ask your principal if there have ever been reports of sexual harassment at the school before, and if so, you could report it then."

That way it would be the teacher's history to blame.

Following the Anita Hill testimony several years before, *sexual harassment* had become a buzzword, and the culture had begun to say we weren't supposed to put up with it, even though Dad had complained how he couldn't even compliment a coworker on her dress anymore.

If Dad had a woman in his life to turn to, she would tell him, "You shouldn't use the word *could*. You're putting the onus on her."

"Kristine is old enough to make the call," he'd say.

"No, she isn't. Not when she's thinking about her teacher, his wife, their baby, and wanting only to protect him. If *you* don't report it, Doss, you're telling her it's okay what he did to her."

My father might say, "A man saying he's attracted to a young woman, momentarily forgetting his age or the difference in position, is an understandable mistake."

This woman would get pissed then. "She isn't a young woman, she's a girl, and a man, especially a man in a position of power, knows better. It isn't a fucking mistake."

Dad could say, "It's not like he harmed her."

She'd try to explain how aggressive and frightening a man's voice can be, even when it's whispered in a classroom or office. When my father stares at her blankly, she might reach for a simile: "It's like oak wilt," she'd say. "The words are the fungus that penetrates the sapwood of the tree. The girl does what she can to wall it off, maybe by laughing, maybe by ignoring, maybe by keeping another guy by her side, but by walling it off she cuts off her water supply and then wilts. You need to understand that the fungus tricks the tree into harming herself."

Dad, ever the literalist, would say, "I've seen oak wilt, there was a stretch of oaks that succumbed to it along the highway to the lake, you wouldn't believe the devastation it can cause, a whole swath of trees that were just brown and dead."

The woman would see only a field of dead women and girls.

In the principal's office, I sweated through my shirt and did my best to hide my quivering fingers by pretending I was cold. Mr. Pesta said there'd never been any reports before, but he wouldn't let me go when I stood to leave.

He asked questions. I answered them, making sure to remove all identifiable characteristics, like the microscopes or the building or the class period.

"Is it Mr. Breytenbach?" he said.

I lowered my head and said yes, uncertain how he could know with all my careful exclusions.

When I asked him what would happen, he informed me, "I'll address it. It's out of your hands and no longer concerns you."

I never learned how he addressed it. I only know that a few years after I graduated, Mr. Breytenbach accepted a position at a bigger, more prestigious high school in Oklahoma, and he continued to coach girls' athletics teams. I look back at photographs from when I was seventeen. He's a chaperone for the prom, and we're slow dancing, his arm around my waist. At another event, we're standing side by side, arms around each other, our cheeks pressed together. At the time, I didn't think anything of this closeness, but I wonder now how many girls went to him with their pain and ended up crying to their fathers or their mothers or alone in their rooms.

My next-door neighbor Ken—he was in his midsixties. We liked to chat in the yard while his wife planted flowers around the tree. One afternoon, when I got home from school and was about to go into my house, he called me over to his garage. He handed me a large painting of

Elvis, one he bought at a garage sale, Elvis in white against a background that appeared like smeared shit. "I thought you'd like this," he said, and then he leaned over the canvas and kissed me, hard, on the lips.

Dad told me it was simple: just don't walk over to his yard anymore.

But the next day, Ken called me from a Days Inn. "I had too much to drink last night and couldn't drive home," he said. "I need a ride to my car. Would you mind picking me up?" He told me his room number and said to drop by when I arrived.

I wanted to help him out. But then I thought of his lips, how mushy they were when he pressed them against mine, and the back of my neck felt wet and slimy and cold, as if my skin were in a dungeon.

When I called my father at work and asked him what to do, he said, "I don't have a problem with you helping him, but if you're not comfortable, don't go."

The woman in Dad's life would once again have to step in: "How can you *not* have a problem with a grown man requesting her presence at a hotel room?"

This woman would wait for an answer. She'd wait and she'd wait, until she could stand the silence no longer.

"Is it because you don't want to ruffle any feathers with your neighbor?"

He'd know enough to answer *no*, even if *yes* felt true.

The woman in Dad's life would demand to know why, why he insists on trusting these men, even after all they do.

The most Dad would give is "I don't know," which likely would be true.

This woman would fill the void with conjecture—maybe it's easier for him if he denies the danger.

Then he doesn't have to contend with the scope of it, the men he knows about and the ones he doesn't—her manager at Sonic who followed her into the bathroom, locking the door behind him; the standup comic passing through town; the artist in Nantucket; his neighbors—all men in their thirties and forties and sixties, each of them wanting to fuck a teenaged girl and acting on it.

Nor does he have to reconcile the doctor, the neighbor, the teacher with the predator. Predators are strangers, are lowlifes, are evil or insane, are men like the ones who murdered his wife; they cannot possibly be professional middle-class men like him. Nor can the men who have helped *him*, who have been friendly to *him*, be the same ones who harm his daughter.

I called the hotel back and told Ken, "I'm just not comfortable" and "I'm sorry" and "maybe I can call you a cab and give them my dad's credit card number."

"Forget it," he snapped and then hung up.

I never saw him again. Weeks later, he was gone, moved out, and for the rest of my years at that house, his wife would never wave to me again, not when I yelled hello after getting out of my car or smiled at her when we were both getting our mail—yet another lesson in how the girl and her body are to blame.

When I think about being fifteen and sixteen and seventeen, when I strip away moments of support, like my creative writing teacher, Cramer, who stayed through lunch to tell me it wasn't my fault Mr. Breytenbach had harassed me, it feels like I was surrounded by men who harmed me, or wanted to, or stood idle and watched.

Dad likes to tell me I can't see the forest for the trees, that I need to step back for some perspective.

So I imagine all those moments in the house, Dad watching the news, listening to his daughter ask what to do. He was probably craving a cigarette, even if it were just one long drag, and wishing for the time I was ten, when I rested my head on his chest and asked him why the ocean has a tide. Back when he knew the answer. He was probably shaking his head and thinking Rolland was so much easier, even when he stole the station wagon before he had a license, speeding and hitting a curb and ruining the tire, or when his girlfriend's mother found their condoms right before they left for prom. Easier because those experiences were like my father's as a teen. Easier because Dad and Rolland were the agents, their actions aligned with what boys are supposed to do.

I think about my students who come to me with their stories. A junior in my Women's Autobiography class stands in my office, telling me about her experience over the weekend. "I don't know what to think," she says, and then she describes how her boyfriend had fingered her even though she was saying no. "After it was over, he told me he just wasn't able to control himself because I looked so beautiful in my dress. I don't understand what happened, why I'm still so upset."

"Because you were sexually assaulted," I say, my voice both unwavering and soft. I know she isn't ready for the word *rape*.

She breaks down then, her knees buckling because I spoke what her body already knows. I hold her, placing my hand on the back of her head as she sobs into my shoulder.

"It's not okay," I say. "And it isn't your fault, no matter what you were wearing, even if you were wearing nothing at all."

Another student tells me how her therapist wrote her love letters when she was in high school and then took her on a date as soon as she turned eighteen. We had just watched *The Tale* in class, a film about a woman who thought she had a healthy relationship with a much-older man when she was thirteen, until she's confronted with her memories.

My student's terrified to report him.

I tell her I understand why she's afraid. I tell her about the doctor with the thermometer, though I make it clear it isn't the same. I tell her about the time I was describing my doctor to a group of my girlfriends at school, and one of them stopped me and said, "It's Dr. Walcott, isn't it?" I tell my student I think about that moment all the time, how I wonder how many other girls experienced what I did or worse, how I wish my father had helped me to report him.

Sometimes I walk these students over to the women's center or counseling services or the Title IX coordinator; sometimes I give them Play-Doh and just listen to their stories. I hold the ones who need to be held and repeat, "This is not okay." I don't think I always get it right, but I can at least name what they've experienced as violence.

At times I think I can do this because I've experienced it myself, but I can also say "what happened to you is wrong" to a student who hears a homophobic slur yelled at him or to a student who must show multiple forms of ID just to buy groceries with a debit card. I believe them when they show me their pain. And I cannot figure out why my father can't do the same, not when I'd tell him I needed to stay home because of cramps and he'd say he trusted me since he couldn't feel what I felt. Though that's my body hurting on its own, rather than at the hands or voice of a man.

My father taught me some things are worth defending though.

My freshman year of high school, in the hallway right after first period, several of my friends ran up to me, each of them in baggy jeans and bodysuits and holding textbooks wrapped in the brown paper from grocery store bags.

"You won't believe this," one of them said.

"Mr. Trail was talking about your mom in history class," another said.

"You won't believe the shit he was saying."

I stopped putting my books in my locker. The four of them were excited, amped up, moving around like flies.

"Did you notice how everyone looked at each other?"

"Yeah, I didn't know what to do either."

They were breathless, caught up in some drama I didn't understand, their bodies buzzing.

"He said it was your mom's fault she got kidnapped."

"What did you just say?" I stared right at my friend, doubting what

I had heard. It made no sense. It was as if she were speaking another language, one I knew only vaguely.

"Yeah, he said it was your mom's fault. I mean, he doesn't know it's your mom. He was just talking about the kidnapping from Shepherd Mall a while back and he said it was the woman's fault for being alone."

"We were all looking at each other and other people started whispering and we just couldn't believe it."

I felt rage then, not because he said it was a woman's fault—I was still years from registering how we shift blame to women for the violence against their own bodies—but because someone was criticizing my mother. He could have said she was terrible at needlepointing, and I would have felt the same need to defend her. But at fourteen, what I hated more was that he had turned me and my mother into gossip.

All day I thought about it, Mr. Trail, my friends, a room full of students whispering about me. I had become the elephant in the room.

I told Dad about it later that night, over dinner at the kitchen table, and described how embarrassed I was to have this teacher talk about Mom in class.

Then I told him, "He said it was Mom's fault she was kidnapped."

He picked up his pencil, turning it end over end over end, stabbing the eraser into the newspaper beside him.

"I'll take care of it," he said.

The next morning, armed with his suit, the school handbook, and a letter of complaint, Dad met with my high school's three principals during first period, while I sat in class wondering what was being said among men. I can't imagine my father argued how dangerous it is to teach fourteen-year-old boys and girls that it's a woman's fault for getting raped and murdered.

I knew by the jabbing of his pencil that his rage was personal. Someone had spoken ill of the dead, of his beloved, but more than that, another man had been talking shit about his wife. I don't how he couched it, but at its root, his anger said, *How dare you criticize what is mine.*

Whatever he said was effective though; the principals made Mr. Trail issue a formal apology for the careless words he spoke about Mr. Engle's wife.

I felt proud of my father for making him apologize, for being a man of action, for protecting my mom from a man who maligned her.

It would be years before I'd notice the contradiction, before I'd wonder why Dad protected the memory of his wife when he wouldn't protect me from men.

I wonder if he would have listened to my mother or a woman in his life, if she had described the oak wilt again, how the damage is on the inside, an entire forest killed by a fungus no one sees. She'd try to explain how the fungus gets passed from tree to tree through its root system, how the actions of Walcott and Breytenbach and Pesta and Ken and Trail are all the same fungus that killed his wife.

I remember a moment when I was living in New York during graduate school, and Dad was visiting me. I woke up angry because I had dreamed he proposed to the woman he was dating at the time, without first talking with me. When I told him my dream, he was drinking his Folgers and feeling overwhelmed by the size of *The New York Times*. He became angry too, at me for thinking he would owe me a conversation first.

Only after I had left the apartment for some space and only after I had returned with irises from a bodega were we able to talk about our reactions.

"It'd upset me if you were going to make a big decision like that and you didn't feel like you could share it with me. We're closer than that," I said. "And I just want you to be happy."

He said my anger came off as my thinking he should get my permission to marry. "Things have changed," he said, "since you've been living on your own here in New York. It's kind of creepy to say it like this, and I don't mean it that way, but up until recently you've been the woman in my life."

And he was right. From the time I was thirteen and he and Brenda broke up to when I was in my early twenties, I had been the only woman around him. He rarely saw or spoke with his sisters, who lived in other states, and he saw his mother only periodically.

I wonder if his advice would have been different if the woman in his life hadn't been a girl who had yet to hear, *This isn't okay.* If instead she had been a woman who understood how every speech act, every kiss, and every bruise that goes unnoticed, unreported, ignored, or excused makes the tree choke off another vein, destroying us from the inside.

But then I think maybe the truth is more disturbing: if one girl reports her experience, then she might grow into a woman who won't accept violence and Dad would have to be even more careful with his speech. Maybe his hedging and his *you could do that* when I asked if I should report the men were as automatic as my laughing had been and serving the very same purpose: to protect the man in power. Not that I think Dad recognized it as such, those moments we sat in the family room and he advised me about what I *could* do. You don't have to know the power you have to be protective of it.

It's easy to think that, had my mother lived, those pads never would have been wrapped in a blanket and hidden; I never would have been alone in the bathroom with instructions about insertion and an interior I didn't understand. I never would have hesitated or doubted what my body knew. We would have had long talks in my bedroom, each sprawled out on the bed, eating something chocolate and decadent and messy. Or maybe just a bag of Hershey's Kisses. She would have taught me to think of my body as blameless and beautiful, to value what is mine. I never would have been searching *The New Teenage Body Book* for clues.

But then I return to the book as an adult and notice what I couldn't see then—letters that show a mother can mess up too: "I have some dark hairs around my nipple," a girl writes. "My mom said that pulling them out will cause cancer." Another one says, "I recently started my period and want to use tampons but my mom won't let me because she says tampons give you a fatal disease and make you not a virgin anymore."

Maybe my mother and I never would have spoken. Maybe she would have bought me a push-up bra when I was thirteen or nodded her head when Dad said, "Don't let your triceps get flabby as you age," or maybe she would have asked me, "Well what did you do to call attention to yourself?"

Maybe the report card from my first daycare, signed by my mother, described the girl I'd inevitably become: "Kristine is weak in confidence, talks quietly, has to be told to speak up, and lets children push her around."

Maybe my mom could not have saved her.

Cleaving To

PART II

✦

I LIED WHEN I DESCRIBED WRITING "SAVE MOMMY" ON THE back of that photograph right after she was taken. The truth is, I wrote it months later. I lay sobbing on my bedroom floor, staring at the picture of us, hurting as if no time had passed.

She was always still missing. Missing from the corner by the floor vent of the kitchen. Missing from the shower, where she'd lather my hair. Missing from the make-your-own-kite competition I would have won, had she been there to help me decorate it.

I wrote it months later because if it's possible to be present in the past, then maybe, just maybe, I could save her still.

I was nine years old and on a date with a boy from my third-grade class. We were watching *An American Tail* at the local theater. His mother sat behind us, eating popcorn, and I kept thinking about my hair, how straight and uneven it was. Mom would have curled it with her hot rollers. She would have feathered my bangs.

Before the movie began, the boy leaned over and asked me if I wanted to go steady. I stuck and unstuck my pink high-tops on the dried soda-spilled floor, afraid to ask what *steady* meant. Yes, I said, and he reached over the armrest to take my hand in his.

In the movie, a mouse named Fievel is separated from his family when they arrive in New York. He's wandering and lost and searching for the ones he loves, and then one night, Fievel and his sister, in different locations, look to the sky, full moon rising, and sing a duet of longing and hope. They're looking at the same star, wishing to find each other, loving each other from a distance.

I saw her, I saw me.

The boy, hearing it as a love song, leaned over and kissed my cheek.

I saw Mom lying on her back in the back seat of the Colt, nothing but open space around her, short grass in a breeze.

I didn't kiss him back. Or even turn to smile.

The men, they're gone. Mom doesn't shake or cry or scream. She's just tired, bags under her eyes, as she stares at the stars outside the window of her car.

The two mice are singing about how they know each is thinking of the other, and I'm in my bedroom in the dark, Barbies strewn across the floor, their high heels lost in the shag carpet. Her teddy bear from her second birthday sits alone on my dresser. I stand at my window, my head just above the sill. I'm not as calm as she is, my eyes watery and red. I stare out and see the same star she's watching at the very same moment. Somehow we know this, we can feel it, and we're comforted.

The movie ended. The boy held my hand as we walked up the aisle, believing me to be his girlfriend, never knowing how I was replaying the scene of mother and daughter separated and connected.

For months "Somewhere Out There" played on late-night love-song shows like *The Quiet Storm*. When the song came on, I'd turn off my bedroom light and stand at my window, looking to the sky. I'd run through the scene again, as if through repetition I could remember differently.

Mom's still out there in the field; it'll work this time.

There must be a version where she comes back to me.

A little over a year after my mother's death, we were told the names of the men who killed her: Travis McGuire and Ricky Martin. I don't remember being told this, but I remember saying their names anytime one of my friends or their parents would ask whether the men had been caught. I knew Travis McGuire and Ricky Martin were half brothers and were in jail for kidnapping and killing a woman from Albuquerque, New Mexico. They had killed her not long before or not long after Mom had died. I knew Mom's car had been found in Tucumcari, which is along I-40, just like Albuquerque is. I knew they found the New Mexico woman's body along the interstate, similar to Mom's body.

Then there was a lighter, the single piece of evidence the police really latched on to. They had found it at McGuire's house. It was gold, and engraved on its side was the name Kathy.

I remember Dad insisted Mom never owned a lighter like that. I remember she used Bics. But the police still seemed to focus on it. And even though the unidentified fingerprint and half of a palm print, recovered from my mother's car, didn't match McGuire or Martin, they told us these were the men who did it. "We're nearly certain," they said. "We just don't have the evidence to prove it in court."

I remember they said a murder like Mom's "isn't a one-time crime." I remember being comforted by that. "At least they're in prison," they said. McGuire for life, Martin for eighteen years. "Technology's getting better all the time," they said. "We can still find a way to nail these two men."

The Distance to You

✦

THE SUMMER AFTER MY JUNIOR YEAR OF COLLEGE, I APPLIED
at a temp agency, and a data-entry position became available at a business at Shepherd Mall.

In the 1980s, we were eyeing puppies at the pet store, stopping
for an Orange Julius before leaving. I remember the TG&Y, how big
it seemed, and the steps inside the cocktail dress shop, three steps up
to a raised platform where the sparkly dresses were, one of which my
mother bought me as a Christmas gift. A dress-up dress, she called it.
Long, lavender, taffeta, and lace.

I remember the tile inside the mall, around the trees the metal
grates, the curved wood benches without backs. I remember eating but-
tered corn tortillas as my meal at El Chico, how the sunlight streamed
down from the roof in angles. I loved the mall. We all did.

But after Mom's abduction, we stopped going there. At times I'd
accidentally drive by the mall on my way to some other location, and at
the stoplight on 23rd and Villa, I would stare at the sign on the southwest corner of the land, turquoise, low to the ground, with an outline
of a sheep on it, and think about Mom and about Linda Thompson, a
woman who was abducted, along with her children, eight months before
my mother was. I thought about Curt Fickeisen, manager of the mall
in 1986, who told reporters, "We have four security people on staff . . .
[and] feel that's more than the average shopping center across the nation
will provide." I thought about Detective Johnson, head of the sex-crime

unit when my mother was taken, who remarked to a journalist: "To say the mall could have prevented this is going way out on a limb . . . You'd have to have armed guards in just about every parking lot, and, of course, that wouldn't be cost-effective."

I tried to understand the term *cost-effective* in the context of that parking lot, of the fear the women felt, of my mother's body rotting in a field, of Linda Thompson's body in a lake. I wondered how the manager and detective viewed cost after Thompson's family sued the mall and settled out of court. I thought of Dad, who, after I asked why we didn't sue like the Thompsons, answered with a question: What amount of money would make it okay, what amount of money would bring her back?

I remembered the people I met as I grew up, people who, despite not knowing my family at the time, said that Mom's abduction affected them personally and they'd never return to Shepherd Mall. Women recalled conversations with their husbands about never going back. They said they didn't feel safe. Shops closed and locked their gates. Stores moved to Penn Square Mall, just a few miles away, as the Shepherd neighborhood declined and city money shifted northward.

The full-time data-entry position paid more than minimum wage, but I hadn't been back since she died. I imagined reentering that space, dramatically different from my childhood. I knew that in the early 1990s, the mall became a mostly abandoned building and stayed that way until April 19, 1995, the day the Murrah Building was bombed in downtown Oklahoma City, killing 168 people. They moved the federal offices to the mall because it was the only building large and empty enough. Acts of violence helped shut it down; an act of violence reopened it, transforming it into an office complex.

But it would always be the place where two men grabbed my mother and forced her into the back seat of her car.

I couldn't decide if the paycheck would be worth it, if I could return day after day and make the space normal again. So I asked my father what he thought.

"For that kind of money, you should try. At least go in for the interview," he said.

"Maybe I'll go up there the day before to see how I'll react."

"You could do that," he said.

I wonder now why this was his answer, when we didn't need the money. How could it not bother him, his daughter about to walk the steps his murdered wife took? Even now, when I'm in my forties, he'll get onto me for not having a campus police officer walk me to my car whenever I teach evening classes. Maybe he thought of it as lightning, that danger couldn't happen to us in the same place twice.

In the middle of a hot afternoon, the day before the interview, I drove to the southwest parking lot, not realizing, until years later, that this was where my mother had parked. I parked my Camry on a one-way aisle pointing toward the mall, the driver's side opposite the brick building, painted cream. I walked toward a long covered entryway, telling myself, *Stay calm, stay, you're okay,* and opened one of the doors. The floor was the same, an off-white linoleum with inset shards of grays and umbers. The iron grates around the trees, their long cuts protruding from the center in circles, were still there. But where was the store where Mom got my dress? Where was the pet store? I kept my arms folded tightly around me, as if the body can contain itself. The mall was tiny. Nothing but a stubby L. There, the benches I remember—curved and slatted. But now in front of the social security office. No Orange Julius. No music playing. No window-shopping. A few mall walkers in tennis shoes. A few people taking an afternoon break to grab a soda at a fast-food vendor. I pressed my forearms hard into my ribs. *I bet we sat on that exact bench once. Mom, Rolland, and I. The soles of her shoes touched this tile.*

Other than the floor, the grates, the benches, I no longer knew this place. I couldn't determine where TG&Y was or Streets, the store where Mom returned the dress the night she was taken. This place was dead. Cold and drab, the way office buildings almost always are. *Maybe I can do this. Actually do this,* I thought. I loosened my arms and headed back to the entrance.

But, as I neared the exit doors, the glass showing the parking lot with only parked cars and no one around, the sun bright off the concrete, I was suddenly afraid. I flung open the door and hurried past some concrete benches and planters, my hand deep in my purse, I couldn't get the keys out, wallet, lip gloss, pens, the keys jingling from somewhere inside, I didn't want to look down to find them, didn't want to take my eyes off my car, four cars away, fumbling, shaking, I grabbed the keys but couldn't separate the right one, keys stuck together, keys falling on concrete, me stumbling, stumbling to pick them up. I couldn't get the key in the hole, couldn't do it quickly enough, *Don't look around, it takes too much time*, I scratched the key along the paint by the keyhole. Then in the car, *Hurry start, lock the doors, reverse without looking back.*

The trip home a blur, fast, along I-40. Just like the men.

Just get home, get home, you're okay, get home. If a cop tries to pull you over, keep driving.

In my driveway, I pulled in so fast I almost took out the hedges, then ran inside and collapsed on the family room floor, sobbing and still not feeling safe. It wasn't a large house, but I felt tiny within it, when all I wanted was a cocoon.

I called Dad at work, my breath heaving. "I'm sorry, I just can't do it, I can't go there again, I'm sorry," I said.

He waited until I calmed down, and then he said, "Darlin', I won't go there."

It jolted me.

"Wait. What? Then why'd you push me to go?"

"I thought it might be different for you."

I think back on this moment and find it hard to understand. So I ask him why he never wanted to go back.

He says it's because he wouldn't be able to stop the images in his head.

I say I find it curious he didn't tell me how he felt, before I went back to the mall myself.

"You were old enough by then to know how you felt and to make the decision for yourself."

In some ways, he is right. I was twenty-one then. But it doesn't feel like much of a decision when he had said, "At least go in for the interview."

I understand he doesn't know what it's like to constantly be afraid, in parking garages, on streets, on walking trails, at gas stations, in bars and in stores. Or what it's like to constantly be grabbed—the guy who yanked my hand as I walked by him and then pressed it into his crotch, the guys who cupped my ass as I passed. So maybe he couldn't see how I'd become my mother as I walked to my car.

But if the images wouldn't stop for him, if Mom's terror would become more real if he entered that space, how could he not tell me that's a risk I'd face?

Maybe I could have been saved from feeling that fear.

Or maybe his telling me wouldn't have made a difference at all.

That afternoon and evening, after I had panicked in the parking lot, I thought about how this was the type of job Dad wanted me to have and I knew he would feel proud of me for working full-time in an office rather than waitressing or working retail. I didn't want to disappoint him. I also thought about Rolland, how he too wouldn't go back to the mall. I remember wanting to prove that I'm stronger than the men in my family.

So early the next morning, I parked on the mall's north side at an entrance I had not used before, a direct entry to the office rather than an entry through the mall. The receptionist, who sat in front of a wall of glass, through which the offices and cubicles were, asked me to sit down and wait. I sat upright, trying to keep my skirt from wrinkling by sucking in my stomach. But I grew more anxious. I tried to watch the people on the other side of the glass instead of staring at my car in the parking lot. But there it was, six cars down the line, facing away from the mall with the driver's side closest to the business door for a faster and easier exit.

It's easy enough to recognize the nerves—fluttering pulse, fingers shaking, heat between the shoulder blades, hair dampening on the back of your neck—but the recognition doesn't mean you can calm yourself down. I looked at the receptionist, who sorted through mail. I looked at the man with steaming coffee. I looked again to my Camry and an expanse of concrete with no visible roads. I knew I couldn't do it. It had been a mistake to think I could. A lie to tell myself that a sunlit parking lot at five o'clock in summer would be different enough than dusk in April and that it would get easier each time I left. I thought about just walking out. Or trying to explain to the receptionist. But I didn't want to. I could say I changed my mind, that this isn't the position for me. But she'd be confused because I'd just been sitting in a chair in a static room. I could say I had forgotten there was someplace else I needed to be and then call the manager later to explain, but then the manager opened the glass door and invited me through.

I followed her into her office, with the slip under my skirt pasted to my body. She turned around, and before she could ask me to please sit in front of her desk, I snapped. My hand went out in front of my body, fingers shaking and spread, my palm saying before I could, *Stop, no more.* "I'm sorry," I said, "I just . . . I can't do this." The muscles in my face were twitching like live wires. "My mother was kidnapped from this mall thirteen years ago, and I thought I would be okay but I just can't do this, I'm sorry, I'm sorry I wasted your time, I'm sorry to do this to you, I thought I would be okay but I can't, I'm sorry you had to see this . . ."

My whole body trembled; I sputtered like a child. And she was scared. I could see it in her eyes when I first apologized. I could see her fear from seeing my body outside of my control. And when I said my mother was kidnapped, I saw her look transform from fear to sympathy. She began to cry. She reached out to hug me, this woman who saw me for what I was, a wounded child. But I knew my body would react if she touched me. I'd shove her right in the chest. So I jerked my body back toward the door. "I'm so sorry," I said again and again, and then I walked out, my legs shaking, feeling like I was walking on piles of stones.

I wish I could go back and tell myself not to apologize, not to play so tough, to let go, to let this woman hold me when no one else did. Better yet, I'd trust that first hesitation I felt and never ask my father what I should do. But doubting our terror is what we've been trained to do.

I stand above your grave. I never know what to say when I read your name. It surprises me still, the permanence of it. Dad didn't give you a headstone but a *pillow marker* of rose granite, a slanted slab that rests just above the grass. How odd to call it that, as if the granite were soft, as if I could rest my head there.

At a nearby grave, a dead bird rests, neck broken, head against headstone, feather and beak, and around yours, loose dirt, dried petals of Shasta daisies. A mound of black earth reminds me you are home, in a cove of soil that isn't red, like it is in Oklahoma.

I am alone, except for the ants—they travel the sleek granite, dip down the crevice of bone, trace the ridge of your name, that deep black ditch. I want to be that small, to crawl inside your *K*, to sleep where the lines meet, no longer a reminder but a refuge, but instead I slide my sandals off, grass slipping between my toes, blades brushing my ankles and the sides of my feet, the distance to you, I know, immeasurably less but comforting.

You tried to describe once, in a letter to Dad, what you felt when you returned to visit your father's grave. I agree it's hard to explain what it's like to be here, in the middle of nowhere in Iowa, the cornfields stretched to the west. I have returned, after many years, and I think of you, twelve years old, your father having just died of brain cancer. You're running around in a black dress and pea coat. You play on the statue, the one "Erected to the Memory of the Soldier Dead 1861–1865," its square block, guns standing high, under the sprawling maple tree, though it was probably much smaller then.

They say memories bleed and blend, like ink through multiple sheets of paper. They give us composites, shadows, reflections, and slivers. They say we can now point to an individual cell, touch it, and plant a false memory there. Maybe if I place my hand on your father's head-stone, if I hold it there long enough, it will be your palm I see.

As a child, I too ran down these avenues of graves, hiding among strange names, this small plot of land my playground, and now, as I read *Wanda* and *Ona Mae*, I remember this scene in winter, a view of frozen cornfields, not the day you were buried, but later, knees deep in two feet of snow—I prefer this memory, real or no—my bare blue hands, digging to reach you.

The object I remember the most is her brown leather blazer. She must have worn it quite often. I loved the smell of the leather, mixed with her Charlie perfume. I remember the mornings, before she left for work, how I would hug her, how the smooth leather would stick to my cheek.

Dad saved the blazer for me to grow into, keeping it in the down-stairs coat closet, toward the back. I knew it was there, but I never touched it.

Until I was home during college, and I hung my coat on a crocheted hanger, and I noticed it there, dust layered on its shoulders. I slipped it out from other old jackets, studying the two quarter-sized buttons, the tag with "Miss Simone of California" written in gold, the permanent creases on the interior of the elbows—her arms bent those creases—the lining with a reddish tint. I held the blazer to my nose. The smell of leather lingered still. The perfume gone. The menthol cigarette gone. I checked the two front pockets. I wanted something to be there, a receipt she had touched, a worn penny she turned over and over in her fingers, a note to remember a particular color of yarn, anything to say a life ex-isted here, in these sleeves. The pockets were empty.

I slid my arms down the sleeves, hearing the sound of dry, stiff leather being stretched for the first time in over a decade; the sleeves didn't even reach my wrists. Even though I weighed 120 pounds and wore a 32B, I had to force the leather across my chest to button the top button. It was tight and would fit only if I didn't wear anything underneath. I stared at my reflection in the kitchen mirror, bewildered, realizing for the first time how petite she must have been, how inaccurate my memory. I tried to explain this to myself: the jacket must have shrunken, condensed, tightened from not being worn, formed to its wooden hanger. Why is it memory holds on to us like this, making us grasp at any reason but the truth?

Even though Dad had told me she wore a 32AA, "barely anything there," in my memory her breasts had been huge. In the mornings before school, Mom and I would shower together, the water pooling toward the back of the shower's seat, staining it red. She lathered my long hair while I kept my eyes covered with my hands, terrified of soap getting in them. As I inched toward the water to rinse my hair, her voice saying, "Keep going, keep going," I peeked through my fingers at her large breasts, her nipples hard and the color of near-spoiled raspberries.

Once I started getting breasts, I would place my nipples in the V between my first two fingers, covering the areolas to compare, but hers were more elongated, protrusive, and the flesh-pink hue of mine has always lacked that deep magenta tint. In my shower, I would hold a mirror at waist level to recreate the angle from childhood, but no reflection or view would reveal her breasts to me again or show me a connection between our bodies.

I ran into my mother in Manhattan, when I was twenty-two, attending graduate school. I first saw her when I was on the R train. She was walking in long strides on the uptown platform, her hair blowing from a train's onslaught of air. I wanted to tear open the doors and follow her. I saw her again in Washington Square Park, where she glanced at me then disappeared behind a tree. At a bar on 1st Avenue, I had just missed her. Her Salems, the filters stained pink, rested in an ashtray beside an empty wine glass. And then, in the doorway of Starbucks on 3rd and 8th, I found her again, this time right next to me. She wore her brown leather blazer, her shoulders narrow and hidden under her hair. I held open the door as she was exiting with her latte. I smelled the menthol, the perfume. I almost called out *Mom*, but the woman looked at me with no recognition that I was her daughter.

Years later, in a Lebanese restaurant in Houston, she sat down with six of her friends. It was her birthday. I couldn't stop staring, her hair thick, brown, a little coarse, with large curls in it, held back by a head-band. I craved to sit behind her, to run my fingers through it, to lean over, my face so close to her head where I could see dry patches on her scalp. I thought of the movie *Memento*, of how Leonard pays a prosti-tute to scatter his dead wife's things around the room, so he can wake during the night and believe she is there, even if only for a few brief seconds. I know that desperation.

I'd go into antique stores, hoping to see her fingers tracing the grain of an oak table. I'd linger where piles of acorns rested under trees; she'd soon be by to gather them for wreaths. I'd see an argyle sweater with a shawl collar in a store's window, say to my husband, Jerry, "Something about that reminds me of Mom," and then go inside to buy it.

He said to me once, "If you were dying and in the proverbial tunnel, your mother on one end and life on the other, I think you would choose to be with her and not to come back to me."

I hadn't always wanted to be with her. In my dreams as a child, yes, I could embrace her—having left witness protection, she'd walk into our living room while I was wrapping Christmas presents, and we'd hold each other—but after adolescence, there were separations between us. I'd dream she was mowing the lawn and I was watching her from a window, telling my father I didn't know how to talk to her anymore. Or she'd show up at a museum wearing a blue tracksuit, her hair a thicket of dried twigs, and I'd run, desperate to find a door to escape.

Then there was a moment in Iowa. I was in high school then, and we visited for my cousin's wedding. Winter, like those Christmases we spent with her family while she was alive, back when we'd go sledding on a golf course, the snow on the fairways tracked with the metal runners of our sleds, and then we'd go back to Barb's house, peel off our snow-soaked clothes in the basement's mudroom, and jump in a hot shower to get warm.

It had been years since we'd been there, the visits growing rare after she died, and we arrived right when a blizzard hit. A whiteout. Heavy wet flakes and two feet of snow.

In my cousin's bedroom one night, I lay on a narrow mattress on the floor and watched the snow fall, dense and slow, outside the window, the flakes so much larger than the wisps of Oklahoma snow, so much softer than our ice. I lay writing, about what, I can't remember. Barb peeked into the room and told me it was time for bed. Her hair was short and permed and lighter than Mom's, her body even smaller. All day I had studied her, and even though they were twins, I could not see my mother in her.

"Goodnight, Teeny," she said, turning off the light, as if I were the child she remembered.

Annoyed but not wanting to defy her, I continued to write in the dark.

I wore flannel boxer shorts and wool socks pulled high up on my calves. I had forgotten how damn cold it is in Iowa. The smell from my uncle's pipe lingered in all the rooms; Barb's penguin figurines, once held in my mother's hands, rested on shelves in the house. Outside, a yellow streetlamp backlit the falling snow, moisture accumulating on the bottom of the window. That snow. Brilliant. From memory. The snow of her childhood, when she skated on ponds, the snow of mine when we pulled a wood sled up a hill.

I was awake. And suddenly she was there. In the room. All around me. A presence I could not see, only feel. I held my pen in the air. Mom, present, here, with me, among me, swirling all around the room. My fingers trembled, the pen in the air, my heart raced, my breath stuck, Mom in the room, where she wasn't supposed to be, when I hadn't sought her, hadn't called for her, when I'd become comfortable with the silence after saying her name. For years I had run my fingers along the yarn of her needlepoints or searched for her hair wrapped around her hot curlers, but then, when I had finally felt her, I was immediately and inexplicably afraid.

I awoke in the morning with no memory of falling asleep, just an unsettled feeling in my chest and my papers strewn across the floor, some wrinkled from my body's weight. I picked up the pages and read on the back of one of them words I did not know I wrote: "Get away from me."

Years later, I'll think of that night, of our snow, wanting to revise the moment she entered the room, telling her instead, "Come closer, touch me, don't leave."

She stands at the top of the stairs, a long pale-pink robe draping over her thin body. It's dark, with no light in the house except from a few small wall lamps turned down low and the moonlight from the windows. I'm standing in the middle of the stairs and looking up at her, her bangs, the tips of them, catching on her eyelashes, her hair disheveled and half pulled back.

"Why did you do it?" she asks.

I know by her voice, nearly hushed to a whisper, that I've upset her, and by the shadows under her eyes, her laugh lines like crevices carved by tears. She keeps looking down at her toes, because she's hurting, because I've disappointed her, because she wants me to change and I'm about to walk away.

"So where are you going?" she asks.

Or maybe this is the time she has disappointed me, when I find out she isn't the woman I want myself to be.

Or maybe it's when we both remember the mother and daughter who played Try to Get Away on the kitchen floor, the daughter hesitating just enough to be caught, the mother not willing to let go, and we know they are irrevocably lost.

Don't mothers and daughters always have a moment like this?

It doesn't matter the reason though, because Talia Shire, in that dimmed light, with shadows on her face and dark hair grazing her clavicles, looks like my mother in her robe. She may be talking to Rocky on the stairs of their mansion, but I can pause and rewind and replay and see my mother standing above me on the stairs of my childhood home. She's beautiful, and she's near. "Why did you do it?" she asks me. "A lot of people live with hurt."

I know where to feel connected to my father when he passes away—in the driver's seat of a V-hull boat, rising and falling over whitecaps on a lake; on an open stretch of road, top down on a Corvette, seventy-eight degrees outside; or in a leather chair, centered in a room, speakers playing Brubeck in the light of dusk.

If ever I lose Jerry, I'll know where to recover him: he's at the stern of a boat or eating apricots from a tree, rocking in a La-Z-Boy or swinging on a glider on an outdoor deck. He's roaming the Temple of Poseidon, griping about tourists who sit on its fallen stones. Or running around forts and museums with weapons and submarines and planes. I'll say, "Tell me again what's so special about this plane," and I'll hear him speak of dual fuselages and maneuverability in WWII dogfights. I'll visit the Smithsonian and see him standing on a bench to sneak a touch of an Apollo capsule suspended from the ceiling. I'll hear him say, in a voice like a child, "I touched something that's been in space."

To feel close to me, you'll find me in the mermaid's tail of the boat's wake, its tiny hands gathering the foam, or on the bow, loving an oncoming sunburn. I'm in the Atlantic, laughing hard at the waves as they crash against me, or in the ink of the Aegean Sea, swimming with sardines shimmering in the light. I'm beside my angel in Central Park, her hand outstretched to touch my head, or in the sunset on the plains, the red earth, the thunder that has time to roll and roll. Listen to a flügelhorn or walk into a closet full of coats, and you'll find me.

But no one seems to know what spaces she loved.

I ask Dad where he would have spread her ashes had she been cremated. "Her grandfather's farm, I guess," he says. "She said she'd never consider herself an Okie unless she lived in Oklahoma as long as she did in Iowa."

But I haven't felt her in Iowa since the winter I was seventeen, not at the farm or her grave or her twin's house. I haven't felt her in a Hobby Lobby or with the sound of yarn being pulled through a plastic canvas. Even at our beloved Lake Eufaula, she isn't there.

Rolland once considered contacting the owner of the oil field to see if we could put a monument where the men dumped her body. I imagined a waist-high thick black marble obelisk, in the field by the tree line, a marker more permanent than those crosses along the highway with their flowers and teddy bears, an occurrence, it now seems to me, that is distinctly rural, that requires open spaces—I've never seen a cross marker for a car wreck in New York, though we do have memorials like the reflecting pools at the Murrah Building and the World Trade Center to mark the physical space of mass death. Then there's the bike painted white, chained to a crosswalk sign on Dunlavy and Westheimer in Houston. I read how these markers are a response to sudden death, to senseless death, to death where a body is disfigured or unrecoverable, to death that is not codified or expected or prepared for. How they offer a ritual that is not bound by time, as funerals are. How they can become instructional—this is the danger of drinking and driving, this is the danger of believing you're safe. How they force us to reinvent our notions of space, where individual grief turns communal and a spot of earth becomes distinctly personal, in a way that cemeteries no longer are, those plots of land purchased and populated by disparate families, with little connection to place.

But the monument for Mom, nearly obscured by grass grown tall over the years, would stand alone in the oil field, viewed only by a male oil-field worker or two, like the ones who found her body. Why mark it? Not where her body is now but where she died, as if that space, where she breathed her last breath, is more sacred.

I've gotten close enough to the oil field. Jerry's grandmother lived in Mangum, Oklahoma, a town whose exit is just twenty miles east of Sayre on I-40. On the way, I forced my eyes closed, though I remembered the landscape from my first time there—you go past the town of Granite, where prisoners were once required to perform hard labor by busting up the mountain for headstones until it was determined to be cruel and unusual punishment, past the small Wichita Mountains and the white wind turbines on the prairie, cows grazing under their graceful and lumbered turning, to where the land is inescapably flat and the grass is a dead yellow all the way to the horizon. It always made me think of the local joke that a man watched his dog run away for two weeks, though I couldn't bring myself to laugh.

Maybe I could feel her in the oil field, in that open wind and creek of red water, but I don't want to know the place where she clenched her eyes with knowledge that the wound would be too deep.

"Would you want me to go to Sayre and collect some dirt from where she died?" Jerry asked me once, decades after her death, as we sat on the couch, watching some movie on TV.

"Where'd that come from?" I asked him.

"I just had the thought last night, when I couldn't sleep. I don't know why. Would you want me to do that though?"

"No."

"Really?"

His disbelief surprised me and made me think I'd answered wrong. It had been an immediate and visceral response, after all.

"Why would I want you to?"

"Because you love Oklahoma's red dirt and there's a chance it still has some of your mom in it."

I had to admit the appeal of having a jar of the elemental, the way a person might feel about an urn of ashes. It'd be different than the rubber banded strands of hair from Mom's first haircut, found later in a box in a closet, the toddler hair dirty and dead and dull, with the texture of worn shag carpet. Instead in the dirt would be a trace of blood of the mother I loved. Blood of the body as I knew it.

"I will, if you want me to."

"No," I said again.

"Why?"

"Because I want no one I love to reenter that space, even if it's to gather the earth for me."

It feels like something will be taken away, something that can't be recovered, as if the land, with its history, will eat like acid what is good in Jerry, destroying whatever is at the center of his yearning to bring me the body I lost.

By thirty, I found myself wanting to return to Shepherd Mall though. At first, I told myself it was about memory. To preserve that tile. Those grates. Those benches. "I must document all of it," I told Jerry. To get it right. When so many details had changed over the years, maybe the memory of the pay phones and El Chico and the dress shop would be closer.

The mall felt different than Sayre. She had been alive there. Terrified. But not like the terror in the oil field. The parking lot still held the possibility that the story could end differently; there, her scream carries both struggle and hope.

So Jerry and I traveled back to Oklahoma from Houston. I told him to park on the mall's west side, where she was taken. We got out and walked toward the entrance. I didn't expect to react to the planters just outside the doors. I hadn't considered them before going, thinking only about the mall's interior and the parking lot. The stuff of memory. A cold case article on Mom's death had changed what I knew though. This is where the men had been sitting, waiting, choosing which woman to take.

Jerry took a picture of me from a distance, with the entire entrance of the mall as my backdrop. I'm wearing a black leather coat and dark jeans and standing in front of a planter, looking down at the dead petunias in them. It looks like I'm in mourning, paying respect at a grave, until you see my clenched hands. I remember thinking the shriveled flowers were a metaphor—what could possibly grow there, in that square planter of concrete they sat on? I imagined taking a flame to it. Exorcising it. Wiping it from history with a sledgehammer. This beginning of her death.

Inside, the light was different, brighter, bleached, where in memory the mall had become shadow and dust. We walked in silence, Jerry staying several steps back, taking pictures of the objects I paused on. The turquoise accents were a darker shade, but the half wall around where El Chico once was and the grates and tile and benches were the same. The pay phones had been ripped out of the tiled wall; holes now pocked its surface.

"Do you remember anything?" I asked him.

"The brick wall and doors of El Chico look familiar."

I sat on one of the benches while Jerry walked around taking pictures of minute details—the ironwork of the stairs, the thickness of the wood used on the benches—until a security guard approached him. Jerry tried to explain why we were there, but taking photographs of state and federal offices, especially after the Murrah Building bombing and 9/11, alarmed the building security.

"You need to talk with the mall manager," he said, weapon on his hip.

At the manager's office, a balding man who looked friendly enough, with a goatee of white hair, welcomed us. I liked that he didn't appear formal, wearing slacks and a dress shirt but no tie or coat. We described the abduction and my need for facts, and, instead of concern or sympathy, he began showing us old photographs of the mall when it first opened and handing us photocopied blueprints, on which he and a maintenance man who had worked at the mall since the 1980s marked where the stores in 1986 were located.

"Where was the pet store?" I asked.

"Right here," they said, marking a room with an X. "It was called Petland."

"And what store had formal dresses?"

"The Jade, right here."

"Where was Streets?"

I stared at the xeroxed blueprints, now marked with the stores of my childhood, and felt no solace from the facts, no closer to the eight-year-old holding hands with her mother as they walked from store to store.

"You know, we were going to change the name here recently. To Shepherd Office Complex," the manager said. "I've gotten so many calls from people mad because we were going to drop the word *mall* from the name. And I get that. It was, after all, Oklahoma's first mall."

I listened to him and recognized pride in his voice. This was *his* space. How odd, this man who saw this place not as I or Jerry or Rolland or Dad or any of our neighbors did. How could he not understand that I wanted it torn down, covered up, not with another retail space, not with other parking lots. And not with residential areas, where a family would be watching TV right where they took her. Turn it back into a lake, I say. Make it unrecognizable, where no one can touch that ground. Silence her scream with water.

Of course, he was not the manager in 1986. The abductions didn't take place on his watch.

We thanked him and left his office.

"Well that was interesting," Jerry said, his voice flat, as we walked toward the mall's exit. I knew he meant all of it, the security, the history, the manager's enthusiasm, the maintenance man's still working there, the people who wanted its name preserved.

"It was," I said as an automatic response, focusing on the parking lot outside. Even though Jerry's over six feet tall and with shoulders so broad people ask if he plays professional football or hockey, and even though I knew he would unlock the car door with his key fob, saving precious time, and open and close the passenger door for me so I spent no moment on the concrete without him next to me, I still, as I stepped through the glass doors, grabbed his hand and clenched his middle two fingers. Nothing could make me forget my female body, small like my mother's, even smaller next to a man like Jerry.

Even now, when I live fourteen hundred miles away on the East Coast, I feel compelled to return. I consider where the threshold is, the dividing line between trying to gain some understanding about grief, trying to pull back a memory from the shrinking universe, the black hole, and self-flogging because I'm addicted to the pain, flesh ripped open to say, *I love you, do you see how much I love you?*

But maybe I'll always be the daughter, retracing her final footsteps to the car, seeing just how close I can get.

Cleaving To

PART III

✦

I WAS TWELVE WHEN I STARTED WRITING POEMS ABOUT MY
mother, in a notebook with "Robby is Scum" and "I LoveD Matt" on
the cover. I should confess, sometimes I plagiarized. I plagiarized songs
like "Remember the Feeling" by Chicago. I wonder if I changed the lines
just enough to make them mine, a translation of a translation. Maybe,
in grief, it doesn't matter if the language isn't true or our own.

But I wrote original poems too, ones no pop band would ever write,
like the one I titled "So Many Questions":

> We were a whole lot alike, and we looked very much the same.
> We had the same interests, and had the same middle name.
> Since we were so much the same, will I also die of crime?
> Will I not see my kids grow up, and will I not live for a long time?
> Will I be taken, into the hands of someone I don't know?
> Will I be forced to go somewhere, somewhere I don't want to go?

It shocks me now. I hear the girl's story as if it weren't my own, and
I ache for her. Because I don't want to reconcile a child and the fear of
being murdered.

I notice how she wrote "We . . . had the same middle name," in past
tense, as if her mother's death implied hers too.

I still don't know the grammar of death.

"I *have* the same middle name" plus "she *had* the same middle name" equals "we . . ."? What tense do you use when one of the *we*'s goes on living?

I feel so far away from that twelve-year-old girl, who believed she would have children, a son and a daughter, just like her mother did. I hear her certainty of a bond between them, "We had the same interests"; the interests she means, I'm sure, are crafts, waterskiing, and eating chocolate, the things important to a child. I envy the closeness she feels to the mother who's gone.

I have my mother's features; even at twelve, I had her long face, her thin frame. I grew up wondering if the men would recognize me, if they'd search for the girl who looks like the woman they killed. I was afraid they'd grab me at my house before I walked in the door or follow us to a mall, snatching me when Dad wasn't looking. They'd whisper in my ear, "You look just like your mother, just as pretty."

In high school, as I became more aware of my body and of sex, I asked Dad if Mom had been raped.

All I remember is his voice, low and heavy, as he answered, "Probably."

The bunny in the grass, seeing the dogs and then running, running until her little heart burst, started to disappear with that *probably*.

In its place another story, written when I was fifteen:

> A breeze chills my body, as I step out of my car. Faint
> footsteps of rubber-soled shoes tingle my eardrums.
> I turn to find the source. Two strange faces grab my
> body, while placing a cold, damp rag over my eyes. As
> they throw me into the back seat, my head crashes into
> the paneling of metal, causing me to black out.
> Upon awakening, I strain to lift my eyes, but the
> rag clamps them shut. Cold numbness tingles my

appendages, making me realize that they have been tied together. As I struggle to free myself, the ropes, tight and stiff, burn against my skin. A wetness, cool and salty, streaks down my cheek. Sweat pours from every pore in my body, causing goosebumps to prickle me. Muffled voices whisper quiet words. Every muscle I have feels the stinging, sharp pains.

Lifted by unfamiliar hands, my body feels limp. Soft grass cushions my aching body, as they lay me down. A faint click sends nerves chilling through my body. With every muscle tense, a sound like a firecracker booms. My pain is relieved.

My creative writing teacher, Cramer, gave me a forty-nine out of fifty and wrote "Keeper" on the top of the page and on the bottom, "Almost too good, Kristine." It had been Cramer who, after I had turned in the first assignment—a personal narrative about the morning Dad told us men had abducted her—had asked me to stay after class. "You weren't supposed to write fiction," she had said. What did she think then, seeing my *I* transformed into the woman in the field, watching my drafts become more focused on violence, as if the versions mapped what it's like to grow up as a woman? And is it fear I hear in her "Almost too good"?

Two men grab her. One of them says, "Be still, bitch!" as she bites a hand and kicks to break free. She screams. They force her into the back seat of a car. They drive to a secluded area. It's night. Headlights and fog. They drag her across dirt. He ties her to a tree by her bound hands. Her arms taut above her head. Her lip bloody. Her eye black. A gash on her right cheek.

This is not my mother.

Or a story I created.

She breathes heavily. Her long brown hair tangled, stuck to her skin with sweat. He tears her shirt with his hands. He rips off her skirt to show her black panties. He runs his finger down the side of her face and whispers in her ear, "I'll tell you what I'll do. I'll leave you tied up here naked. First it'll just be the bugs eating at you. One day, maybe two. That sun's going to cook you. And animals . . . they'll pick up your stink. They're going to come looking for something to eat."

This could be my mother.

It doesn't matter that the woman is Sandra Bullock in the 1996 movie *A Time to Kill*. Or that she's surrounded by thirteen members of the Ku Klux Klan or that the tree is part of a wooded area rather than the flat plains of Sayre. It doesn't matter that her hands are tied above her head and not behind her back. It does matter, though, that she was cut down from the tree to heal in a hospital bed; the movie is, after all, fiction.

I watched the film in my dorm room my freshman year of college. I was alone that night when I heard Kiefer Sutherland say "pick up your stink" as a precise translation of "exposed to elements." I thought of ants scrambling over the sweet nectar of a peach, clumps of hair strewn across a field, the woman's stench smeared on the tree.

Only then did I realize my father had lied to me. She wasn't sleeping, her clothes wrinkled but unsoiled, her eyelids softly closed, eyelashes interlocked like the hands of lovers, her nails dry, cracked, but clean, her skin white from winter and early spring, her exposed earlobe soft like a petal and nearly as pink. Of course. What else could I expect but a lie? My father, at forty-three, wife murdered just two weeks before, looking down at his eight-year-old daughter who asks the impossible question—Why can't I open the casket? Why can't I see?

If I were to accuse him now, he'd say it wasn't a lie, that she *could have* looked like she was sleeping, that he never identified her body to know its *exact* condition, but still he knew she wore no clothes—the coroner told him there would be no reason to dress her—and that a dead body won't look like a body after a week outdoors, that she could be identified only by her teeth.

I had accepted it. Accepted it for years. Long after maturity and experience should tell me otherwise, the way we take things in our childhood at face value. He could no longer water it down, disguise the horror behind "she was in nature for about a week." Even *decomposed* no longer felt accurate.

The sentence became stripped down and real: Animals ate my mother.

I thought of ants and whether a dead body responds to their stings, of raccoons and their claws. I thought of roadkill, rabbit fur in the breeze, a beak deep in sinews, how the hawk hesitates to move, even as a car approaches at seventy miles per hour. He has claimed the torn muscle. I thought of her body being circled by coyotes, how birds would fight over the fluid of her eyes. And for the first time I wanted something of it. To fight for what I remembered the most: her fingers, her chewed, cracked nails. If her body wasn't intact, if I couldn't believe in a peaceful death, then I wanted a piece to guard and keep, to be able to say, *This is mine.*

In May 1999, when I was a junior in college, Rolland asked *The Daily Oklahoman* to write an article about my mother's case and how we hoped the Oklahoma State Bureau of Investigation (OSBI) would perform DNA testing to confirm or deny Ricky Martin and Travis McGuire as the killers.

In the May 2 *Sunday Oklahoman*, Rolland says, "The detectives have told us they've ran down every other lead they have . . . This is it. It either points to them (the suspects) or it doesn't. If it doesn't, we can put behind any hope of prosecuting anybody. To us, it's closure either way."

We were naive then, thinking of hope and closure as simple things.

The story worked though. Several months after the article appeared, the OSBI tested for DNA on items in the car.

I was sitting on the couch in my college boyfriend's room—bunk beds, posters of Coors Light on the walls, *8 Seconds* and porn on VHS—when Rolland called. My boyfriend handed me the phone, both of us uncomfortable because Rolland had never called there before.

"Hey, Goof," he said.

"What's wrong?"

"Sorry for calling you there." His voice was weary. "But I have the DNA results and I want someone to be with you after you hang up the phone."

He told me the DNA didn't match Travis McGuire or Ricky Martin or anyone else in Oklahoma's database. Just like that, the assurances from the police, who'd told us, for years, they were likely the killers, disappeared. It wasn't as if anything had changed, and yet everything had. I could no longer hold on to the comfort, however tenuous it was, in thinking we'd eventually have enough evidence against them. Then Rolland said he had received a report noting the specific pieces of evidence that were tested.

"Do you want to know?" he asked.

I knew it had to hurt because he was asking, but I didn't want him to know more than I did. And I didn't want him to endure that pain alone.

"Yes," I said.

He told me there was a male's DNA on cigarette butts and a Pepsi can, Mom's DNA from blood samples, and a mixture of a male's and Mom's DNA in a semen sample. I began to shake, my hands, my arms, my breath all tremoring. My boyfriend placed his hand on my shoulder while I covered the receiver and cried.

Rolland then said the words going through my mind: "I always figured she was raped, but the semen cells confirmed it. It destroys any possibility of imagining otherwise."

I tell myself not to go there again. Not to see the fist hitting her temple, the punch of a knuckle against muscle, the bruises, blue and immediate.

I tell myself I won't sleep if I do this, the muscles in my legs and shoulders tensing. Don't feel her hands go dead and the cramping of her shoulders, don't hear her hips crack when her legs are forced open.

I know Rolland imagined what happened, but I don't think he ever saw it in the first person. Or wished for it to have happened to him.

Don't jerk from the cigarette burning her cheek. Don't hear the words *bitch, cunt, whore*. Don't feel the jaw stretch wide, the ram against tonsils. Don't gag.

It's nearly impossible to stop the images and sounds once you start down this path.

Don't watch her look out the window to see her house as the car passes exit #138 on I-40. Don't hear the silence while the men rest or listen when she says she should not have gone to the mall, that she should have known better, why did she go.

Another woman says she wants to know what happened to her murdered mother so she can prove to herself she can survive each time, but that doesn't feel right to me; something else is here.

Don't say she thinks of her family, hoping her son won't clench his pain, concealing it in an underground pocket, that her husband will find someone else to love, that her daughter won't ever want this.

Don't watch the men turn onto an isolated road and park. Don't watch her kick and fight to stay in the car because she knows it's safer than the field.

What comes to me is this: I don't want Mom to be in the field with no one there to bear witness or to feel what she felt. I don't want her to suffer alone.

Maybe I'll search for alleys with no lamplight, keys held as I was taught—one slipped between each finger, a set of claws—though I know I will drop them when the forearm chokes me, my hand flexed flat, the clink on pavement.

I won't reach for the eyes, no quick stab to snap the larynx, and when I scream, the pitch will be an echo waiting years to be heard.

Maybe I'll crawl into the back seat of a car, vinyl slick against my skin. Maybe I'll ask for a beer to appease my thirst.

No matter the route, interstate or highway or back roads of dry red dirt, I'll tell them to find the abandoned oil field, its pumping units frozen in a stalemate memory, and demand for my hands to be bound behind my back.

Then with my shirt ripped open, shredded threads, bra pushed up around my neck, the night can be in déjà vu, the stars recounting each curse. Let every tear and every bruise swell with knowing.

Don't listen to us call out for the ones we love. Don't think we're praying for them to sleep, to play as they always played. Don't hear us plead that daughters never know just how badly we hurt.

There's a gorgeous line from Mark Doty's *Heaven's Coast*, a memoir on grief and losing his partner to AIDS: "I think that when people die they make those around them feel something like they felt; that may be the dying's first legacy to us." He goes on to say, "I've had friends who died in confusion or rage or terror, and the living who knew them felt, then, confusion or rage or terror."

It isn't as if Mom had cancer like her own mother, who gifted us with acceptance when she let us gently pull the hair from her scalp. "It doesn't hurt, and it's just going to fall out anyway," she had said. It isn't as if Mom's words jumbled like her father's, even before they took a piece of his brain, leaving everyone around him confused. It isn't as if Mom aged into poor health, like my father, her lungs and her hearing and her legs and her hips deteriorating, little by little, our pain parceled out over a decade.

What is the legacy of the ones gone missing? Is it to keep searching, through evidence and facts and memories and stories, filling in gaps with details we've imagined or stolen or experienced ourselves?

What is the legacy for the deaths we cannot know?

Truly Innocent Victim

◆

I'M NINE, AND MY FRIEND AND I HAVE TAKEN A BREAK FROM pretending we're cheerleaders, splitting the time each of us gets to play with one metallic silver pom-pom—it sparkles in the sun and rustles like leaves. We've left the pom-pom on the driveway and now we're picking blooms from the honeysuckle bush, grown tall, concealing half of the front windows of my neighbor's house.

Lee, my neighbor's son, is home from college. He comes outside and shows us a trick with the honeysuckle, how you pick a bloom and pinch its green base and slowly, slowly pull out its thread and then, there, at the end, a drop of nectar to taste, sweet, so sweet. My friend and I pull out thread after thread, drop after drop, until the grass in front of the bush is speckled with white blooms.

"Now twirl me," I say, with my hands fluttering toward Lee. This is, after all, the reason I love when he's home. He laughs and takes my hands in his and then starts spinning, fast, so fast, my body like a helicopter's propeller, my feet somewhere out in space, he spins me around and around until I'm dizzy and laughing and screaming and flying. Already I have a crush on him, his strong hands holding on to mine, keeping me tethered to the earth.

My babysitter's mother made me a Halloween costume to wear to school: a poodle skirt, a petticoat, and a turquoise shirt that buttoned up the back. I twirled around in my skirt, layers of white netting thinning out as

I spun. In my elementary classroom during our free time, a boy sprawled out on the floor, reading a comic book. He wasn't my boyfriend, but he wanted to be. When I stepped over him to get to the teacher's desk, he smiled, because he could almost see up my skirt to glimpse my white panties with tiny rainbows on them. My skirt billowed and swooshed as I walked. I stepped over him to sharpen my pencil across the room. I stepped over him to get to the cubbyhole. I stepped over him to get a book from the shelf. I knew the petticoat, with all that white, would hide me. How is it that by nine years old, I had learned the art of the tease, though I didn't yet know what sex was really, only that the boy wasn't supposed to look and I wasn't supposed to show? Why is it I felt such power then, stepping over him in my petticoat, like Scarlett O'Hara with her shoulders showing, saying "I wore this silly old dress for you," in a movie I watched with my friend while we ate no-bake cookies we had made? Though I was years from articulating what I felt then, I wasn't that different from women in college, who, when interviewed for a study on sexual teasing and consent, said they tease to feel powerful and in control, to feel attractive and desired, where more men in college said they tease to see just how far they could take it. What power can this possibly be, when it's connected to wanting to be desired, when the need for control shows how little we actually have it? Why is it I couldn't see the tease didn't work out for Scarlett, pining for men who say they don't give a damn? Instead I liked what I saw in the boy's eyes, the way he grinned. How he stayed on his back, waiting for what I would not give.

By the time I entered high school, Lee's mother had moved out of the house next door, and Lee and two of his friends, Brandon and Richard, moved in. They liked to drink Bud Light and hang out in their driveway whenever they were finished with work. Brandon worked for grocery stores, so if a friend dropped me off after a movie or shopping, he'd motion for me to come over and take the free Oreos and crackers he had in the trunk of his car.

I liked hanging out with the guys in the yard. I also liked to lay out in my driveway in my pink velvet bikini or wash Dad's Bonneville to get a good tan. When one of them stepped outside, I'd bend over for cleavage, what little cleavage I had, and let the soap run down my thighs, something I learned from the posters selling beer that had hung in Rolland's bedroom. I'd suck in my stomach, even though I was already thin, and smile when one of them would walk over and ask, "Am I next?"

Lee was the one I knew best, since his mom had lived for years in that house. I recall Dad telling me a story of how Lee's stepfather, drunk one night and standing in the backyard, pointed a gun at my mother, when she emerged from our house, though later Dad would say he doesn't remember this. "He just liked to get drunk and shoot moles in the yard," he said, but why would I remember a gun aimed at her body, if Dad had not told me this?

Lee was short and muscular, with full light-brown hair, styled with pomade. He wore tight Gold's Gym T-shirts and cargo shorts on weekends when he mountain biked or took his boat to the lake. I had had a crush on him since middle school, back when my friend and I would watch him mow his lawn, his shirt off, his chest muscles sculpted like the men's in the Chippendales posters that hung on my bedroom wall.

I have a photograph of a boy I went out with when I was middle school; he's standing in my bedroom next to the calendars and posters, the boy's smooth body dwarfed by the man on a workout bench, whose dark chest hair and pecs peek out of his tank top. I think about how Dad wrapped my birthday present in beefcake wrapping paper when I turned thirteen and of the posters Rolland once had in his room, like Samantha Fox, her white dress falling down, how she crossed her arms to squish her breasts together. The men in my posters weren't famous like Fox; the men could have been living next door.

Lee had been a car salesman and then a salesman for running boards for trucks. He worked from home, so I'd see him more often, especially during the summer days when I was at home and Dad at work.

My senior year was about to begin, and we had been flirting for weeks, me standing in front of his house where the honeysuckle bushes once were, my hands in the back pockets of my jeans.

On a hot August afternoon, he took me to used-car dealerships because I needed a car for my senior year. We bypassed the usual hassles and pitches because everyone knew him. I stood to the side of cars and watched him bend over and check engines and ask about scratches and gas mileage and tires and discounts. I liked that he was taking care of me. We sat in a Camry, me in the driver's seat, him in the passenger seat, me studying the clutch and just where to put my feet.

"But I don't know how to drive a standard," I said.

"It's not hard to learn. I could even teach you."

I looked at him and grinned. "So you're saying you can teach me how to handle a stick?"

"I could definitely teach you that," he laughed.

A salesman poked his head into car and asked how we were doing.

"Fine," I said. "I'll need to come back later tonight with my father, so we can look at it again."

Back at Lee's house, as we waited for my father to get home from work, I sat facing Lee on his couch, resting my elbow on the back cushion and leaning my head against my hand. I remember my body position as deliberate; I wanted to appear casual and attentive and open. I was seventeen, and somewhere I had learned a tilted, lowered head and eye contact were seductive.

He sat next to me, his knee nearly touching mine. I noticed tiny scars along his jaw and wondered if they were from years of shaving. A nick here. A nick there. A few gray hairs in his sideburns glistened in the afternoon sun that shone through his front porch window. He was sexy in the way *People* magazine's Sexiest Men Alive were—older but not old, men in their thirties and forties, like Richard Gere and George Clooney, men with thick hair sprinkled with gray, with laugh lines, with small wrinkles on the backs of their hands.

He said, "Do you ever think of me?" and I answered, "Of course," with a slight shoulder shrug, as if I were not afraid of what the question could lead to.

When he ran his fingers through my hair, then held it back and kissed my neck just below the hairline, my flesh goose-pimpled in one sweeping wave down my body. He kissed my ear, my jaw, my lips. Slow. And with no hesitation. I liked how he held my head so secure in his hand.

He didn't feel wrong the way my teacher, my doctor, my manager, and my other neighbor did. Those were old men, bald men, men with wives and children, men with grandchildren even, men who were supposed to look after me.

Lee kissing me felt wrong in the most exciting of ways; it was sexy and salacious and taboo.

None of my high school friends were dating men who threw parties full of gorgeous women in their twenties and thirties or men who owned their own boats, their own Harleys.

His hands were tugging on my hips, pulling me into him, his hands were grasping my shoulders, grasping my head, I could smell his Obsession when I kissed him back, and I remember thinking, *I should tell him to stop, I don't want to get pregnant, I won't know whose it is.* I remember thinking he had been with many women, that the pill could sometimes fail, but never in my life would I have asked him if he had a condom. Never would I risk interrupting or ruining his desire.

I was afraid of what it would mean if we had sex—it would mean I was a whore. Even though I had only ever been with my high school boyfriend, *whore* kept reverberating in my mind. I didn't grow up going to church, but I still breathed in and internalized its language, its judgment.

I remember thinking I should say, *I can't,* but then he took off my shirt and bra and paused to admire my breasts. This man who had dated so many women. Who had seen so many breasts. When he moaned, it made me think mine must not have been as ugly or as young as I had feared.

"I want you," I said.

We had sex on the floor in front of his couch.

Later that evening, Dad and I met Lee at the dealership to buy the Camry. I worried about smiling too much, but Lee performed well by focusing on the car, pointing out to Dad the touched-up scratches on the air dam. They talked as if I weren't there, inspecting the engine, the radio, the tread, then remarking about Lee's Celica, the one he sold to Rolland for his first car, how it lasted forever. "That was a great car," each said with nostalgia, a history shared between them. I remember Dad thanking Lee for getting the commission removed and then shaking Lee's hand, thumb and fingers gripped in this sign of respect among men. Dad was probably thinking, as I was, *Here is a man who looks out for us.*

Lee is beautiful, don't you think?

He's much too old for you.

Can you see how, when he skis, his body laid out, pulling against the boat, when he cuts across the water, across the wake, when the spray from his slalom arcs left and right, high into the air like a crashing wave, he moves like a work of art?

He just wants to fuck you so he feels virile and young.

Can you see how his arms are so strong, when he grips the rope with only one hand, his body at a thirty-degree angle with the water, his hip just inches from its surface? I like when those arms hold me, his hand gripped around my shoulder.

He likes that your tits are firmer than women's his own age, still developing.

Can you see the couple of gray whiskers on his face? How his skin, just next to his ear, is looser than a high school boy's? There's something so sexy about those tiny folds of skin. They're soft and tender, exposed next to the stubble.

He'll never revere the vulnerable parts of your body the way you do his.

Can you see how nicely his hand rests on my hip as he sleeps?

No, but I can see how he shoves you against the wall with those
hands.

Do you remember how he held the honeysuckle to my lips? I was nine
then, when he showed me the beauty of that drop of nectar, how it
caught the light in a single spark.

I remember how he liked to watch you suck.

Did you see the picture his sister decoupaged for him? A collage of photographs of all the women he has dated. At its center, a photograph of
him and me, kissing in a hotel room. He hung it in the entryway of his
house. It makes me think he loved me the most.

You were no doubt his greatest trophy.

He moves like art on the water.

You keep saying that.

He begins on his back, his feet wrapped around the rope while the boat
is idling; then the boat takes off at full throttle and he rides the water
on his back, *on his back*, for minutes, as he waits for the boat to reach
top speed, and all you can see is a fury of splash and spray until the wake
thins out to a line and he pops up, so quick, so sudden, and he skis the
water with his bare feet.

What does it mean that you love him the most when he's seventy
feet away from you?

On a warm night when Lee was out of town on business, driving running boards to a dealership in Kansas, his roommate Richard took me
to a bar, three years before I should have been at one. For weeks, Richard had been running his hand down my thigh when Lee left the room,
or Richard would suggest I'd ride with him on his Sea-Doo while Lee
pulled skiers on the other side of the lake.

I think about how good and terrifying that danger felt, Richard
stopping the Sea-Doo in an isolated and empty cove, how I unwrapped
my arms from around his chest and he'd twist to kiss me, deep and

hard, with the force of a river that's been held back. How powerful I felt then, his desire for me strong enough to risk his friendship with Lee, strong enough to break them apart. I'm reminded of the dam at Broken Bow Lake, how each morning you hear a siren before they open the gates, how quickly the water rises in the river, how fiercely it flows. Pitted against each other, Lee's and Richard's desires were dangerous the way an eddy line can be. Sometimes I think I just brushed the downward spirals, the current mere inches from where I was standing; other times I think, no, you were pulled under, tumbling in the dark depths of water.

Richard was just shy of thirty and wasn't as well-built as Lee, but I liked his pronounced jaw, how he wore suits like my father's and carried a briefcase of mutual funds, that briefcase its own type of power.

It's hard for me to understand the attraction Richard felt for me though. I had just been to my prom, had just given my valedictorian speech, and was busy carhopping at the nearby Sonic drive-in, shielding ice cream cones from the wind with my jacket, like so many other teenagers, while he was educating adults on how to plan for their retirements. I can't understand the shift from talking *net asset values* and *securities* and *capital gain distributions* to taking a teenaged girl to a bar with an outdoor deck and a rowdy crowd. I can't remember or even imagine what we talked about then. Maybe newly released films we had seen, like *Sabrina, While You Were Sleeping, First Knight, The Bridges of Madison County,* or *The English Patient,* all films where one woman is torn between two men.

Harleys lined the parking lot of the bar. I wore a red satin crop top, my stomach flat and smooth. Richard asked me what I wanted to drink, and I said a vodka collins, the drink Dad always said I would like, when I was old enough to go to bars, because it was sweet and sour enough to hide the taste of the alcohol. On my second drink, my stomach burned, my neck dampening with sweat.

Richard leaned over and said, "Go to the bathroom and take off your bra."

Married grown men, like my teachers or managers, had all trembled when they stepped beyond speech to touch me, their fingertips shaking, the muscles around their mouths twitching, their bodies betraying them, revealing to us both that their touch was wrong. But neither Lee nor Richard ever quivered, and I was drawn to the certainty of their bodies and their speech, how they spoke and grasped and groped without flinching.

I think now of the men at Shepherd Mall, waiting in the parking lot for a woman like my mother, how I doubt their fingers shook when they grabbed her.

I didn't go to the bathroom like Richard instructed. Instead, I unfastened my bra at the table and pulled the straps out the sleeves, one at a time, and then reached down the front of my shirt to draw out the red lace, as if to say, *I'm no amateur, you know.*

But I was. I was a girl playing the role of what I thought a thirty-year-old woman, perhaps a colleague of his at the investment firm, would be like: confident, sexual, secure in her body and her desire. I wonder which part of my body shuddered and betrayed me in that moment; maybe it was my smirk, a little girlish, or maybe it was the red lace demi-cup from Victoria's Secret, bought to appear like an Angel.

I was dancing at our table, with Richard behind me, grinding against my backside. He turned me to face the bikers, one in particular—a man in his late forties, with long hair and black chaps, who had been watching me and ignoring his date dancing by the stage. Richard reached around me, unbuttoned my shirt, and slowly spread it open.

He pointed his finger at my body, as if to say, *Do you see what I get to fuck?*

The biker stared at my breasts as I kept dancing. I loved how he watched me and not his date. I loved the way he smiled and shook his head, how his lips looked wet.

Years of watching the boys in my school turn and talk and grin when girls like Jen Maclimore walked into the classroom, her breasts far larger and more developed than mine ever would be, were momentarily erased with Richard's pride and this craving, my firm and small breasts, on display in the hot humid air.

When Richard went to the restroom, the biker called me over with his finger.

"You're *amazing*," he said, as he handed me a slip of paper with his number on it. "I'd like to take you for a ride sometime."

I didn't see it as a man giving a teenaged girl his number. Or as a man sneaking his number to another man's date. Or a man giving his number to a girl when his own date is dancing by a stage. A man telling a teenaged girl, I'd like to take you *for* a ride sometime, not *on* a ride sometime. None of that mattered then. Only that men and not boys were amazed by the sight of me. It's what I ached for, that feeling that my body was the gates of the dam, in control of the water's course. If only someone had shown me what I see now: Richard reaching around me, unbuttoning, how it was his fingers and not mine pulling open the gates.

I wore a sky-blue shirt dress, buttoned up the front, and Steve Madden sandals with a chunky heel, my feet caged in twenty strips of leather. I had recently purchased both in New York when my father let me skip school to join him on a business trip.

I think of that dress whenever I remember that night. My sky-blue dress with pastel flowers, how proud I was to own it, a dress bought in SoHo, and how proud I was for knowing SoHo meant "south of Houston" and that Houston was not pronounced like the city in Texas.

Lee was out of town again, and Richard wanted to take me out on what I thought would be a date. I couldn't just walk next door and get in his Land Rover though, not when my father was home, so Richard suggested I drive my car on a dirt road behind Circle K, to a field, half a mile from our houses.

I wasn't thinking of my car abandoned in a field, of how a cop or someone might travel that dirt, see my car deserted, and call it in. I wasn't thinking of a phone call to my father, the familiar terror when a policeman asks if he's the owner of a 1991 Camry, of the hours he'd spend panicked that his daughter, like his wife, had been abducted and killed.

I'm livid at myself for risking that. For being so wrapped up in going out with man who carried a briefcase.

My shirt dress. Richard's SUV and collared shirts and suits.

I can almost see the flowers on my dress. I search for a type—they weren't roses, weren't lilies, they may have been peonies—as if the flowers matter.

I want to see the dress again. Sky-blue, buttoned up the front.

Richard took me to a bar after we abandoned my car. A bar in some other part of Oklahoma City, where no one he knew would be, where only a couple patrons sat in a dark corner in the back.

We shot pool, and I made hand job gestures with the cue in my hands. He told me I like a big stick; I used the word *shaft*.

It's hard to imagine worse dialogue and actions than this, so full of porn clichés, but I suppose that's the only language we had for a relationship like ours.

I racked the balls; he ordered vodka for us both.

I loved that with my heels on, my eyes were level with his jaw, chiseled like a cliff. Lee never liked it when I wore heels. He'd always tell me to change into flats.

"We can go to a friend's house nearby," Richard said. "He won't be home. I have a surprise to give you."

The first time I wrote about this night, I was in graduate school. For weeks, I couldn't eat, couldn't sleep, and when I did, I saw Richard in my dreams. I think now of that writing as a purging from a virus, the sweat on your neck, the swallowing. How you know it's coming and you cannot stop it, how every fiber and every cell tightens into constrictor knots. I purged the story and what emerged was a girl a reader could leer at. "I feel like a voyeur," a classmate said when he read that version of the story.

But how can I write the story differently, when I haven't been trained to gaze at anything but my own body?

My sky-blue shirt dress with pastel peonies. How short it was.

Every time I write what happened, my sentences disintegrate into subject and verb and object: *We walked into the house. Richard carried a brown paper sack.* Memory gets stripped down to actions, rather than the texture of experience, how it felt when I sat down on the couch and Richard kneeled in front of me, how it felt when he pulled a box from the sack, two steel balls connected with an electrical cord, wrapped in packaging like a curling iron would be, what I thought when he said, "I bought this for you," or how I felt when he unbuttoned my shirtdress, opened it like a robe.

It's only when I lean back in a chair, spread my legs, and imagine a man on his knees between them, that I begin to remember.

How cold the balls were when he pushed them inside me, how heavy the cord hung. How Richard held in his hands the controller at the other end of the cord.

I'd never used a sex toy before, and I remember thinking, *No toy should ever feel like ice. Or make you feel like an appliance.*

I had loved Richard kissing me when he shouldn't, those moments in the coves of lakes. Those moments when he'd bite me with the intention to bruise, a way of claiming my body when Lee was in the other room. I loved the pursuit, the foreplay, brief seconds of touching when nothing more could happen. I loved being the body he couldn't fully have.

But I had said yes to the investor with a briefcase and Land Rover. I had drunk the vodka collins and stroked the pool cue, both of us smirking. I had watched his palm grip the cue harder because we were in public and he couldn't touch me as he wanted to.

Though I could not have expressed this then, I had learned it wasn't fair to tease a man and offer nothing in return. But only in the tease did I feel valuable and strong.

I understood that Richard had brought me to his friend's house for this. This was the price of feeling desired, the transaction that patriarchy teaches us all to expect.

Even if he had asked me, *Do you want this*, I would have answered yes. Because no would mean *are you sure*, no would mean *what the hell*, would mean *you're such a fucking bitch*, would mean *find your own way home then*.

I know this now, and I knew it then, in my body, in the fear it gripped on to. I think of the weight on my toes, as I kept my legs braced, of the pressure on the pads of my feet, how my body drove into the earth everything I could not do or say. If I said no to the balls being pushed inside, the rejection would be mine, not his, and what worth would I have as a girl trying to find her way back home?

So I arched and squirmed and moaned. This was what I owed him, not just sex but a performance. *Look how good your toy makes me feel*, my body was supposed to say, but the performance felt ridiculous with a cord protruding from my vagina. So I reached forward, kissed him, and said, "I'd rather have *you* inside me."

It wasn't a lie. I hated the steel vibrating inside me, how my body swallowed its sound. I hated how clinical it all felt, him sitting with a controller in his hands, studying my responses from a distance.

I'd rather have you inside me. I want to stop the story there.

I don't want to be in this body anymore, to remember its history.

Not when he presses off and then pulls on the cord, pulls harder and harder, as if in a tug-of-war with her body. Her muscles gripping the balls without her wanting them to, his fingers gripping the electrical rope. Her vagina feels like a Chinese finger puzzle, with no side giving way. Until the snap. His body falling back. His hands holding one ball and a broken cord, the other ball staying inside her.

It's hard to believe the timing still, how in the silence of the shock, both of them staring at the severed cord in Richard's hands, his friend came home.

They ran to the bathroom, her sky-blue shirtdress open like a robe.

In fiction, the scene would be comical. Until you paid attention to her dress.

If I reenter that bathroom, it's a panicked animal I see, a girl's nails and fingers clenching a grown man's shoulders. She isn't in a corner, she's on the toilet, but that's the texture of it—a rabbit in a corner of a room that's flooding, it keeps jumping and jumping, desperate to find any tiny ledge to grip on to.

"You've got to relax," he says, as if a drowning bunny can stop her own terror. He's trying to pry open her body like a fist, but his fingers keep slipping.

She's rocking and hunching forward, her arms wrapped around her stomach as if it were cramping, she's imagining a room full of doctors and nurses, all of them laughing, all of them telling the story for years of that woman with a steel ball inside her.

Though maybe they would have seen a panicked kid and the adult man who brought her in and they would have been tender with her instead.

I can't help but wonder how many women enter emergency rooms with something lodged inside them. For the aunt of one of my boyfriends, it was a banana her husband used. I wanted to know but never asked, peeled or unpeeled, because I couldn't understand either one, but now I think, why does that even matter? A woman suffered the humiliation and trauma of a banana stuck inside her. And why is it that men, even men we love, think it's fun to shove objects inside us?

"I don't know what to do," Richard says, exasperated.

She doesn't know either. But she asks him to leave her alone in the bathroom.

She keeps rocking and clenching and praying to someone or something, *Please, please, please get me out of this, please get it out, please,* her fingers pushing inside, spreading, slipping across the steel. She's begging for her mother to help.

I think now of the histories of our bodies, of what my mother may have known in her bones, what her muscles may have held on to. I think of how she was hemorrhaging during her pregnancies, how much she may have gripped to keep me in her womb. I want her to have been in that bathroom, her hands and chewed nails gentle on my quaking shoulders. To have her voice, lost within a year of her death, telling me softly that it will be okay, to breathe until my muscles go slack. To hear her say, *Your body is strong, it can hold on to what it wants to and can push when you need it to.*

But finally, in the quiet, with just my body in that fluorescent light, I felt the instinct to push. To use muscles in a new way. The metal ball slid down slowly, easy and smooth, gliding into the palm of my hand. I clutched the still-warm steel and whispered, "Thank you, thank you, thank you," to God if there is one, to Mom if she had been there, to my body for knowing what to do.

I had chills from all the sweating, my hair pasted to my neck. I stood up from the toilet and stared in the mirror. "Calm down," I said. "Breathe," I said, as I wiped the mascara smeared under my eyes and lifted the hair from my neck. I buttoned my shirtdress back up, with flowers like peonies.

When I opened the bathroom door and stepped out into the living room, Richard and his friend were on the couch, bottles of beer in their hands. I remember they were laughing.

And I felt ashamed of the panic I had displayed. A woman Richard's age would have known how to push out a sex toy, how not to break it.

Richard wanted me to drink some more, so he gave me his beer.

I hated beer. But I guzzled it to forget the girl whose body trembled.

He told his friend to turn the stereo on.

"Why don't you strip for us?" he said.

I don't remember what I felt, having Richard say this so soon after I emerged from the bathroom. I see the memory in third person, as if I'm sitting next to Richard and his friend on the couch. I think now of the trauma the girl has just gone through, of how she's already pushed the pain and fear aside, of how she doesn't know how to say *I can't* or *I won't*

do that for you. I'm sitting on the couch, afraid to hear her say this, afraid
of how the men next to me will respond if she tells them no and *I want
you to take me home.*

Her shirtdress is pasted between her shoulder blades from sweat.
It's sky-blue with pastel flowers, it's short, it's made from cheap polyester.

It's a dress of a teenaged girl.

I must leave the couch. I can't sit here with adult men and watch her
strip, this teenaged girl in a teenager's dress. Who can't hear the echoes
of her mother.

Sometimes it's easier to hold on to the first person, to the past
tense, to those moments where I felt I had some control, swaying when I
wanted to, crouching low without being told to. I stood in front of them
and danced, taking my time with the buttons of my dress. I remember
being afraid they'd notice my cellulite. But now I think about how I was
five foot eight and weighed 115 pounds, how I had freckles rather than
age spots on my skin.

I walked over to Richard and straddled one of his legs. I bent over,
then pulled away when his mouth opened. I rubbed my thigh against
his hand, then pulled away when his fingers moved. I loved watching his
hand reach out for me, my body no longer failing.

If only I could pause those seconds when I possess what a man
wants but cannot have. If only I could button up my dress, leave the
house, take my own car home rather than have it abandoned in a field.
If only I could hold on to his hunger.

That's the word I keep thinking of when I remember how Richard's
mouth followed mine when I pulled away. And maybe it's because he
resented this hunger that he wanted to see how far up a longneck can go.

I didn't understand, until that moment, how the origin of *vagina*
could mean *sheath.* Because a bottle is concave, the skin tries to follow
the contours, like a cloth of a Molotov cocktail. The skin gets pulled.
The skin splits open.

Richard took a sip from his beer, then pressed the glass to her
mouth. "Here," he said. "Taste yourself."

I remember the night as snapshots without transitions—how or when they took off their shoes or their clothes, if they undressed at the same time. I want to know what was in the in-between, between the moment Richard said *Now lie on the ground and touch yourself* and when my shins were flat on the couch. I can say what it felt like to be in my body. I feel the objects acutely still, that hard floor, the cold steel, the solid and unforgiving bottles, but I have no memory of what their bodies looked like, how they moved, what kind of force they used. I remember how Richard enjoyed bruising and think something in me must have burned the snapshots of their touch.

Then the girl's on the ground, her knees becoming raw, Richard behind her, his friend in front. She's trying to synchronize, she's trying not to gag or bite down, trying not to show how much it hurts. Whatever power she had felt in their wanting is gone.

Richard's friend loses his erection.

She thinks, *My body is too ugly, too fat, too young, too small, too loose, too much like a child's.*

But then Richard says, "What the fuck is your problem? You go limp with a woman like this in front of you?"

Woman—not *girl.*

I like his rage, the defense of my body.

"A woman like this," he said.

I want to hear it again and again.

His friend is trying to get it back, skin through fist, Richard is rolling me over to finish, and I just keep replaying his shock that a body like mine could make a man go soft.

I don't remember getting dressed or saying goodbye to his friend. I don't even know what would have been said between them, a man and a teenaged girl.

During my senior year, I thought I wanted to be a writer. Or a teacher. Or a shrink. Maybe an architect, even though I didn't notice the angles of a room or the scrollwork on the entrance of a church or realize how a curve in glass shapes the light. I didn't care about the thermodynamics of brick versus concrete versus stucco or about how in design, like in literature, form follows function. But I had told Rolland I wanted to study architecture, and he said I should call Jerry because that's what he was majoring in.

I'd known Jerry only as my brother's best friend, the smart and tall one who kept changing his major and who had two small gold hoops in his left ear. He and Rolland used to get drunk together, especially at the lake. They liked to watch hockey and college football and NASCAR. They liked to play tennis and golf.

One afternoon, Jerry came over to the house, carrying models and poster board and books. We sat on the floor of the formal living room. The couch where my mother liked to nap had been moved to another room, so the two end tables framed nothing but an empty wall. Jerry spread out the color wheel and shading strips, showing me how a midnight blue changes depending on the color it's placed next to. The fluidity of color. Its dimensions and weight. How the color wheel is not flat at all but a cylinder, white on one end, black on the other. Complex and beautiful. He explained why you end up with a rectangular door and a square room, after hours and hours of original designs, how architecture is a mind game.

He said, "When a person enters a building, they automatically open their mouth."

He said, "Imagine a tall building, all glass on the first floor, all concrete above. Structurally, it's sound, but people won't trust it because they see heavy materials on top of a fragile one."

He talked with his hands—large, beautiful, pointing to the slope of the living room's cathedral ceiling. My brother's best friend, wearing worn tennis shoes and light-colored jeans and a T-shirt from a sports bar. My brother's best friend, with his eyes becoming dark brown and his nose now narrow at the bridge and wide at the nostrils.

"What other tricks do buildings play?"

"You see that landing at the top of your stairs? It appears like it's unsafe because there isn't any support, like a column, under it."

I stared at the landing. Eighteen years in that house. Lying on the living room floor while I talked on the phone. Playing weekend-long Monopoly marathons with Rolland in that room. Getting in and out of the closet under those stairs. Eighteen years of knowing which bricks appeared like they had been baked longer in the fire, which banister rung was splintered, which plank of the wood floor had a loosened nail, and Jerry, my brother's best friend, pointed out something I had never seen before.

I began to love him then. Even though I was already sleeping with Lee and Richard.

It would be a year before I flirted with Jerry by stealing his baseball hat off his head and placing it on mine, before he would ask Rolland for permission to date me, before he would kiss me while I wore a red silk sweater, still kept in my closet to remember. It would be four years before I stopped messing around with other guys and accepted it was Jerry I wanted. But it started then—at least in my memory, it did— Jerry becoming something other than my brother's best friend, as he sat crossed-legged on the living room floor.

Because he talked to me. Because he taught me what I never knew about blue and the perceived dangers of my stairs. Jerry, who had stood in my kitchen with me and Rolland while detectives placed our hair in baggies, who remembered my mother, remembered stapling pictures of her to telephone poles all along I-40—he was just thirteen then— who had two earrings and an ankle tattoo of Calvin and who laughed when my father gave him shit for them. Jerry, who had stood in that living room with a tuxedo on, red cummerbund and bow tie, for prom pictures with my brother and their dates, now teaching me about the curves of an Ionic capital. About the flying buttress, how it allowed in more light in a church and made people feel closer to God.

Jerry gathered all his materials and left. I waved goodbye from the front porch, and when I reentered the house, I thought about the light in the living room, the power of it, how in memory Mom's face was lit by the sun as she slept on the couch, of how memory is like those buttresses, reshaping experience with light.

During the summer after my freshman year of college, Lee called late one night, waking Dad up, who answered the phone with a groggy hello a second or two after I did. "I've got it," I said, as Lee remained silent for a moment.

"You coming over later?" he asked.

"Yes, I'll be there in a minute or two."

I left through the back sliding door, a sound Dad could associate with my letting the dogs out. In only a T-shirt and underwear, I traveled barefoot the familiar path—the sidewalk Dad poured when we moved into the house, to the rose of Sharon along the cyclone fence, its pollen powdering my skin as I passed, through the gate I'd quietly latch.

Lee's bedroom window was on the side of his house, separated from my house by only eight to ten feet. I had the habit of stopping to peer inside, to see him curled under his comforter, asleep with the TV on. I liked watching him this way, with the pane of glass between us.

Once inside the house and in Lee's room, I took off my shirt and slipped into the king-size waterbed, trying not to make too many waves. His body rose and fell anyway, and he awoke to call me *sweetheart* before falling back to sleep. After two years of seeing each other, we no longer had sex every night, and I liked when I could just slide next to him and listen to him breathe.

I woke up a few hours later and did everything in reverse. The moon was thin, making the exposed roots of the maple more difficult to traverse, but it was a walk I had done dozens of times, sleeping in Lee's bed a couple hours each night. When I reached my back porch and went to slide the door open, it was locked. I saw the latch down, and that wasn't a latch that just fell on its own. But nothing looked different inside the house. The TV wasn't on. Dad wasn't at the kitchen table. The dogs were still curled in their chairs. I walked into the garage to open the door to the house. It too was locked.

Then I knew. I would have to ring the doorbell and wait for him to let me in.

But I had no shorts on. I had no bra on. Just a T-shirt that reached to my thighs.

So I ran back to Lee's house, went back into his room, turned on his light, and began rummaging through his dresser drawers.

"Lee, wake up, I need your key to our house and I need a pair of shorts. Short ones."

"What? Why?" he said, still half asleep.

"Dad's locked me out of the house. He knows I'm here."

He jumped out of bed, his Labrador barking, suddenly excited by the commotion in the room, and found the key to the house and a pair of cut-off jean shorts.

"What are you going to say?"

"I don't know yet. I'll call you later."

Back outside, I stumbled over a root, and in the short amount of time between Lee's driveway and mine, I thought about how I wasn't a kid anymore, I was nineteen after all, a college student, living away from home during the school year, and, like so many others before me, I thought my age gave me some amount of power, meant I was no longer young.

As I started to turn between the houses, I saw a shift in light from the front porch, a shift in shadow. There, in his faded robe and his tighty-whities, he sat rocking in a chair, intentionally moved to the front of the porch for full view of my going and returning.

I can't remember everything we said. I know I told him Lee had called and asked me over because he wanted to discuss the possibility of dating and then we had started watching a movie and I had fallen asleep. I know I kept my shoulders hunched so Dad wouldn't notice I didn't have on a bra and that I kept Lee's shorts from falling far below my shirt, so Dad could tell himself he only thought I didn't have shorts on when he watched me walk back and forth between our houses. I know the conversation moved from the porch to the kitchen, where we both stood on opposite sides, until I sat on the counter because my legs grew tired. I wonder if he felt powerful then, his adrenaline outlasting mine. I know I didn't apologize for going over there—there's nothing wrong with two adults having a conversation about dating—but I likely apologized for falling asleep.

I know he said he wasn't comfortable with my dating Lee. "It's just not something I'm comfortable with," he said, the same wording I used when I told the old man next door I didn't want to pick him up at the hotel. Why is it that we water down our fear and make it about comfort or ease?

I know I deliberately pivoted to a logical discussion about dating someone older. "When I'm fifty and he's sixty-four, it won't matter," I said.

I knew, even then, that he'd prefer (we would prefer) denial, to push away the complexity of it all, of a daughter needing something from an older man that she herself could not understand. So I offered my father an analysis of numbers, and he, in return, never asked if we were sleeping together.

I wonder why and how he held back from that question.

I started dating a guy in college, and his mother, curious about my mom's death, paid to read all the archived newspaper articles from *The Daily Oklahoman*. I told my boyfriend I'd never read them, so the next thing I knew a stream of emails, with copy-and-pasted articles in them, flooded my inbox. I was a sophomore, sitting in a dark room in a sorority house at one o'clock in the morning, the computer screen blinding. I wasn't certain I wanted to read them, but there they were, right in front of me, and it felt strange that someone, my boyfriend's mother no less, knew more than I did.

I learned there were eyewitnesses who heard her scream and saw her being dragged to her car.

I learned about her body in the field—she was left substantially nude and face down, her hands bound behind her back. Dad would later say, after I asked him why this detail was hurting so much, "Because it's the final insult."

And for the first time, I learned of mistakes in the case:

> More than four hours elapsed from the time witnesses told Oklahoma City police that two men kidnapped Kathy Sue Engle from Shepherd Mall until state troopers were asked to look for the vehicle, police records show. Officers felt they should first verify with Engle's husband that she was indeed missing, but it took them 3½ hours to locate him.

I had remembered Rolland's saying there was confusion over city limits, that because our house lay on the dividing line, where our mailing address was listed as Yukon but we technically lived in Oklahoma City, the OKC and Yukon police kept passing the information back and forth, arguing about jurisdiction. But I had no idea that it took nearly four hours to get it right. Four fucking hours. When Dad was home the entire time.

I read more:

> State representative George Osborne expressed outrage at the delay, saying "I don't know that if we have eye-witnesses seeing a woman being dragged screaming into a car that we need to wait four and a half hours to contact the husband." In responding to Police spokesman M.T. Berry's reply that "Teletype information [is] hard to call . . . back if it's wrong," [Representative] Osborne said, "I don't care if they had to stop every little yellow car on the road and shine their lights in it and say 'Is everyone in here all right? We just had a

kidnapping and it was a little yellow car.' I don't care if
it bothers people or not. It wouldn't bother me."

I couldn't understand why a state representative would be com-
menting on her death—I didn't know then how easily death can be
politicized.

But before I could fully process that the police had fucked up, I read
another article that said, "Kathy Sue Engle's main mistake, police say,
was walking back to her car alone. Because she did, Engle became another statistic on an ever-growing police case list of investigations into
kidnappings and murders of women."

My hands began to shake. I could taste blood, my teeth piercing the
skin on the inside of my lip.

It was Mom's *mistake*.

Because *she* walked alone, she was to blame.

Because *she* walked alone, she *became another statistic.*

Just a number on a *list* of women.

As if Mom and murdered women are not human, instead mere in-
conveniences for the police, the way they accumulate, the way they resist
being solved.

I couldn't breathe. I wanted to hit something. I wanted out of what
felt like an increasingly tiny room in a huge dark house, most everyone
comfortable or sleeping. Even with over ninety women in the house, I
felt no one could understand this rage. I left the room. I left the house.
I ran across the street to Theta Pond, thinking I would just sit for a moment. Get a breath of air. Watch the swan sleep. Cool off. But I couldn't
sit. I kept walking, searching for dark areas along campus. I kept walking, each step a pounding of the word *mistake*.

I wanted someone to fuck with me.

I thought, *I'll use my nails, I'll dig my thumbs in, stretch the sockets,
gouge out their eyes. I'll bite pieces of skin off their face like the animals did
to Mom's body. I'll show them the only mistake is a man's not knowing the
rage I hold.*

I kept my shoulders tensed to brace a blow, my hands in fists.

An Oklahoma State University patrol car slowed beside me. A male cop rolled his window down. I kept walking.

"Are you all right?" he said from his car.

"I'm fine," I said.

"You know, we encourage our young women not to walk alone at night."

I didn't respond. Instead, I cut through the center of campus, staying under trees as much as I could. I walked over to the union, deserted at night, and sat on a bench on the front lawn. I felt empowered sitting there, late at night, alone, thinking of how I didn't let that campus cop rescue me, of those times I postponed Walmart trips till daylight, those times I promised Dad I wouldn't go shopping alone. I remembered the times my dates and I left malls after a late movie, the dimly lit and empty lots, how uneasy I'd feel, even with a guy there. But not anymore. Not that night. That night I wanted to park next to a van and dare the driver to take me. Would Dad and Rolland and my boyfriend and the cops understand that I felt entitled to fight?

> Why can't you remember conversations you had with Lee, after
> two and a half years of dating?

I remember a few. Brief ones. Fragments. He said he'd be a successful businessman one day. A millionaire.

> You never believed him.

I know, but I found it endearing that he believed it.

> What else?

He said it was ridiculous that I was drying the underside of my damp hair so my hair would remain straight all night. Couldn't I see I was holding his friends up for dinner?

> You were just trying to play the part well.

He said he didn't like it when I wore heels.

That should have been a sign for all the ways you'd grow to be
taller than him.

He said he liked to jerk off while standing at the bathroom counter. He
said he liked to imagine me sitting there in front of him.

No, he liked looking at himself in the mirror.

I don't believe you, he said, when I told him I couldn't have sex because of
an accident I had in my dorm room. I was standing on a chair and lost
my balance and came straddling down on the back of it.

That does sound far-fetched.

And I had an inch-long cut on my labia and heavy bruising. I couldn't
walk for a few days. Even at his house a week later, I had to take care
sitting down on the side of his waterbed. He said, *Show me*. So I pulled
down my pants and underwear and carefully, tenderly, spread.

What did he say after he saw the pus and blood?

I think he said he was sorry.

That's it?

I think he said, *I'm sorry, sweetheart*.

What would it have been like if you had just been believed?

He said he felt sick to his stomach the morning after I caught him having sex with that woman from the gym.

Her name was Jarolyn.

I still hate that name.

He knew you would be sneaking over that night, and still he had
sex with her where you could watch from his window. And then
you let him fuck you after he said he was sorry.

I had slept with Richard by then, so I deserved it.

It's not remotely the same thing.

Midway through our relationship, he used lyrics from "Get Closer" by
Seals and Crofts to tell me he was upset that I didn't want sex as often.

You were beginning to see he couldn't give you what you needed.

Your mother felt so far away still.

I met a guy in college that I liked, so I broke up with Lee when I was home one weekend. He called me in the middle of night and yelled at me for kissing someone in front of my house. But I had been in bed for hours. *I just saw you through the fucking window, don't you fucking lie to me*, he said.

Drunk, like usual.

No, there was something really delusional about him then, something that moved beyond drunk. I even walked downstairs and stood at the kitchen window to show him I was in my pajamas. *You changed awfully fast*, he said. And then, the next morning, when Dad was at work, Lee stood at the bottom of the stairs and screamed about how he saw me kissing that guy in the driveway, and then, when I had had enough of swearing to him that I had been in bed, I told him to get the fuck out of my house, the first time I had ever said something like that to him.

I'm proud of you.

He stood there, shocked, his face transforming to that of a boy, as he cried and said, *But I love you*. It felt good to stand at the top of the stairs and stare down at him.

You only said it because you had a new guy at college to return to. I know, but it was the first time I'd ever felt powerful with him.

I was twenty-one when Dad, Rolland, and I were seated in a conference room at the Oklahoma City Police Department, meeting with a detective. We sat at an elongated dark table, one that felt ridiculous with only four of us sitting at one end. The week before, Rolland had received the DNA results that exonerated Travis McGuire and Ricky Martin in my mother's case and gave us the evidence, the mixture from the semen stain, that destroyed the ability to imagine a death without rape.

Dad and Rolland asked a slew of questions about evidence, what it would take to recode for CODIS, the federal DNA database, whether technicians can separate male and female DNA from mixture samples and secreted fluids. I listened to the men's language, how they used science to distance us from rape, while I was shaking my leg, trying not to knock the underside of the table, a question reverberating in my mind.

For a week, I had practiced the wording so as not to incriminate myself, but the words were getting muddled as my chest tightened.

"Do you have any more questions?" the detective asked.

I placed my feet flat on the floor, leaned forward, and said, "I have one." They all looked at me, and in memory there is a long pause, the men waiting for a question, me feeling like a child afraid to speak. I turned to my father and said, "But the two of you may not want to hear it."

Neither Rolland nor Dad moved.

I wanted them to leave the room. I wanted time alone with the detective in the secrecy of that space, where the only light originated from a few windows. I wanted a private testimony.

"What type of fluid from my mother's body . . . ," I said and then hesitated, "was on the beer bottle?"

The detective answered immediately, saying, "Saliva," as if there were no other option.

"Okay," I said as lightly as I could, trying to suggest mere curiosity.

I felt relief then, knowing that for her, a beer bottle was just a beer bottle. The detective kept on talking, but I was picturing a bottle against her lips, her taking a sip, and I leaned back, releasing my hands from clenching each other. I breathed and sighed, even with words like *bloodstains* and *smears* lingering in the room.

On the way home it changed though. I sat silent in the back of Dad's car, as Rolland and Dad dissected the information given to us. I stared out the window—interstate traffic, billboards, chain restaurants like Applebee's—and longed for a body of water, an open horizon in front of me and dampened red earth. I felt heartbroken, as if someone had held out an object I loved and I had watched them walk away, knowing I would never get it back.

In the three years since Richard and his friend, I had tried transplanting the memory of me with one guy in front, one guy behind, to the back seat of Mom's car, vinyl instead of an area rug, brown hair for blond, but the space was always too tight, the circumstances too different. I didn't want Mom to know the pain of a bottle inside her, how the skin gets pulled inside, but for a week, I had felt close to her, as if we had the same scar on our pinkie toes from jumping off railroad bridges into rivers. For a week I had believed I had felt something she had felt, something few people know, something she, like me, would have kept to herself, but the detective had ripped her away from me when he answered with such certainty *saliva*. A beer bottle could have been the secret we could speak.

For years after this meeting, I'll think of bottles and of Mom—beer bottles and bottles of her Giorgio and Charlie perfumes and bottles of gray Riesling and bottles of Heinz, how she'd place the ketchup in my stocking each Christmas. I'll think too of messages sealed within bottles, of the mother of a thirteen-year-old who writes, "Forgive me for not having known how to protect you from death. Forgive me for not having been able to find the words at that terrible moment when you slipped through my fingers." Of the twenty-four-year-old woman, dead from cancer, and the child who found her note, three years and 6,190 miles later, of how her story had been bleached by the sun because the bottle was clear. Of the first known message sent in a bottle—Theophrastus and his search for the inflow of the Mediterranean, a message not of lament but a need for the source.

I'll imagine finding a way to reseal a bottle of Heinz with a note within it, to weight the bottle and send it to the bottom of Lake Eufaula. I'll learn it's the pressure of the water, on the outside of a bottle, that protects the messages inside, the water like a body holding on to glass, concealing the love and pain between mothers and their daughters, guarding their messages like a womb.

It was sunny in Jerry's apartment, but my desire for metaphor, for the emotional truth of that day, makes it stormy, the sky green in the distance and full of hail.

Jerry loved to watch tornadoes. A siren would go off, and instead of going to the centermost room of his apartment or house, he'd go to the balcony or roof. Because there's a terrible beauty to those storms.

It was the summer after my sophomore year of college, and my college boyfriend was at home in Colorado while Jerry and I spent most weekends making out on Jerry's couch. Or on the floor in front of the couch, while rented movies played in the background. *We can't keep doing this to him*, he would say, and I would agree, but then he would massage my shoulders and I would tilt my head until my hair fell to the side of my neck. *I want you*, I would say, over and over, knowing he wouldn't have sex, partly because I had a boyfriend and partly because I was still Rolland's little sister. That *want you* felt simultaneously safe and true. Then we'd grind against each other for hours, my bra and shirt on the floor, his shirt tossed on the couch, until the credits to the movie were rolling.

The destructive force of a tornado is a marvel. It can level towns and make the landscape appear as if a forty-mile-long bomb has gone off. In May 1999, an F5 ripped through Oklahoma City, not far from Jerry's apartment, and had, at the time, the highest recorded winds on earth at 360 miles per hour. In some areas, nothing remained but the foundations of houses. If Jerry had been home, he would have ignored the warnings about the mile-wide funnel, choosing instead to go outside and wait for the sublime.

We sat on the floor of his living room, me cross-legged, him facing me, the shades of his balcony door open. The trees a bright full green swaying in the sun. He said, *Two, but I barely count one of them because it was only one time, and we were interrupted after just a few minutes.* Then he looked at me for an answer, and I felt the pressure outside drop.

I remembered how Dad and I were watching *Friends* once, the episode where Monica tells her boyfriend how many guys she's slept with, an amount considerably more than his two. "If you ever find yourself in this position," Dad said, "don't ever answer. Even if the number is one, you lose."

I wanted to ask him, But what do you say when a guy doesn't accept silence as an answer?

I've had nightmares about tornadoes ever since Rolland left me in the middle of a storm. I was ten, and he gathered a blanket and a radio and a phone and laid them in the centermost room of the house. "If you hear the siren," he said, "or a sound like a jet engine, take the dogs and go into the laundry room. I'm going to my girlfriend's house," he said. I stood crying with the patio door open, the sky gray, leaves coming down from the maples, while I listened for anything that resembled an airplane.

I'm afraid to tell you, I said to Jerry.

They used to tell people to open the windows during a tornado to equalize the pressure. If you don't, they said, the sudden drop in external pressure can make your walls explode, causing the roof to fall on you.

You don't need to be, Jerry said. *I won't judge you.*

But I remembered when I first told my college boyfriend. I was lying on the couch in his fraternity room, burying my face between the cushions. I wanted to lose myself like a pair of keys. When I told him not only the number but also about Lee, about Richard, about Richard's friend, about how violent they sometimes were, he stood up, walked away, and began pacing the room. He sat in the papasan chair next to the couch, staring ahead, and reached his hand, just his hand, across the space between us.

I thought of my shame and fear uncoiling, the exhaustion of my body from trying to keep it all in, of how little he wanted to touch me then, the great distance between us.

I remembered too how I cropped my hair and he kept running his hands through it, a huge smile on his face. I thought it was because the cut looked good, but then he said, "Now the hair on your head has been touched only by me, none of it by Lee."

They tell you now to keep your windows closed, because they discovered the winds of a tornado can sweep through a window and lift the roof off your house. It's hard to know what is myth and what is true. Hard to decide between a roof caving in and a roof flying off, between being crushed or sucked out.

Jerry's laundry was scattered in piles around the room. I wanted to start sorting and folding, clearing all the debris from the room. I told him about each guy. *You already know about Lee*, I said, and he flinched at the memory from the summer before, when I was still wrapped up in Lee, when Jerry had planned an entire weekend of teaching me how to Rollerblade and of making me dinners and watching movies, only to hear me say, twenty minutes before he was supposed to pick me up, that I was going to the lake with Lee instead.

Often there are multiple small funnels in my dreams. They drop down here. They drop down there. They occupy the sky, where there's no safe direction to turn. Sometimes I am driving, trying to dodge and outrun them, though they tell you never to do this because a car becomes a steel death trap in a storm. Sometimes my father is driving but instead of fleeing, he drives straight into the funnels, finding pleasure in spinning and then driving out, spinning into another and then driving out, while I scream and scream for it to stop.

I didn't know how to tell Jerry about Richard. One neighbor was bad enough. I didn't know how to tell him about Richard and his friend at once. Or how to admit that I couldn't even remember his name. I knew not to use the word *threesome*; that sounded more like a choice and more like I had wanted it. So I just described that night, the drinks, the strip tease, the bottles. Jerry reached forward and placed his hands on my shaking shoulders. *Don't touch me*, I said, my head buried in my knees.

I grew up with a tornado siren going off every Saturday at noon—a test and a way to keep birds from nesting. I think of a mockingbird building a home during the week, straw, string, grass, twigs from our maple, until a siren blasts it out.

Don't touch me, I said. *I don't deserve it.*

My college boyfriend liked to describe his plans to take a baseball bat to Lee's knees or force Richard's mouth to the curb and slam his teeth. I read his anger as validation that what they did wasn't right, but I was the one who had to calm him down, always begging, "Please, please, please don't." Then I'd apologize, because it felt like there was no way for him to assuage that rage and I knew I was the one he was angry with. He had already shown me through my cropped hair that the only way to be loved is by removing every part of me another man had touched.

Jerry put his arms around me, even as I tried to push him away. *I'm so sorry,* I said.

You have nothing to apologize for, he said.

There's a path in Oklahoma City that tornadoes seem to always travel. We call it Tornado Alley, a local version of the larger swath of land that spans several states of the plains. I don't know why people keep rebuilding there, knowing it's just a matter of time before another funnel rips through.

Jerry held me until I calmed down. We sat on his living room floor, the pressure inside, the pressure outside leveling; he pulled his body back but kept his hands on the backs of my arms, as if to say, I'm not turning away. Then he asked me, *Was there any part of you that enjoyed it?*

I couldn't believe his tone, without judgment, without condemnation. The way he looked directly in my eyes, his own eyebrows lifted just slightly, as if to say, I am just curious here. He wanted to open it up, unwrap any of my shame.

Was there any part of me that enjoyed it?

Had I ever let myself consider that?

I remembered how it made me feel desired, how Richard had said "a woman like this."

Yes, I said to Jerry, with a big breath out. *I liked being the object.*

He kept his hands on the backs of my arms; he touched his forehead to my forehead and just held us there.

Sometimes a tornado does the unexpected—takes a dock with three boats tied in their slips, lifts them all up, and flips them all over, dock and boats now floating bottom up, each boat still tied, each boat still in its slip, the world entirely the same, just turned upside down.

Dad and I were once again standing in the kitchen, my acceptance and rejection letters for graduate programs stacked on the counter, their envelopes neatly sliced with a letter opener. I'd decided on NYU, craving the sounds of trains and traffic and even of paintings, though I didn't yet know how Pollock can make you feel like you're standing in beautiful noise.

Jerry and I had talked about whether he should join me. He had said it'd be good for me to be alone, since I had never been alone, always going from one boyfriend to the next, relationships overlapping. "Part of me wants you to have that experience of independence," he said, "so you know you don't need someone else."

But we also knew the city would change me in ways I couldn't yet realize and knew we wouldn't make it if he didn't change with me.

"Jerry and I want to live together," I told my father in the kitchen.

He was leaning back against the sink, his hands on the edge. He wore Dockers and a knit shirt, rather than a dress shirt and tie, which meant it was a weekend.

"I won't support that," he said.

He meant both financially and personally, but I was already prepared for the former, having considered all the possible objections he could make.

"I'll be using the trust fund from Mom's death and student loans. Jerry's going to bartend so he can pay down his credit card debt. I'll pay for the apartment, since that's an expense I'd have anyway."

"He can stay here to work on his debt," he said, backlit by the window and afternoon sun.

"I'm in love with him," I said.

"No, you're not. You're in love with the man he could be," he said, referring to what Jerry might accomplish if he ever figured out what he wanted to do and finished school.

I knew Dad hadn't seen us together, hadn't listened to us talk about art or film or literature or history, about how the pyramids in Egypt are unlike any other structure on earth or about how the Bible was constructed by a council of men.

"I'm in love with the man he is now," I said.

"I'm just not okay with it. Yeah, you may do things I don't know about, you may even stay at his place sometimes when I think you're elsewhere, but if you live together, you're just announcing to everybody that you're sleeping together."

"Everyone can get over it," I said.

"I just find it immoral. People shouldn't live together before marriage."

"Do you call having an affair with a married woman *moral?*" I asked, shocked by the words from my mouth, by how quickly and easily they came, by how good it felt.

He winced. He too never anticipated this. But I didn't know if it was my awareness of his affair that stunned him or that I'd lobbed his history at him.

"Your mother was the one who broke her marriage vows, not I."

"That's a cop-out."

"But it's true."

I was shaking my head and rolling my eyes, dumbfounded by how, even when it comes to the love of his life, a woman is to blame, and maybe it was because he thought we'd reached a stalemate, or through my sighing or the stiffening in my body he sensed his daughter wouldn't accept hypocrisy or authority this time, that he said, "If you do this, I won't come visit you."

It broke me. There in the kitchen with the newly tiled floor, Mom's linoleum brick pattern removed, but with the strawberry hand towels she had touched still hanging from the cabinet rack, I succumbed to tears.

"You really mean that?"

He just shrugged his shoulders, as if he were tired and there were no more words to cast.

He stood there, arms still braced against the counter, and listened to me cry with my head in my hands, until I left the kitchen and went upstairs. Just like that, I had become a child again, twenty-two years old, crying on my bed, my stuffed monkey Toad still sitting on the shelf.

I was grabbing something out of my car one evening when I saw Brandon next door in his driveway. The Oklahoma wind swirled dirt in the air. I tucked my hair behind my ears and walked through the yard, stepping over the maple's roots, always protruding in arcs from the ground.

"Hey there," I said.

"Hey, I haven't seen you in a long time. How was New York? You look really skinny."

Two years had passed, just like that, my trust fund run out, Jerry's debt no lower, but I had my graduate degree. Dad had visited New York multiple times, our need for each other and Washington Square, with its chess shops and The Blue Note, outweighing the immorality of being shacked up. He'd even say, after talking to Jerry for hours about aircraft carriers and the Dead Sea Scrolls and *Stargate SG-1*, "I see now why you love him."

Jerry had been ready to leave the city, exhausted from being anxious all the time, planning escape routes for the next terrorist attack after 9/11, the memory of how our throats burned from smoldering buildings and bodies with us constantly. So we had moved back to Oklahoma, still unmarried, Jerry into his parents' house, me into my childhood home, our life from New York packed in boxes and stacked in Dad's living room.

Brandon and I chatted for a while, about girlfriends and boyfriends, marriage and jobs.

I needed to say something to him, something I'd been thinking about for months. Maybe it was because I was twenty-four and had come to see seventeen as young, or maybe I still remembered my answer to Jerry—*I liked being the object*—and was beginning to see *object* as a problem, especially after professors in their sixties ran their hands down my back, saying things like *I just wanted to feel the lace on your shirt*, or a random man grabbed my crotch in our corner bodega.

"There's something I want to talk to you about," I said to Brandon. "Well, not really talk about but say to you. But this may not be the right time," I fumbled, looking at the beer.

"Oh, it's all right. Go ahead and tell me."

"Well, I just wanted to say thank you."

"Thank me? For what?"

"For when I was younger. For not being physical with me. I don't know if you remember the times I was drunk over here and Lee wasn't around and you and Richard were. I know we flirted, but nothing actually happened with you."

"Of course I remember. I actually regret that all the time." He laughed and took a drink of his Bud Light.

I hadn't anticipated *regret* and had no idea why that could be his response. I imagine I looked confused as I searched for the next words to say.

"Anyway," he continued. "I wanted to be able to say we didn't do anything in case Lee ever asked me about it, which he did once. I could say to my best friend we never messed around."

I wanted to know why Lee would have asked him that, even though I knew it didn't matter. I wanted to say, "You weren't a fucking saint," as I remembered how Richard lifted my shirt to show Brandon my breasts and how much Brandon enjoyed it and how Brandon made me the screwdrivers that got me so drunk that I spent the next day puking and trying to remember what Richard had done to me.

Instead, I said, "Well, whatever your reason, I just want to say thank you. It would have made things worse."

"Yeah, you were pretty vulnerable," he said.

He took another sip of beer and asked if I wanted any of the Oreos or crackers from his trunk. He said he and Lee rarely went to the lake anymore, that Richard had settled down, married, and now went to church every Sunday.

I said no to the food, said it was a shame about the lake, said I would see him later, and walked back to Dad's house.

Somewhere between driveways I began to think about the word he used—*vulnerable*. I remembered how I could turn every object into a tease—pool cues, gearshifts, Blow Pops I bought while they were fueling the boats. I remembered my postures, the head tilts, how I would lower my head and look up at them and grin. Hadn't I appeared nothing but confident and mature and sexual and certain? Hadn't I played the part perfectly?

I thought I had hidden every fear, every doubt, only to learn they knew I was vulnerable and touched me anyway.

They saw that the bunny's foot was broken and still they made her run.

I wish I could go back and take steps toward Brandon, stand just inches from him, glare into his eyes, and say, with an unwavering voice, "How intoxicating vulnerability and youth and power must be when you're taught they're yours for the taking."

You were seventeen. Lee was thirty-one.

I know.

You were eighteen. Richard was twenty-nine. Who knows about his friend.

I know.

Can't you see how fucked-up this is?

I think of Lee as licking at some wound that could not be reached. Lee, years after we dated, injured from working in an oil field, collecting workers' comp. Then drunk in the afternoon, watching *Wheel of Fortune* in his garage and swearing to me he was going to buy a house with acres of land. With a face so thin it scared me. Having to sell his boat. Having to store his ski. Having to get rid of his Harley.

> He fucked you in the ass without discussing it with you first. Or using lube.

Please don't remind me.

> And he only stopped when your crying became too loud.

But.

> But?

It's hard to hate a person whose brokenness you see.

> Richard likely wouldn't have broken you if Lee hadn't done it first, one man giving permission to another. Like the men who killed our mother. You can't separate these, as much as you want to.

But Richard's an asshole, more than Lee ever was.

> Really?

Violent. Aggressive. Asshole.

> What about when you were standing by the maple tree in our front yard? It was night, and you had been listening to some song that made you sad about our mother.

"So Far Away."

> And Richard saw you and walked across his yard and asked you what was wrong.

I don't know why that song makes me so sad. The lyrics have nothing to do with her.

> And you told him you were feeling sad about our mom. And he hugged you.

I started feeling an emotional attachment to him then.

> And while you were in his arms, he asked if he could do anything to help.

I don't remember what happened after that.

> You probably looked up into his eyes and said, "No, I'm fine really, and isn't there something else you'd like to help me with?"

That does sound like me.

> You want him to be a monster, but even he showed you kindness at times. You have to hold the violence in all lights.

It's different with him though. Lee became more and more vulnerable as the years passed, but Richard married, had children, became a managing partner, attended charity events all dressed up with his wife. Sometimes I imagine seeing him again in a restaurant or a bar. Sometimes I imagine that I tease him—I'm still ten years younger than he is—and I say, I want you, and then walk away.

> You want to finally feel power over him.

Sometimes I imagine asking him what he would think of a twenty-nine-year-old man pulling his eighteen-year-old daughter—yes, he has a daughter—around in a club by the belt he took off then cinched around her neck like a choke collar.

> You liked it.

Or what he would think if a man lifted his daughter's shirt in front of another man and said, "Doesn't she have great little titties?"

> You liked that too.

I know. I liked the adrenaline rush of it all.

> It was so much more than that. When grown men wanted you, when they showed you off to each other, when Richard called you a *woman* and yelled at his friend for losing his erection, you felt beautiful, feminine, more secure than you had ever felt before.

It was fleeting though. I always returned to shame—such a whore for liking when Richard tied my wrists to his bed—and then I'd go back, wanting to feel desired again.

> Why do you hesitate to call it rape?

Lee or Richard?

> Both.

Statutory rape in Oklahoma is sixteen. Cross a border and it turns to eighteen. Cross another and it turns into a difference between the ages of perpetrator and victim.

> Your point?

It's not so clear-cut.

> Yes, it is. You were a kid. They were adults.

I didn't get close enough.

> With Richard you were always drunk. The Oklahoma statute says, "Rape is where the victim is intoxicated by a narcotic or anesthetic agent administered by the accused as a means of forcing the victim to submit."

I knew what the drinks were for.

> You never thought about what you wanted. It was always about them.

That's not rape. That's called not knowing that I mattered.

> When you hear about a young woman going through something similar, you call it rape.

It is, for them.

> Or if someone did this to Kenzie.

I would fucking kill him.

> But why not when it's you? Remember when your ob-gyn said he couldn't perform your annual exam because you were too tense and tight? "What's happened to you?" he said.

I couldn't explain that I forced the entry.

> You may not have said no, but they tore your body up, each time they fucked you.

Please stop.

> Skin splitting open. Muscles ripping. Cuts.

Please.

> In legal language, they're called *lacerations*.

I didn't know sex wasn't supposed to be painful.

> They knew.

Maybe I hid it well.

> Not when he calls you *vulnerable*.

Maybe I secretly wanted the violence. Maybe after months or years of imagining what she went through, I wanted to know for myself.

It isn't as if you said to Lee or to Richard, "I want to understand what she experienced, will you help me find a safe way to do this?"

You were way too young to know what you needed and why.

A detective once said to us, "It's very rare to have a truly innocent victim like your mother."

It doesn't matter how much you wanted to feel connected to our mom or liked the attention or craved what you'd been taught to crave (maybe it was never about our mother); they were men who never should have touched you. Men who knew what our mother had been through. It doesn't matter that you enjoyed some part of it; it doesn't make you less innocent or less of a victim. Besides, you forget that even with our mother, police said she was to blame.

It's not the same though.

What about assault?

I wasn't dragged screaming to my car.

What about abuse?

Okay, it was abuse.

A pamphlet from a women's center says, "Sexual assault is a crime, whether you call it rape or abuse."

I didn't know her pain.

Please just call it rape. It perpetuates the problem if you don't.

There *is* a difference though.

A difference in circumstance and details, but it's still rape.

I don't want it to be labeled the same. I can't let it be.

Why? Why can't you just say, "They raped me"?

Can't you see? To call what happened to me "rape"—no, to say, "My neighbors raped me"—cheapens her death. It feels like it betrays her, makes her rape so very ordinary. When she's not here to speak her story, I want to quarantine it from every other story, to respect that silence by saying her experience is not mine. I don't know what it's like to shake and bleed and scream; I don't know what it's like to have my hands bound with fishing line, what it's like to fear for my life—think about that phrase. I felt afraid I wasn't pretty enough, feminine enough, worth enough. I was afraid about many things, but I was *never* afraid I would die. I know we don't have the language to show this difference, and I know it's important to label my experience and to name the other thousands, hundreds of thousands, millions of rapes. But I also need to honor her story with some distance, to give that terror its own space.

Why do you keep thinking of the sky-blue shirtdress?

My dress, with flowers like peonies, in a polyester that didn't breathe.

Why is this the detail you hold on to?

I want it back. I want to hang it in my closet, next to Mom's brown leather blazer.

Why?

I don't know why.

> Yes, you do. Because sometimes you still hold on to "a woman like this," and you need to remember, *This is the dress of a teenaged girl, not of a woman Richard's or Lee's age.* Even with all the distance you try to create, you want the dress and the blazer side by side, reminding you, like my voice, that despite the differences here, when it comes to violence against our bodies, Lee and Richard and the men who killed Mom are the same.

I'm in my midthirties, and I've come home to Oklahoma to visit family. I'm staying at my father's new house, no room familiar or my own. We're eating a "snacky night" dinner, just the two of us, cold cuts and crackers and cheese and ranch dip laid out on his kitchen island. He builds a sandwich with pepperoni, salami, and Muenster on white bread saturated with mustard, while I sit on the barstool and eat Kellogg's new cracker chips.

"These are pretty good," I say.

It feels like the right time to talk to him. Jerry's back in Pennsylvania, where we both have new jobs and more stability than we've ever known, me as an assistant professor and him as a user-experience researcher for IBM. Classes are out for the summer, so Dad and I have plenty of time to spend together.

Lately I've been going to doctors and physical therapists for pelvic-floor dysfunction, which means that for years (since the beginning?) my pelvic muscles around and in my vagina have been so tight they rip apart. After years of painful sex and male doctors telling me it wasn't a big deal—"You don't have to worry about that until you want to have children"—I found an ob-gyn who said, "Yes, this is a problem," and "No, you don't have endometriosis," and "Due to trauma your body learned that tightness and pain are normal. You'll need to learn to let go."

I had heard her say this, heard the physical therapist repeat it while her hands were inside me, slowly stretching the muscles to release their tension, but I hadn't really processed it. Not until I lay alone in my room one night, lights off, Enya's *Watermark* playing from my phone, me on top of the covers, naked from the waist down. I held the dilator the therapist had given me to stretch the muscles myself and when I pushed it inside me, my body reacted. I had been completely relaxed with Enya singing about distant shores, until that thing, a little bigger than a tampon, closer to a penis, was inside me. That thing that I was controlling with my own fingers. I wanted it out. No, I wanted it in, but my body wanted it out. It pushed, while I tried to hold it there with my hands trembling.

Then it hit me, and it was every bit as violent as the word *hit*. For the first time in my life, with no one but me in the room, with a dilator and not my fingers or my husband's, without Jerry's skin against mine, without his lips pressed to my neck, without his breath, heavy and arousing and warm, to distract me from my body, I felt the extent of the trauma. My body knew it. Had known it for twenty years. And now its memory was fighting my hands.

Only then, as I cried and felt my body rejecting touch, did I understand. I am a victim.

And now I've come home to claim the word.

It seems right to tell Dad now, to explain the history of my body. I'm writing again and needing to know his perspective. I've also told him about my muscles, and to his credit, he's been asking how therapy is going, but he doesn't want the details about how the therapist has to spend an hour with her hands inside me, and we haven't talked about why my body is holding memory in its fibers.

I'm prepared to tell him everything, to say, *It's not your fault, Dad.* To say, *I just needed her.*

I remember a conversation we had in Houston, years ago, after having dinner to celebrate his sixty-third birthday. We reminisced about the dumb things I did growing up: shoplifting a sexy black bikini and getting expelled from seventh grade because I gave a Miller Genuine Draft to my friend at the bus stop and she took it to school and drank it.

"Those weren't the moments that made me really worry," Dad said. "It's the other stunt you pulled," referring to when I was fourteen and said I was staying the night at a friend's and we stayed at a boy's house instead. "That was the moment," Dad said. "The time all that stuff came up—raising a daughter without a mother. I thought you were gone. I was sure I had failed."

I could hear the heartbreak in Dad's voice. I didn't understand why that moment was different than Rolland's sneaking out and stealing the car or why my father felt like he failed, but I could hear his pain still.

"But I turned out all right, Daddy. Because of you."

"But I didn't know that then."

I asked him if he hadn't known about that night and I had told him later, after he knew I survived, that I'm okay, that he did well as a father, would he still feel like he failed.

"Yes," he sighed.

Now he's standing right next to me in the kitchen, spooning ham salad onto a plate, and I'm wondering if I'm ready to hurt him. But what do we do when the truth starts pulling on us, when the need to tell outweighs any pain it might cause?

"What were your thoughts, then and/or now, on my relationship with the neighbors?"

There. I asked it, and I can't turn back.

"To be honest?" he says. He sets his spoon down and looks right at me, as if he's been waiting years for this. "I'm just going to be quite pointed about it. That was when I felt the most disappointed in you. And absolutely the most deflated as a parent."

Disappointed. In me.

"Why disappointed?"

"Because you knew I would think it was wrong, and you defied me. That this was happening right next door. With a man I talked with, cut lawns with; he even helped me move."

Disappointed.

"I remember three to four instances," he says. "The time you went to the lake in Arkansas, the night I waited on the front porch, the time I busted through his door and found you."

"I don't remember the bursting-through-the-door moment."

"I walked over to Lee's and the blinds were open where I could see everything. Now you weren't having sex, but it was clear it was commencing. You popped up and came to the door and tried to block me from coming in."

"Why?"

"Because Lee was trying to zip up his pants. And I pushed around you and there was Lee, standing there all smug."

I doubt Lee was *smug*. More likely he was scared shitless and tried to pass it off as nothing.

"I really don't remember that," I say.

Dad sits down next to me at the island and grabs some more crackers for his plate. We're not looking at each other, father and daughter side by side—him sinking his teeth into spongy white bread, me staring down at my sandwich and chips.

I'm still stuck on *disappointed*, still trying to figure out memory and how I could have forgotten a moment when Dad, Lee, and I all stood in the light of Lee's living room. What did we say at that moment? And if it was clear we were having sex, why didn't he do more to stop us?

"Now I know about young women's sexuality," Dad says, "and that it is natural to seek answers from a safe environment, but I just couldn't believe it was happening next door, I mean *right* under my nose . . ."

"That's not what that was, Dad."

I fidget with my glass of water, placing the base of the pilsner on the dark spots in the granite, trying to line up the edges. I don't know what to think about Dad's saying he knows about women's sexuality. About girls seeking answers in safe places. Where would he have gotten that? In a book with a title like *How to Raise a Daughter Alone*, written by a man who consulted no women?

My fingers shake as I lift the glass to my lips then set it back down on the black spot in the marble.

"You know so little, really," I say.

"Well, you just asked what I thought."

Dad moves across the kitchen to get more cheese. When he steps away from the counter, his oxygen hose catches on the knob of a drawer. "Damn it," he says.

"So it was because Lee was our neighbor, but what about his age?" I ask.

"Well, that was part of it too. I certainly lost all respect for Lee."

"Why didn't you tell him to stay away from me?"

He looks up from his plate and stares right at me. "He was a grown man, outside my control. Besides, my problem was not with Lee. My problem was with *you*."

He is pointed when he says this. It's sharp, angry, bitter. Meant to jab. And it does.

"You still sound upset," I say.

"Well, I am. I felt absolutely the most defeated."

Defeated, disappointed, deflated, defied. I realize they are terms of power. It all comes down to Dad, not having the power to stop me.

I don't think to point out that the men who killed Mom were grown men too, outside his control, but he wants to kill them nonetheless. Instead I'm stuck on *disappointed*. I keep returning to the word. It says the fault was mine. It says I had the power to act otherwise. I tell myself not to succumb to it, that I've come too far to return to shame, to wrap myself in it again.

He begins cleaning up the kitchen. Puts away the salami, the pepperoni, the shaved ham with layers of green mold, the ham salad a grotesque pink. He places a knife in the sink.

We move to the living room. On any other night he would turn on the TV, turn the volume way up, and pick food out of his teeth. On any other night I'd get my laptop out and scroll the news. But here we are, facing each other, me sitting cross-legged on a couch, tissue box in front of me.

"Even though I've told others this, I'm afraid to tell you," I say, starting to cry. "Especially because you're probably going to feel even more disappointed in me."

But then I think about how, years before, when he and I were talking about Sandusky's sexually abusing children, or maybe it was the Catholic priests sexually abusing boys, Dad had said, "Things like that happened in my town when I was growing up. But we *never* talked about it." There had been something in his voice then. Within a memory, perhaps a longing for a way to speak.

Dad keeps his arms on the armrests of his chair, his body open, while I slump and curl into a ball. My lip is quivering. I run my finger back and forth on the bottom of my lower lip and look across the room rather than at him. I tell him everything then—about Brenda and the pubic hair and how I flirted for the attention of the neighbors, about how Lee and I started having sex when I was in high school and how, when he started kissing me, I was afraid to say no, because I wanted to be seen as a woman, to be desired. I tell him about Richard, about that night, about the sex toy and being terrified and his friend's coming home and the threesome and the beer bottles and how much I wanted Mom.

I throw it all at him, my voice shaky, my body tense, while he watches me with no expression on his face.

We sit in silence then.

I stare at the painting called *Jazz Lady* hanging above the fireplace, a gift from me and Jerry. His chess sets are displayed on tables, including the one he bought when we were in New York. All around the room, there are objects and memories of us, but those times feel so far away now.

I break the silence and ask, "Are you angry now that you know?"

"Oh, sure, now that I know it wasn't quote, unquote *consensual*." He pauses. "I wish I had seen the warning signs. I was constantly looking for signs that we needed counseling. I tried to tell you that you could ask me questions. I know it's natural to have questions and seek answers."

I don't know why he's returned to this, after all I have said.

"I did my best to hide it from you, Dad."

I detail how Lee and Richard were abusive, how they didn't respect me or my body, how my body did say no, how everything was so tight and painful and that I didn't know that pain wasn't normal.

"Did you think I was abusive to your mother?" he asks.

"Um, no . . ." It's such an odd question, one I do not understand.

"Then why couldn't you work that in reverse?" he says. "Where you recognized that not all relationships were abusive and that what you were experiencing wasn't normal, so that you could get yourself out."

"Because that requires distance, Dad—to use the logic that my father didn't abuse my mother so Lee shouldn't abuse me." I detail all the steps I took to hide my trimming of my pubic hair. "That's not exactly a rational mind," I say.

He nods.

This isn't what I really think though. It wasn't my mind that was the problem. Burying hair in the trash can or wrapping my arms around Lee and saying "I'm sorry" after he shoved me against the wall or thinking a bruise is an exciting way for a man to claim my body is exactly what I had been *taught* to do, by a world that doesn't value women.

"Do you think things would be different if your mother had lived?"

"I don't know. There are so many stories about young girls, my students even, who have had experiences like mine and they have mothers."

He keeps his arms spread over the armrests. I'm amazed he's been able to keep his body so still. But then he looks to his shoes and flexes one foot and says, "What, if anything, do you want or need from me? Was writing and your condition just an excuse to get this off your chest?"

The question trips me up. On the one hand, it's kind and supportive, but it's also delivered in such a matter-of-fact way. His *if anything* makes it seem like I shouldn't want something, his *just an excuse* an accusation.

"I didn't have any expectations really, but I guess if there's anything I want from you, it's that I want you to be angry at Lee and Richard."

"That's understandable."

That's all he gives me.

I didn't even know what I wanted until this moment. I want him to feel not anger but rage toward Richard and Lee. To say, *I want to shoot them, starting with their toes.* I want his fury to be bottomless, uncontainable. Like ours is with the men who killed Mom.

I want, most of all, for him to say, *I was wrong to feel disappointed in you. You were hurting. You were lost. And I'm sorry. I'm sorry you went through this. I'm sorry I didn't know how to protect you.*

I ask him, "If I had told this to you back then, would you still feel disappointed in me?"

"Yes," he says.

"You wouldn't feel angry?"

"I'm sure I would. I might have railed against you."

I didn't mean *angry at me.*

"That would have made matters worse and reinforced my shame," I say.

"You can't be doing that!" he says, an edge back in his voice. "You're talking from a position of hindsight now. You can't go back and know how you would have reacted then." His hands grip the edges of the armrests.

He's worked up again, and I don't really know why. I think about telling him it isn't difficult to know, because thirty minutes ago I felt shame, and if I feel it now I would have felt it then. Some things don't change. I've always been the daughter, scared of being rejected.

But more than this, I want to knock him off his power pedestal where he thinks he knows more than I do.

"Railing against me or the neighbors wouldn't have changed much. We would have gone around any roadblocks you put up."

"That's probably true," he says. "It's just a matter of biology and men's primal nature . . ."

But before he can finish, I'm raging myself, about biology and sexuality and cultural definitions of men and women and about studies of female sexuality and how women are not the receivers that society says they are and that even if you want to argue primal nature then you have to consider the fact that men have more fully developed brains than other animals and that they can stop their own biological impulses and say, "Okay, I'm going to lay off . . ."

"Whoa, whoa," he says. "You're off on a soapbox now. And that ain't gonna work. I was going to say, before you interrupted me, that if there is a woman in a revealing dress and a woman dressed like the Amish, it's just a matter of biology that a man will make a pass at the woman in the dress."

And so it begins, an argument like many others we've had. I should say, *I guess Mom should have been wearing a burlap sack that night.* But instead I keep slamming my head against the same granite wall, arguing about adornment and nature and what women should expect from men. We're getting worked up. We're going in circles. I know we'll get nowhere, but I won't let it go this time.

"So you're saying it was my fault because I wore a bikini in the driveway."

"No I'm not."

"Yes you are. If you take your position to the extreme, that's exactly what you're saying."

"Now you yourself said you flirted with the neighbors."

I stand up. I walk off. I go to the guest room and pace in tight loops, trying not to shatter something. I can't let that be the last word though. I won't let it be. I want him to see there's violence here, that a pass is not what we experience.

So I return to the living room and fume, "It shouldn't matter what a woman is wearing. She shouldn't have to hear that her tits look great."

"Why are you only considering the vulgar comments?"

"Because you have no idea what it feels like to be harassed, and I'm sick of men thinking they're entitled to comment on women's bodies."

"I don't make vulgar comments, your brother doesn't make them, I bet Jerry doesn't make them, so would you say that we're entitled?"

I bite my lip, take a breath. "I agree you don't use vulgar language toward women, but I don't think you're outside the patriarchy."

"Patriarchy? Now you've totally gone off!" he says, throwing his hands up so they slap back down on the leather armrests. "So you want matriarchy, then?"

"No, I want neither," I say.

"I feel sorry for you," he says. "Because you're going to live an unhappy life."

"Don't," I say, recognizing we'll never speak the same language or understand power the same way.

"I have to do my breathing treatment," he says, standing up and turning away.

I go back to the guest bedroom livid, thinking of how he had said, "Outside of rape, a woman has the most power because she can say no." Mom's glass boxes rest on the dresser, easy enough to break. I feel trapped in the room but know I shouldn't drive, not when I'd want to push his Vette on a corner, test the limits of my rage. I can do nothing but stand in this room and all this tension within it, wind up the rocking horse music box and long for the Toyland back, *Toyland, Toyland, little girl and boy land*, even though it tells me, *once you pass its borders, you can ne'er return again.*

I call Jerry, who says, "He said he was looking for signs, well, sleeping with your neighbor was the sign," and "I'm sorry, baby."

I don't sleep. All I do is rehash the argument, thinking of everything I should have said, of how quickly the conversation turned toward what was easiest for him—let's talk about men and about women and not about you.

The next morning, I leave early, before he's come out of his room, taking the Vette to a lake and then to have coffee with my mother-in-law, who rails against my father.

"It was not your fault," she says. "And how can he possibly think your much-older neighbors were *safe* for you?"

I think about the men who were supposed to be safe, those doctors, teachers, managers, and neighbors, how they would have been, had they never touched me or expressed their desire to, had they seen my age or my dead mother or their position of power or the fact that I was *vulnerable* as a reason never to act, or, in the case of Brandon, to stop his roommates from harming me.

"Maybe your dad can't accept it's rape because then he'd have to admit to himself that he failed to protect you."

I don't know that my mother-in-law is right. But I want to hold on to this.

Later I'll think maybe he can hate Mom's killers and not Richard and Lee because I survived. Or that when I spoke, he heard a confession, that my crying and shaking were from guilt I felt. Or maybe it all comes back to that *Show me*, how without a wound on display, we won't be heard or believed or seen as innocent.

Maybe I had wanted to get something off my chest. Maybe no matter the reason, I would have been right there, in his kitchen and his living room, trying to let go by saying, *I want you to see me and know me. I want you to understand the truth.*

Cleaving To

PART IV

+

I GREW UP PREPARING FOR A PHONE CALL OR FOR THE PO-
lice to show up and say they had a fingerprint match. I'd imagine detectives arriving at my school and pulling me out of class. Or I'd be riding
home on the bus, ready to watch MTV and eat Fruit Roll-Ups, and
instead cop cars would be blocking our driveway and street. Even living
in New York in my twenties, I rehearsed potential scenarios: Rolland
could call while I was getting into a cab or in the middle of the night to
say they had a DNA match. We'd hear the answering machine first. Or
he'd call while I was sitting at Bethesda Fountain. People would hear
me scream and then watch as I climbed in and tried to scale the angel's
body, because I needed her hand to touch my head. *Protect me*, I'd say.

Then 9/11 happened.

Jerry and I were supposed to be at the World Trade Center that
morning, to pick up some forms because he still hadn't filed his income
taxes, but we had overslept, and instead of running from the ash, we
watched it all unfold on TV, as if we lived anywhere but in the city. Until we walked outside that night and witnessed people looking lost and
walking down the middle of carless streets. Everyone spoke in whispers
in a city turned silent, except for the sirens. And then the faces of the
missing began lining the subway walls. The faces of the dead. I kept
thinking of the flyers of Mom that people had stapled and displayed all
along I-40, but here was pain multiplied by the thousands.

The search for the two men seemed insignificant then. All those
poems I wrote about wanting to kill them, all those times I stared into

my reflection in the shower's tiles, the water streaming down my back, and practiced exactly what I would say during the sentencing of a trial, all of it in vain. Time wasted. I wanted to give up, to accept, as Claudia Rankine in her meditation on forgiveness puts it, that this *happened, happens, will happen*, to feel a nothingness, a void. But I needed a gesture, a symbolic act of emptying, so I decided to write the men a letter, just as I had desired, at eight years old, to write my mother a note while she was missing and to release it in the wind outside my bedroom window.

I didn't enter Grace Church on Broadway and 10th for God or the representations of Christ or the scripture, resting in the back of the pew, with its words of forgiveness read to me long ago by a woman who looked like a witch. I was nine then. My friend's parents had taken me to their church on a Wednesday night. They had led me to a room in the basement while the rest of the congregation snacked on cookies and punch. The room was small and gray, with two chairs opposing each other. They shut the door, leaving me alone with the old woman with the large nose, who talked to me of forgiveness, while I stared at the carpet like I was in trouble. She said I must ask forgiveness for my sins.

"It's the only way to see your mother again," she said. "She's waiting for you in heaven."

"But why did God let my mom die?" I asked.

"Because God has a plan for everything, even if we don't understand. And being saved is part of that plan."

I didn't really understand why I needed divine forgiveness for lying about taking two Hershey's Kisses instead of one or for prank calling my first-grade teacher during a slumber party, but I wanted to be reunited with my mom. I didn't feel comfortable praying in front of the old lady though, even after she gave me the words to say. When I told her I would pray that night before bed and ask forgiveness then, she said the devil would come to my room and convince me not to pray. "Every night he will visit you because he wants you with him instead. You will *never* see her again."

I imagined his fork at my throat, his tail that kept me snared as he dragged me farther and farther out of Mom's reach.

So I dropped to my knees and I prayed and I asked forgiveness for all the wrong I had done and I asked to be saved.

My friend's parents then paraded me down the center aisle of the church, everyone clapping and cheering. In my memory, they held me up in the air, as if I were that much closer to my mom.

But later that night, I huddled under my sheets and shuddered, waiting for the shadow of a man with horns. I heard the earth cracking open. A deep fiery hole. The flames danced outside my window.

I went downstairs and entered the family room crying, curling myself into my father's side, as he sat on the couch. He was furious with my friend's parents, tried to convince me that the devil would not come for me, that the old lady was wrong, but I waited, all night and nights after, for his clawed hand.

Nor did I enter Grace Church because of the words of the youth minister, who spoke to me at sixteen about forgiveness. We sat in the gym while my friends played basketball, so many balls vying to enter one hoop. I had gone, then, to ask for an answer on how to handle my hate and anger, strengthening from my growing awareness of the horrors of my mother's death. I described the murder and said I wondered if church or God could help me heal.

Wearing jeans and a white silk blouse, keeping it casual to connect with the youth, the young woman told me I needed to forgive the men who killed her. Then she detailed a fight she once had with her sister, how they didn't speak for a year, how she repeatedly asked God to help her forgive. "After time, he answered my prayers. I forgave my sister, and I felt so much better afterward," she said.

My leg stopped shaking, my body suddenly stiff. She had said this with utmost sincerity. At first, I didn't know how to respond, but then I leaned forward to say, "I'm sorry, but I don't see how this is the same. A fight you had with your sister, no matter how serious, is not like the men raping and killing my mother."

"It's all forgiveness," she said quickly, her voice soft and certain, her head tilted slightly to the side, as if to say I should understand this already.

I shook my head and bit my lip. I should have ended the conversation there. I should have seen the basketball court as a metaphor, the lines dividing what is in, what is out, what thresholds can't be crossed. But instead, after a short time of staring at the boys playing ball, their armpits sweaty, I asked, "How can I forgive when they haven't apologized?"

"My sister didn't apologize to me."

The sunlight through the open gym doors was bright. I leaned back in the folding chair, the slight screech of metal on concrete. "Okay, but how can I forgive them when I can't understand what they did?"

And then that ultimate answer again—"You aren't supposed to understand; you're supposed to accept that God has a plan for you"—the answer that shuts down the conversation. I hadn't yet learned to see the answer as a narrative, one we have invented because living without a cause, without a reason, is too difficult to bear. We want to walk on earth that is firm, made steady by the stories we create.

I didn't tell her this. Instead, when she asked if she would see me at church the next week, I answered, "We'll see, you've given me a lot to think about," and I stepped out of the gym into the Oklahoma wind.

No, I didn't enter Grace Church on Broadway for forgiveness or to forgive. I passed the gates for the architecture, the exterior wood, scored to look like stone, the yard of bright green grass, the only full grass for blocks, the pointed archways, the spires reaching like my mother, on tiptoe, for something just beyond her fingertips. I entered for the groin vault, the chandeliers, dimmed during the day, the dark pews like my mother's antique pew along the wall of our family room. I entered for the silence and the light, described by Jerry all those years ago in the living room of my childhood home.

I sat on the right side of the sanctuary, pen in hand, the paper, textured and tan, bought specifically because it appeared weathered, an embodiment of grief. I already knew the first two lines I'd write. I had recited them in my head for weeks, hearing them as I passed the faces of the dead on the subway walls, as I passed the bare walls later, after a city worker had torn off the tape and thrown the flyers in the trash.

To the men who killed my mother . . .

I held my pen to the page, ready for the line to appear. But I hesitated, my hand beginning to shake, lip quivering. I pressed the pen down again. I didn't want to cry there, not where people could see. I didn't want them to ask me if I was okay; I didn't want to try to explain. My sniffling seemed to echo through the nave; a woman turned to look. I told myself I should have brought tissue; I should have considered it might not be easy.

For over an hour, the page remained blank, except for the first line and the dots where I kept placing the pen's tip in an effort to begin, the light in the church growing dimmer, until my hand finally steadied enough to write.

I'm letting you go. For sixteen years I have held on to you, fists clenched. I have dreamed of finding you, my life spent in thoughts of hurting you—the first: to stomp on your toes and kick you in your balls while your arms were chained to charcoaled walls. As I learned the extent of her pain, of her rape and her suffering from fear, I wanted to hurt you more. I wanted to make you bleed where wild animals could smell your stench, to watch as they ate you. And then it was simply lethal injection, to your blank stare and my head against glass—all of this for closure to my loss.

What I didn't realize was that you were controlling me, my thoughts like obsessions, my memories tainted with sadness. My suffering has been long—the hope of justice always giving way to disappointment.

I am opening my fists, fingers stretching to let you slip. And though I am afraid to see my palms, empty and open, I am in control, my thoughts of her not clouded by her death, my memories innocent again, not because I have forgotten what you did but because I can remember joy—the way we laughed as I repeatedly tried to crawl away and she snatched me up again and again, encircling me in her arms, pulling me close to her body.

Do not think that I have forgiven you—I cannot forgive what hasn't been apologized for—and even then I would not give you the satisfaction. This is my testimony that you will no longer be a *you* to me, that though I still hope for justice, my time, energy, and care will not be given to searching anymore.

I will drop this in the East River, not so it will find its way to you, but for me to watch it drift away.

After I finished, I walked toward the East River through Alphabet City. Jerry joined me. We were bundled up in our heavy coats and scarves, my fingers no longer feeling the paper because of my gloves, the wind sweeping through alleyways and streets. At the river's edge, Jerry stood behind me as I leaned forward over the rail to place the paper in water with my ungloved hand. I held it there, the paper darkening, briefly stiff under my fingertips, then softening until it rippled with the water. I let it slip from my fingers and watched it drift, dipping in the current, the ink smearing, my words running together, being washed away, until it disappeared in the wake of a barge.

I felt relief then, as it left me. I could now fall asleep without imagining the men being pulled from a cop car, without wondering if every middle-aged man was *the* man. How lovely it felt to know they were gone, sinking in murky waters.

That's how I had imagined it, anyway.

At the river a tall chain-link fence, stretching as far as we could see, obstructed our passage to the water. I stood watching the current, the water thick and tinted a brownish green. I wrapped my fingers around the diamonds of metal, placed my forehead against its rough grain, until the cold wind off the river made me turn away.

"What do you want to do, baby?" Jerry asked, his arms around me.

"I guess go back home."

We walked away from the water with the letter in my pocket, protected by my coat. It's with me still and, just like the men, never far-enough away.

In the film *The Interpreter*, a character describes an African ritual to end mourning where, after a year has passed, a murderer is bound and then tossed into a river to drown. The family of the victim then has the choice: to remain on the shore, their feet firm in the sand, or to swim out and save him.

If they choose to let him drown, the character says, they will have justice but no peace, but if they recognize that life is not always fair or just, the act of pulling him from the depths can take away their sorrow. "Vengeance is the lazy form of grief," she says.

I was watching the movie with Dad, and I turned to him and asked, "You would let him drown, wouldn't you?"

"Damn straight," he said. "No, on second thought, I'd castrate him first. Then let him drown."

There's relief in hearing him say this, his unapologetic hatred that has no veil. Growing up, I never heard him cast judgment, no "You should try to forgive," no "It isn't good to have those thoughts." Instead he offered an understanding and a comfort.

Years later, I dream I'm on a boat with my mother's killer. He's been in prison for years, and an elderly woman who defines herself as a humanitarian has gotten him out, to live the rest of his life on the Caribbean Sea. He's standing, cramped in a birdcage, arms to his body like a straitjacket. The humanitarian emphasizes it isn't full freedom here.

"Tell me he doesn't get to fish," I say.

"No," she says.

Then he's out of his cage, he's jumped over the side of the boat, and I, the omnipresent witness, follow him down, the blue darkening from turquoise to cobalt to navy. I hear his voice, that this is what he wants. The humanitarian dives too, arms reaching out to save him. They're screaming back and forth, voices gargled and bubbly and loud.

She's kicking hard, her hands extended for his jumpsuited body, and he's thrashing to quicken his descent. And I am descending with them both, wondering just how far she will go, if she'll die in an effort to have him live.

I've always been moved by the story in *The Interpreter*, of a hand reaching down into cold, clear water for the body of the undeserving, how it erases a person's sorrow.

I don't want to choose the lazy form of grief.

But in the dream, it isn't my hand that's reaching out to save him.

The One That You Love

✦

I MADE A DEAL WITH MY FATHER AFTER MOM DIED. IF AIR
Supply ever came to town, he would take me to the concert, even if it
were at two o'clock in the morning and I had school the next day.

Mom would listen to Air Supply's *Greatest Hits* on Dad's turntable
while she cleaned the house. Once, when she stood on one of the kitchen
chairs, its oak legs crackling under her weight, while she Windexed the
hanging lamp, its four panes of glass, I sang "The One That You Love"
to her, trying to hold the notes and hit the pitch, high even for a child's
voice. She held crumpled paper towels in her left hand, her body backlit
by sunlight. I sang from the family room, its walls covered with paintings and latch-hooks and needlepoints of trees, the carpet a golden shag.
When the song reached my favorite part, I ran toward her, dropping to
my knees and sliding, singing with my arms stretched wide, *Here I am,
the one that you love*, returning my hands to my chest, *Asking for another
day*. When the song ended, I walked to the stereo in the corner, my
knees chafed with carpet burns, and lifted its needle back.

For years after her death, I would lie in my room and listen to their
albums, hearing the songs as duets between us, me saying *I can't let go*,
Mom saying she'll come back for me, *when the time is right*. With all our
home movies being silent ones, it was the only voice I had for her.

I waited for Air Supply to come.

I even sent them a letter when I was nine years old, but they never
replied.

But then, when I was twenty, I heard on the car radio they'd be in concert at Frontier City, Oklahoma City's amusement park, and I called my father.

"It's time to keep your promise," I said.

Frontier City is a pathetic version of Six Flags, its rides outdated, its roller coasters small. But when that's all you have, you think it's pretty wonderful, spinning around in The Tumbleweed and getting pasted to the wall when the floor drops out. The concert came free with admission and took place at a small outdoor stage in July, with about twenty rows of chairs in front. We didn't get there in time to grab chairs, which surprised me; I didn't know that many people would remember Air Supply. Dad and I sat on the grassy hill and looked down on the stage. The grass felt dry at the first touch, but after we sat, moisture penetrated the fabric of our shorts. I smelled the funnel cakes from a nearby vendor.

When Air Supply started with "Sweet Dreams," it sounded wrong. The cassette I listened to in childhood had been stretched from playing it too often; the voices were faint and low. Dad had to splice the tape, and when I listen to "Sweet Dreams" now, I still anticipate a break in the music at three minutes, twenty-one seconds.

Dad walked up the hill to smoke a cigarette, and "The One That You Love" started. With its repetition of a single note on the keyboard, its volume increasing with each strike, with Russell Hitchcock hitting the high notes for *hold me in your arms for just another day*, I hugged my knees tightly, feeling the pain just under the surface. But the song is short. I didn't have time to stay with the memory—me sliding across the carpet, arms held open, begging my mother for more time.

The band announced "All Out of Love" as the final song and suggested that people slow dance in the aisles between the chairs or up on the hill. The guitar started. *I'm lying alone with my head on the phone*—I grew up ignoring this line—*thinking of you till it hurts*.

Dad reached down for my hand.

There on the grass, on the awkward slope, I pressed my cheek against his cheek and closed my eyes as we danced, hearing the words *I'm so lost without you*. I didn't care if they sang to a lover. Their songs were about longing and loss, loss of a beloved, of a Jane, of a Sandy, who were all my mother.

Normally, when Dad and I danced, he'd move me all around a dance floor—"a woman should never be able to anticipate where you're going to lead her," he would say—but this time, on that hill, in the Bermuda grass, with the smell of cigarettes on his shirt, we simply rocked back and forth. Then he asked, "Are you okay, darlin'?" and there was something about his asking this out loud, about acknowledging that I might not be okay, that made me sob into his shoulder.

The song ended. The applause ended. People were leaving, passing by us on the hill, my head still buried in his chest.

"I won't let go till you're ready," he said.

A year after the Air Supply concert, Rolland, Dad, and I went to a Bob Dylan and Paul Simon concert in St. Louis. On road trips we took when I was young, the cassettes alternated between Air Supply for me and Paul Simon for Rolland and Dad, electric guitars and synthesizers shifting to the South African rhythms of *Graceland*. We sat in the last row of the amphitheater's seating, and as Dylan played, we watched old hippies sway on the grass hill behind us and we took bets on how long it would take the drunk man holding a cup of beer in each hand to fall down the hill. It happened within a minute, but he didn't spill the beers.

After the sun had set, Simon performed, and we forgot about the people on the hill. I think now of the three of us, singing and nodding and dancing on that warm night, how connected we were then, my father and his two grown children, fully present and in rapture over the percussion and horns. Then Simon began "Bridge over Troubled Water," his voice, never the majestic sound of Garfunkel's, truncating the words and yet still carrying the quietness of the original, his left hand moving as if it were skimming the surface of water. It's a song of sacrifice and presence; even as the girl is leaving, the *I* is near, ready to comfort when needed.

I knew it was Dad and Mom's song. They danced to it at a party once and "had a moment," he had said. But I didn't know hearing Simon perform it would make him cry.

He had only cried in front of me three times in my life—when he told us she'd been abducted, at Rolland's graduation, and then while making a toast at Rolland's rehearsal dinner, when he had said, "Kathy couldn't be here." I've never known if he cried alone, or if the decision to be stoic and strong for his children followed him into every room, even behind closed doors.

So when he stood there, sniffling, the muscles in his face tightening, his hands buried in the pockets of his slacks, trying to keep the emotion in, the memory contained, I didn't know what to say or how to comfort him, this man aching for the woman he loved. All I could do was place my arm around his waist, rest my ear on his shoulder, and sway with him to the song Simon describes as a hymn. When the song ended, I held on to Dad until his body relaxed, until he moved his arms, signaling he was ready to be let go.

Cleaving To

PART V

✦

MOM WAS ABDUCTED ON A WEDNESDAY. DAD TELLS ME ON that Friday afternoon, as he stood in our front yard, alone, the maple providing shade from the spring sun, he felt her die. A man prone to rational explanations, he simply shakes his head, knowing reason cannot provide the answer this time. "I just felt a burden lift from my shoulders, and I suddenly knew she wasn't suffering anymore."

For years, I struggle with thinking she suffered for two whole days, as I fill in the nearly forty-eight hours with every possible way they could have tortured her. But then I'll read over the newspaper articles again and notice the car was found early Friday morning, making the timeline conflict with Dad's story. I don't tell him this, though. Maybe they left her in the field alive, and she died hours later from her injuries, or maybe Dad's memory is wrong, and he stood under the maple on Thursday. Even if forensics could conclude she died just a few hours after the abduction, I don't want to alter the peace he felt then, the certainty he has.

I want that certainty as my own. I still have dreams where she returns and we say we always knew, knew there was a mistake, another body, knew that the coffin was filled only with air. I'm tired of imagining scenarios, of learning detail by detail, fact by fact, the versions of her death, twenty years spent revising. I have imagined her case file—black binders filled with minute details, the photograph of her left toe, the exact description of her scream—as a means to a still life. To know it all. To destroy possibilities—the blow to the face or the blow to the stomach or the blow to the head or no blow at all. To live within a stable story. That's what I want. I tell myself the answer lies in the binders.

Or does it? The file won't tell me why they did it or even the cause of death. I could eliminate certain possibilities, but it also could mean knowing the worst. Maybe there's a freedom in the boundlessness of imagination. Her body may still be sleeping, her eyelids softly closed. I can see her this way. Popcorn salt on her fingers, the mother with dark sunglasses still smiles beside the blond in the stroller. The case photograph of a woman's face will take away the mother in the picture from the zoo. And there is a gift in seeing her on the streets, in bumping shoulder to shoulder in the supermarket, in smelling her at the café as she passes by with a slice of chocolate-ganache cake.

I just wish someone would tell me which is easier.

So I turn to James Ellroy's memoir *My Dark Places*, a memoir that might as well be a homage to misogyny, but I'm desperate for answers from someone who knows. Ellroy's mother was murdered when he was ten, and he worked her unsolved case later in his life. Faced with the badly maintained case file, he imposes order on it, organizing the fragments into a manageable form. I know this longing, what it's like to search for a form for grief.

He examines the case file and evidence, holding the nylon stocking used to strangle his mother, studying the photographs of the autopsy, her deformed nipple, the blood on her lip. He holds her dress and bra to his face out of desire to feel her body. I know this longing too.

After viewing the pictures, his mother's skirt pushed up around her hips, the shot of the pubic hair that he must quickly shove away, he says to himself, "Now you know. You thought you knew. You were wrong. Now you know for real."

I recognize the way the mind divides the real and the imagined, how the fact that her nails were clean, rather than filled with the blood and skin of her killer, destroys the story he had built, of his mother as a tigress fighting the man who strangled her.

This is the risk of knowing.

But Ellroy doesn't tell me if it was worth it. I wanted him to say, "Kristine, I prefer the tigress and should never have looked," or, "I promise you, if you flip through the binders of your mother's case file, you will be happier knowing the one, true version."

Instead, when he states the details of his mother's autopsy, her scalp cut, flaps pulled back, the top of her head sawed off, I hurl the book, shocked I had not thought of this, the damage done *after* my mother was found, and I am back at the funeral, shaking my head at the girl in purple, who believes she is on her side, intact, in jeans and a blouse, sleeping as she slept on the living room couch. But no one tucked her hands under the pillow, her hair behind her ear, no one clothed her. "There is no reason to dress her," the coroner told my father, since the casket would be closed. I think of how our coroner's wounding is somehow worse than what nature did, how purposeless, since he failed to determine how she died.

They sliced Ellroy's mother's stomach open, found whole kidney beans, shards of meat, masses of cheese, agreed she ate Mexican for her last meal, and I'm jealous he knows this, can make death real.

I need something this concrete, a detail to hold on to. I want to know my mother's stomach was coated with chocolate, contained a tag from a Hershey's Kiss and slivers of foil. When every version keeps making her death more horrific, I just want to know that on the last day she lived, she was able to taste something she loved.

In 2004, just after Jerry and I moved to Houston, me for a PhD program, him to finish his undergrad, Rolland called. We were watching the playoffs, the Yankees against the Twins, and I had just finished cussing at the couch, or, more accurately, at the slipcover that kept falling on the floor.

Rolland spoke to Jerry first, without forewarning him, and then asked to speak with me. He babbled about the TV show *Lost*, telling me to watch it sometime, and then his voice cracked. "I called the police to check on the case again," he said.

I should have known this was coming; he worked on roughly a two-year cycle.

The detective told him they had recoded the DNA evidence for the sixteen points of reference needed for CODIS, the federal database. Like with the local database before it, CODIS returned no matches.

I acted normal on the phone, asked questions in an indifferent tone, and listened to Rolland's voice become scratchy, as if tired. I wanted to say, *What the hell?* It had taken them five years to recode the evidence from the local to the federal databases. Five years we had waited, after learning McGuire and Martin weren't the killers. I didn't understand, and still don't, why the OSBI didn't just process the evidence for the federal database to begin with.

After I hung up, I buried my head in my knees, and when Jerry asked me what was wrong, I could barely say, "It's over."

I hadn't realized the hope I still held on to until Rolland said the detectives had done all they could do and still came up empty. I thought, *There's nothing more. We'll never have justice. I'll be walking the streets for the rest of my life, wondering if the man who bumps into me is the one who bound her hands behind her back.*

But another part of me felt relieved, wanting the phone calls from Rolland to end, wanting to let the story rest rather than constantly adding new details to it, like sperm cells, like a beer bottle.

It felt like we'd been playing, all these years, the game Marco Polo, the men just beyond our reach. I'd felt the force of water when they moved, splashes when they dashed away, but when I opened my eyes, no one was there, just ripples spreading out over the surface.

I wondered how I was supposed to let go, to give up. I felt scared. Eighteen years of wanting to know. It felt like a part of me by then. Who was I without the fantasies and questions, without the rewritings of her death?

I remember thinking, as Jerry held me and tried to steady my shaking body, *I failed you, Mom. I'm sorry.* As if I, and not the detectives or the people in forensics, had done something wrong.

But I hadn't done anything at all.

Maybe that's where I felt like I had failed. Rolland, after all, was the one who always called the journalists and detectives while I did nothing but tell stories.

For four years, Jerry and I worked on our degrees, as we racked up student loans and discussed whether or not we could afford to eat out for dinner. I'd begin writing about Lee and Richard for the first time, losing sleep for weeks as the scenes returned to me. We'd learn Jerry has ADHD and anxiety, something that helped explain the failed classes and impulse buys on credit cards and why he had to touch the oven's burners every time we left our apartment. We'd swim in the murky water of the Gulf, warm like bathwater, and eat burgers and fries along the beach. He'd be half-annoyed and half-delighted, watching as I lifted fries in the air for the gulls. I'd pull all-nighters grading papers or writing papers and drinking cheap black coffee from the Mr. Coffee we got as a wedding gift. We'd get a puppy, name her Shasta after Mom's favorite flower, and be awestruck as she leapt the banks of the bayou with grace. We'd learn that hurricanes are not like tornadoes, with days of waiting for a storm to arrive and clouds appearing not as walls but as bands. And that Houstonians liked to boast about diversity until refugees from Katrina moved in and lived in trailers. We'd watch the Waugh Bridge bats emerge in the evenings, ribboning across a violet sky, and we'd watch as Shasta carried a dead one around as a trophy. So much energy and flux.

Except with the case. I had no new films or books or data from police to revise the story. I'd begin to feel the versions of her death become static, preserved with the past and the words I was writing.

Until March 2008.

Another phone call from Rolland, who said he'd been "farting around on the Internet while at work" and stumbled across Cold Case File on *The Oklahoman*'s website, a series where a journalist writes about cases in an attempt to produce new information and to influence the cold case unit, newly created by the OCPD, to review case evidence. Of course, Rolland contacted the journalist, who agreed to write about Mom's case, both in print in *The Oklahoman* and for the website.

The article appeared online and then on the front page of the Sunday paper. I couldn't believe it was on the front page, after twenty-two years. But we are white and middle-class and Rolland grew up to become a judge and I was working on a PhD.

Jerry and I pulled up the website on separate computers, him in the small living room of our apartment, me in the bedroom, because neither of us could wait for the other to finish or keep from interrupting the other as we read. When I opened the page, my mother's picture emerged—the family portrait of the four of us but zoomed in to include only her. I hated it. I've always hated her picture in the paper, her picture now online, the sole reason behind the photo: her death. But it was the image of the Colt that shocked me most. Two decades later and there it was, boxier and tinier than in my memory, with tires like a golf cart's. You could see the license plate number, CXX-6737, in green on the "Oklahoma is OK" tag, a large silver back bumper, "Colt" in silver along the side—I had forgotten that but recognized it then. My mother's car. My hiding on the floorboard. My staring out the passenger window directly at the sun, describing to her, as she drove to KinderCare, the way it becomes a purple Certs rocking in the sky.

In the photo, you can see through the hatchback's glass to the interior of the car, no detail, just the lines of windows, seats, and dash. I felt the urge to zoom in, to imagine what happened inside, but I told myself there'd be nothing but pain to find in there.

This didn't spare me though. I clicked on the article and began breaking with the first new detail I read:

Roy Hinther doesn't know what attracted his attention. It may have been a flicker of motion or the sound of a struggle. Whatever the case, he glanced up to see Engle with the two men. One stood at the front of the car. The other was with Engle near the trunk. "She received a blow to the back of the neck from the guy who was with her, and then they opened up the back door and pushed her in."

I had only known the men had dragged her to the car. Not where they stood. Not that they hit her on the back of the head. Then I read about how the car had "bolted from the lot. Moments later, a man fixing his truck at NW 1 and Villa saw a yellow Colt slam into a curb, then stop. Two men were struggling with a woman inside the car, and one got out briefly before moving back in to control her. The car sped off again." I wanted to punch anything near me, the wall, the computer screen, my own thigh. I couldn't understand how a person could see these things and do nothing but watch, how they couldn't find a way to follow the Colt. Then I read what the police found inside the car—the back seat was bloody, Mom's knit blouse was smeared with blood and had two cuts in it, Mom's bra had been sliced from her body. I was shaking and pressing the back of my hand against my face and biting its thin skin with my front teeth, anything to stop the images of cutting, but what made me seize, my body cramped tight, what sent me falling to the floor and Jerry rushing in to hold me, was the description of her body: "insects had accelerated decomposition, and much of the head, neck and genitals already were obliterated."

Her head *obliterated*, her neck, her genitals *obliterated*, the most tender tissue, understandable, but also the most personal, a foot nothing, a hand, even the fingers I love, easier, more manageable. Her head obliterated. I shut my eyes and saw the word. The emptiness of the O.

Obliterate: to blot out, leaving no clear traces; to cause to disappear from view; to completely conceal; to erase, efface; to cancel to prevent further use; to completely get rid of from the mind; to do away with; to destroy.

My origin erased. None of this ridded from my mind. No clear trace of Mom's narrow face. Her smile that was more like a smirk. Obliterated.

There was nothing to say but to repeat the word.

It was days before I could sleep through the night, and even then only with sleeping pills. Dad and Rolland seemingly felt nothing. Rolland said to me on the phone, just after reading the articles for the first time, "I didn't read anything that surprised me. It's basically what I've already imagined." But the imagination is different than the words *head* and *obliterated*. Even with all the scenes I had created over the years, I never imagined her body without her head or with her genitals destroyed. And I couldn't understand how Dad, who won't return to the mall because the scene would be too real, could act as if these details weren't every bit as brutal as standing in that parking lot would be.

I felt like they wouldn't understand if I told them I couldn't let go of the word, how I kept repeating it in my head, as I walked the dog in a field or lectured my students on the uses of imagery.

Though maybe that isn't fair. I think of how Rolland, after attending a reading of mine, where I read poems about Mom's death, had said to me, "I'll never do that again. I think the same things you think and feel the same things you feel; the difference is, I don't say it." Neither Dad nor Rolland seemed to realize how their silence made me feel deserted and wrong and utterly at a distance.

I couldn't tell them about the bunny I'd come to believe: a scene in early spring, with helicopters spiraling down from maple trees, and a bunny nibbling on grass, her brown fur shiny and sleek, her ears twitching. A dog approaching. She freezes, hunching toward the earth, her belly against the ground; even her eyes stay still. But the dog, with his hackles rising in a wide swath down its back, grows nearer. The bunny darts toward the faraway fence, to a hole she thought was there, but she becomes trapped in the corner of the too-high fence, the dog inching closer. I saw terror, I saw thrashing, her heart clenched in the dog's mouth.

I had stopped trying to describe what I felt, ever since I had flown home from New York a month after 9/11 and sat on Rolland's couch and cried and said to him and to Dad, "I know you can't understand what it's like to live in New York right now, but I had to come home and tell you I love you, I love you both so much," and Rolland had replied, "You talk too much."

I couldn't tell them how I stayed awake at night, staring at Mom's picture from the article, how I'd reach out to touch her face, hoping to feel a part of her there, hoping to restore what had been taken. I knew well enough they'd change the subject.

Jerry would validate what I felt though. Over dinner at our favorite Tex-Mex place, he'd say, "I didn't sleep last night either. All I could think about was how your Mom's body was treated like trash." I'd watch his leg shake under the table, his body amping up with no way to lessen his rage and sadness; my body felt that too. I wondered if it was because he knew my mom, because he remembers his own fingerprints being taken and Rolland's sudden distance in the months after her death, how much Jerry missed his best friend, who needed separation to grieve. Or if watching his own mother being beaten, when Jerry was a child, was what made him able to say, "It makes sense why you wanted to touch her face." Maybe it was the long conversations he grew up having with his mom—about the abuse, about why she had yelled at him after burning her finger (it wasn't about him but about pain, she had said), about why his best friend had to pull away—that made him unafraid to say, out loud, that he hurts too.

After all of this, and just twelve days after the cold case story gave us the Colt and body bag scenes, I found out through an email to our entire family what Rolland could never say to me:

I know the news story probably surprised most of you . . . I have felt a responsibility to try and keep the investigation going. I don't think I want to do this again. It was extremely difficult to go through the interviews and see the story in video. I expected to have a feeling of accomplishment and purpose afterwards. Instead, I felt very depressed and angry . . . While I still want her killers brought to justice, I think it is time for me to accept how it is.

I'm not going to lie, it enraged me. I couldn't understand how he could sound so nonchalant on the phone and then write that he was depressed and angry. Perhaps it's because he married a woman who thinks crying or expressing emotion is a weakness, especially in a man. Or perhaps he was trying to emulate our father, who when he heard the psychologist say, "Children who've gone through trauma need stability," had seemed to translate that as *I must be stoic at all times.* Or maybe Rolland saw nonchalance as a way to protect me; after all, no matter how much I age, I'm still the little sister.

I thought of the pressure Rolland had felt, though I'm not sure where it came from. He was the one who pushed all those years, pushed what I imagine to be a shipping container, bright blue, with all his weight, and inside of it—her body and her killers and fables of white knights and the history that is masculinity, that is the son. Rolland who had wanted to contact *Unsolved Mysteries* when we were young, Robert Stack walking through the darkness to speak Mom's name. Rolland who had wanted to sue the mall. Who went to law school, worked as an assistant DA because there were other women and families to save. Who'd make sure those binders never became too dusty. Twenty-two years of phone calls and meetings with detectives and interviews for the newspaper, and now it was time to give up.

I thought about how different our grief would have been, had we known, from the beginning, what had happened to Mom. The details had been parceled out over decades, and so in some ways, while her absence was sudden, her death was slow. Or maybe it's more accurate to say she died multiple times, each death more graphic and more violent and more difficult to bear.

Now I could begin to imagine the shipping container rusting and abandoned in a field, its original spot having moved only an inch. Grass and weeds will sprout and cover its sides, concealing it. Then Rolland, his hair graying, can let his blistered hands heal, and I can search for a type of silence that offers a balm instead.

Motherline

+

WHEN I WAS SIXTEEN, I WENT SEARCHING FOR THE BAD
Mother.

My aunt Alice, my father's sister, had mailed me the book *Mother-*
less Daughters, and I sat on our family room couch, reading and high-
lighting passage after passage that explained to me who I was and said
exactly what I felt:

> There is an emptiness inside me—a void that will never
> be filled. No one in your life will ever love you as your
> mother does.

> Lately I've had the almost uncontrollable urge to walk
> up to people I barely know and say, 'My mother died
> when I was seventeen.' . . . I imagine saying this as if
> it could explain everything there is to know about me.

> I am always painfully aware of . . . the awful fact of
> never knowing her as an adult, only as a child; never
> able to relate to her intellectually on an equal level.

So many passages of turquoise, yellow, and pink. And a dog-ear for
the section about mourning the Bad Mother. A daughter must grieve
fully, it said. She must hold on to the mother's splendor but also her
faults. If she doesn't, she grieves for a woman who did not exist.

I remembered Mom's drawing a happy face in chocolate pudding. The rocking horse ornament she made. How proud of her I felt for getting a new and better office. Had she lived, even for one more week, she would have had that office and a business of her own. But I didn't know who the Bad Mother was.

My father sat in his leather chair, his legs propped up, his eyes closed and head tilted back, the evening sun streaming through the half-lifted shades. He tapped his feet, still in his oxfords from work, to the sound of Eugene Wright's strumming a base.

"Tell me something bad about Mom," I said.

"What? Why?"

"The book Alice gave me says I'm supposed to grieve for the good things and the bad things."

He shook his head, annoyed at the existence of self-help books, at his sister who always sent them.

Maybe this was when he told me Mom left her clothes piled high on a bench, let the dishes pile up in the sink, or refused to squeeze the toothpaste from the far end. "Tremendous trifles," he called them. Or maybe he closed his eyes, staying silent in the dulling light.

I know I didn't feel any closer to the imperfect mother, so the next time I visited Alice in Texas, the two of us having lunch at La Madeleine, where I ate quiche lorraine and strawberries piled high in a glass, I asked her to tell me.

"She was a workaholic and a chain-smoker," she said. "I didn't really know your mother that well. She didn't like me very much."

I remember staring out the window at her Mercedes, with its one large windshield wiper that, for some inexplicable reason, reminded me of a big bushy eyebrow when it moved, and feeling torn between two women I loved, the aunt who spoiled me with new clothes and mailed me books of poetry, and the mother who had painted my fingernails red.

When I returned home to Oklahoma, I told Dad what Alice had said.

"Your mother wasn't a workaholic. She loved to work, but not too much. And I wouldn't consider her a chain-smoker either. To me, a chain-smoker is someone who lights the next cigarette before the first one is finished. Your mother wasn't that bad."

It felt like playing the game Memory, placing the cards face down, in tidy little columns and rows on the linoleum floor of our kitchen, flipping them over one by one, but none of the cards were matching.

I'm doing that still, spreading the cards out, searching.

I remember "Iowa Corn-Hick" was her call sign on our CB radio. I remember how she forgot to trailer up, and the lower unit of the boat's engine carved into the concrete of the road, leaving a scar in the metal. How she stayed in the water behind me, helping me to keep my ski tips straight, and then pushed my butt up as the boat took off. How she named an inflatable boat, big enough for just one person to sit in it, *Her Majesty's Ship.*

I remember she played bunco with a bunch of screaming ladies and pretended not to notice when Rolland and I sneaked downstairs to snatch M&M's from green plastic bowls on the card tables. How she loved peanut M&M's and Hershey's Kisses, but she ate Junior Mints at the movies. How she told me never to have a drink or food in my bedroom, even a glass of water for a friend.

I remember she made us make loose fists, hit the sides of our heads, and say "Ding-Dong" before we could eat one of the cupcakes by that name. If I had had a child, I would have made her do the same.

I remember she made meat loaf and goulash for dinner. Or we'd eat Chicken in a Biskit and Easy Cheese for snacky nights and watch TV, *Miss America* or *Grease* or sometimes our silent home movies. I remember she told me to close my eyes when Rhett kissed Scarlett and left her behind on a road, the sky a burning red.

I remember she made a small ceramic square with an open hand on it, for saving our chewed gum; it said, "Stick it here, Kathy." How disgusting that is to me now, my watermelon Bubblicious hardening next to her Juicy Fruit, how we'd pop them back into our mouths after dinner.

Dad said she'd studied in Mexico, but it wasn't until she was pregnant that she came to love Mexican food. He told me she'd been a math teacher for a year, though she majored in languages. That she was tiny from the waist up, had large hips, a flat butt, really great legs. He said she wanted to buy an old home and fix it up; I remember her driving us to old houses, how she admired them from the street.

He said she'd suffered from polio as a child. I want to ask her if she remembers quarantine, the tape across the door of her house.

He said she'd break out in poison ivy, even if someone was burning it miles away.

That she, while pregnant with Rolland and hemorrhaging at the hospital, lay in the bed smoking a cigarette. She then convinced the doctor to let Dad bring their terrier to the hospital that night.

Not long after Kenzie's birth, while I was home visiting from graduate school, Rolland mentioned that he wanted to see baby pictures of himself, so he could compare his daughter's looks to his own. I, who have snooped around Dad's house for photographs of Mom, for the clothing she once wore, the designs she stitched, knew exactly where the pictures were: tucked away in a large rectangular cardboard box with the characters from *Peanuts* printed on its sides, toward the back of the guest-bedroom closet, its ceiling heavily sloped by the roof of the house, where I could navigate more easily than the men in my family. The last time I had sifted through this box, I was in high school, and I replaced the lid after just a few glances, because the box seemed to contain a life from before I was in it.

Late one night, I rummaged through the box for Rolland, finding baby clothes, knitted blue, and a baby album that records Rolland's firsts—turning over, a smile, a crawl, the first cut of his fine hair, the emergence of teeth.

I found her family's chocolate chip cookie recipe; two red leather books: her childhood diary—my mother at twelve years old—and an autograph book; and pictures of a house party with all women—Mom in a plaid suit, holding a cigarette and a cocktail, her hair long like it was in the 1980s. One of our neighbors is flipping the bird to the camera, another is screaming, and a cop with a boom box is stripping down to a G-string. I would have liked to have known this Kathy.

I found another photograph. She's in a hospital bed, with a pillow stuffed behind her, white sheets and blankets covering her legs. She's wearing a light-blue hospital gown, its neck rimmed with paper lace. She holds me in her left arm, feeding me with her right, a squatty bottle with a red rubber nipple. Her hair is black and short, like I've never remembered, a Dorothy Hamill cut that exposes her right ear, a round stud earring. She looks tired, she isn't smiling, but there's something about the way she's looking at me, brand-new baby born early, that brought tears to my eyes. In the box lay her hospital bracelet, cut near the ID tag, from when I was born. I held it and wondered if her sweat was still on the plastic. I wanted to touch my tongue to it, to taste the salt of her body from when I came into this world.

Deeper into the box, a stack of envelopes lay slipped between crocheted blankets. *My god, her handwriting*, I thought. *So much like mine, our K, our f.* In high school, I had deliberately sculpted my handwriting to appear more feminine, practicing different scripts and angles to represent a self I longed to be, never realizing I was recreating hers somehow.

My hands flipped rapidly through the envelopes, postmarked between 1969 and 1971, some addressed to my father's home in Ponca City, Oklahoma, others to Fort Polk, Louisiana, where he fulfilled his time for the Army Reserves. She signed some of them Kathy Bruce, her name from her first marriage, others Kathy Engle. Fifteen letters from my mother. Two from my father. I wanted to read them. I had to read them. In the stuffy closet with poor lighting, surrounded by Mom's homemade wreaths and picture frames stacked several deep against the wall, I began to pull the paper from an envelope, but I hesitated. Maybe they wouldn't want me to do this, the letters too private or revealing, but I couldn't resist my mother on paper—unfiltered and closer, the layers of perspective scraped away.

This isn't the mother I wanted.

It isn't a brunette I imagine but a bleached blond, wearing black pants and a cheetah-print blouse. She sits at a hotel bar in Cincinnati on a business trip for Conoco. Normally she wouldn't be able to wear pants on a Wednesday, given the rule that male execs at Conoco instituted: women could wear pantsuits only on Fridays, and only if the blazers, which had to remain on, covered their asses. She deliberately left the blazer in her room.

At the bar, a man named Art sits next to her. "What do you think of the new applications for COBOL?" he says, but she acts aloof. He tries again: "Did you hear about Sue and *the minority guy* at work, you know, the one you've been training?"

She twists toward him and says, "Noooo, tell me," though she knows not to become too involved in company gossip. After all, she's been the subject of it herself, with her recent affair and divorce. She searches through her handbag for her pack of Salems, her hangnail catching the lining of the purse.

After finishing her cigarette and a glass of gray Riesling, she leaves Art at the bar and returns to her room. Picking up a hotel pencil and the Sheraton-Gibson stationery, she tells herself to remember her coin purse for the six-cent stamp and writes, *"Boy am I with a bunch of ding-a-lings. I'm used to being with a gentleman (you) who orders for me & lights my cigs. Once and awhile, Art lights my cigs, but you know how he is—not too sincere—only doing it too impress me. Am I impressed! He's such a country bumkin—it's embarrassing. I can hardly wait to get back to my worldly gentleman—boogie bear."*

I want to sit with her in a booth in a dark corner of that bar, Art flirting and failing with another woman across the room, and ask her what the difference is between lighting a cigarette sincerely and doing it just to impress someone. I want to know why she thinks my father is worldly when he's lived only in small towns in Oklahoma and Texas and traveled just a few times for work. More than this, though, I want to know why she prefers a man who orders for her, even as I fear her answer.

She signs her letters Kathy, then Kath, then Kat. A cropping of her former self.

Years later, when working on a profile of her, I revisited the words she wrote, spreading the letters and pictures and diaries in front of me on my bed, hoping I could finally construct her and stitch together a woman cohesive and whole, but too much was missing from the pages and photos. One letter, in particular, kept perplexing me:

> For the most part I enjoyed being home. Friday we went to where my dad is buried. It's been three years since I've been there. I'm glad I went. It's hard to explain the feeling I get when I go there. I hope you'll let me go after we're married. I could never make Thomas understand how important it was to me. It's funny Doss, in a way I felt strange and sometimes lonely at home. I guess the reason is that for the last 2½ years I wasn't "allowed" to be a part of my family and also that I'm not able to share my feelings for you with them. I just felt kind of out of it part of the time.

I called my father to ask about the tone in her letters, how it seems she needed permission to go home.

"You're right," he said. "Thomas was a very domineering person, a very controlling person. He could not be dominant around her family because when he was with them, he didn't have all the knowledge and therefore did not have all the power. He didn't necessarily forbid her to see her family—it didn't go quite that far—but he wasn't close to his own family in Iowa and therefore had no reason to go back to Des Moines."

"Why'd she marry him then?"

"Oh, you know, you think you know somebody but you don't. In a different situation, under different circumstances, they change. In Ponca City, he ruled the roost. He determined who she saw and where they went. It really was the crux of their marriage problems. Even between she and I," he said, "our conception of who we were before marriage changed. She considered me a party person. While that was the scene while I was single, it wasn't when I was married."

"What was the difference you noticed in her?"

"The thing about parenting. She wanted to go back to work when you and Rolland were babies. I didn't agree with that, but we compromised. The reality afterward didn't quite jibe with me. That was a surprise, me being more of the parent."

"In one of the letters, she seemed so excited about possibly being pregnant, and you guys started trying for kids so early."

"It's one of those things where you never know until you try. You don't know how you're going to feel until after it happens. And you can't go back."

So the woman in the letters is also false.

I thought about the stories my father had told me over the years, how she had called him at work one day and told him to come home to "break in" the bed that had been delivered. When I asked if he went, he said, "Of course I did." About how she had called him while he was at home on a weeknight, having put us to bed, and told him to meet her at the bar. About what he most often said: "She was a better wife than a mother." I didn't ever ask him why he sees wife and mother as opposed or where on his spectrum the professional, the daughter, the sister, the friend were supposed to go. Or why he doesn't make room for the self, the woman who exists on her own.

Over the phone, I said, "The weird thing is, as I read over these letters again, I can't reconcile these people. I can't reconcile you, my father, with the boy writing about how much he misses his lover. You even used the word *bitchin* and you hate cuss words. And I can't reconcile the mom of my memory with this other stuff you've told me. Even the fact that she was working late the night she was taken. She wasn't there for dinner. She wasn't there to tuck us in. But I remember her being there. I remember a woman who played dress-up with me and was homeroom mother and did things for my class and had an ornament-decorating party for me and my friends."

"You're not wrong really. She was very attentive to your wants and needs when you were school-age. The difference was more when you were babies. Her point way back then was, and you need to put this in your book somewhere because I remember it so clearly, she said, 'You can only talk to the baby and the dog so much. They don't talk back.' She needed intellectual and social interaction, and that I can understand."

"Is there anything else about the differences between you two?"

"Just her nail-biting. She had beautiful hands. I remember using bribery with her. I told her it didn't make sense to buy her rings when her nails detracted from any attractiveness. That spurred her non-nail-biting, but only for a time."

After we hung up, I stared at the slices of wedding photographs—my grandmother cut Thomas out of every single one so Rolland and I wouldn't see this other man—and noticed for the first time that all of her smiles are closed-mouthed, sometimes even looking forced. Only when she looks directly at her uncle, her father's brother, the one who walked her down the aisle that day, does she look at ease.

When I asked her twin sister Barb about Thomas, all she would say was that they dated in high school and college, that everyone else liked the match. "We were part of the same church," she said. "And everyone liked the thought of a Kathy Meffert and Thomas Bruce wedding. She married him just because that's what was expected at the time."

I stared at the fragments and artifacts and felt a tightness in my chest, the same tightness I felt in the closet of my childhood home, when reading the letters for the first time—my body heavy with longing for my mother's voice. I want that moment between us—me, mixing the oatmeal into the chocolate chip cookie dough, her, reaching in the bowl for a bite, as she explains why she married him, when he changed, how it isn't okay if a man holds power over you, what it is she really wanted.

It never goes away, really, the pain of knowing she should have been able to tell her own story.

I was twenty-six when I married Jerry, the same age my mother was when she married my dad, though I didn't realize this at the time.

In the months leading up to the wedding, we planned details like Easter eggs in code—a *K* on the bottom of the invitation, Hershey's Kisses in bowls, the stained glass of the chapel an echo of her needlepoint—so not only our life together was present but Mom was present too.

I felt apprehensive about getting married though. I'd never again have the adrenaline that comes with first kisses and uncertainty, and I knew I'd always be, in some way, the girl who wants affirmation from men. I went to my father and asked him, "You've always told me people don't change and I've never once been faithful, so how can I possibly get married?" He told me then that people can change, if they always remain conscious of it, every second of every day spent aware of how they want to be different. I've always wondered what my mother's answer would have been.

On the day of our wedding, before I pulled on my beaded dress and shimmied into the petticoat, before I slipped on the gloves Mom wore in her wedding and danced with Dad to a song called "Memory," before Jerry sent down a partially-eaten Reese's and before I took a bite and sent it back, before I walked a bouquet of Shasta daisies down the aisle of the empty sanctuary and placed it in the front pew, I stood in a classroom in the chapel's basement, wearing a black skirt and yellow blouse, my clavicles exposed and sharp. My back was to the door, and I stared into a mirror, messing with my hair, pulled back in a low-do on the nape of my neck. I thought, *A life with Jerry is better than hunger, and besides, I never really felt better after a man's hand gripped this neck out of desire.*

Then Rolland, already in his tux, peeked into the room. When I turned to face him, he looked disoriented, as if he had just walked into the wrong room and was lost in some kind of labyrinth. He shook his head and left.

A minute or two later, he called me out into the hallway, his eyes full of tears, his face twitching and red.

With a voice that was cracking, he said, "I thought you were Mom. I don't know if it's the day or your hair, I've never seen her in you before, maybe I've never let myself see it, but I swear I thought you were Mom."

He hugged me, his shoulders trembling, and I didn't know what to say. In the weeks leading up to the wedding, I had fallen asleep to daydreams of her returning, of my seeing her in the corner of the church, how she'd try to be anonymous and cloaked, but I'd chase her into a room she couldn't escape from.

But Rolland was the one who saw her. And it caused him pain.

He pulled away. "I'll see you in a bit," he said, before he turned to walk up the stairs, the moment as brief as that.

Back in front of the mirror, I kept searching my reflection, wondering if I was the woman of her first or second marriage, wondering why I can look at her high school pictures and see a little of me in her or a person can walk into a room where I'm standing and recognize her, but never, as I study my face or even catch a glimpse in a window I'm passing, do I find a trace of the woman they can see.

Dad tells me she loved writing computer programs, solving a business's needs with logic and code. I go online to find what the classic program

Hello World! looks like in COBOL, the language she used. It's dreadful and dry, with its DISPLAY "Hello World" and STOP RUN and MAIN-LOGIC-EXIT. *How could anyone love to program?* I think, until I read Vikram Chandra's book *Geek Sublime: The Beauty of Code, the Code of Beauty,* in which he describes how even though languages like COBOL may be less flexible and less forgiving of ambiguity than English, coders still grapple with language, manipulating linguistic structures and tropes, searching for expressivity and clarity. Perhaps Mom and I could have connected over poetry and code.

When Jerry went back to school for his undergraduate degree at Houston, he chose to return to computer science, which he studied before architecture. He hung out in the student lounge of the computer science building, playing the game Magic with a bunch of computer geeks, all of them wearing T-shirts with jokes on them like /*no comment*/ that only geeks would get.

This isn't the man I'd fallen in love with, I'd think, the one of color wheels and flying buttresses.

At our apartment, he'd sit in the leather chair we took from Dad's house and code in C++ and Java and Visual Basic, lines of incomprehensible language spitting out programs. *How did I end up married to my parents?* I'd wonder as I listened to him explain object-oriented languages and compilers, how a capacitor gives a bit a charge.

I was working on my dissertation then, a collection of essays on grief, meditating on the violence done to my mother's body versus the slow losing of my father from aging, on not knowing one parent while knowing the other. It started in a nonfiction class, where I wrote about Shepherd Mall, a profile of Mom, and the morning I woke up without her. A mentor had said, "Now cut up every paragraph from all your pieces and rearrange and braid them, until you find a structure for grief."

I loved the act of rearranging those paragraphs, printed and laid out on the floor. *Let go of chronology,* those fragments were saying. *Don't try to fill in the details you can't remember; let the white space say what's missing.* I relished the control of shaping the pieces. I suppose that's why I started writing in the first place, all those years ago when I filled a notebook with poems. When it felt like I couldn't control Mom's next death or Dad's swollen and near-weeping legs, I could at least have power over those words on the page.

Sometimes I think Mom and I are no different, each of us wrestling with language and form and function, but I still cannot grasp how the number 3 translates to 00000011 in a bit of memory, how language can disassemble into electricity.

I tell Dad I wish Mom were alive to watch *Mad Men* with me, because I'd love to hear her perspective on the women characters who try to break into men's professional roles. After all, she had once worked her way into the world of men.

But Dad doesn't seem to be considering this history when he says, "I don't want you to get the wrong idea about your mother. She never had any career aspirations in terms of being successful or powerful. She just really loved to code."

I don't doubt she loved the logic gates, the Boolean constructions, the functions calling on functions calling on functions, but I don't trust she had no career aspirations, not when, just before her death, having worked for a man who refused to pay her for her work, she had decided to start a programming business of her own. And not when Dad's former secretary writes to me and Rolland and says:

> The cold case story about your mom took me back to a different time in my life. I remembered that your mom and dad were mentors to me, a young, naive, country girl just starting my life in the city. I reminisced about the very first time I met Kathleen Sue Engle. I had been on your dad's staff for a week or so. In walked this tall, very pregnant, professional lady with bouncy hair and a pretty smile. I knew she was his wife before

we were introduced, because both their eyes twinkled when they saw each other. It was very apparent they loved each other very much. She and I talked many times—often several times a day—for five years. We had a common bond, take care of your dad. She taught me that you could be a working professional, as well as a wife and mother. In a time when it was not popular for a woman to do so.

I didn't realize I don't want to share the power over language and the story of her death until I reread the cold case article weeks after it first appeared, and found myself shocked not by the details but by the writing itself. The journalist writes,

> It was April 23, 1986, and things were about to turn deadly.
>
> Kathy Sue Engle, 41, got out of the Colt. The brunette, a married mother of two, was thin and almost as tall as the men now watching her.
>
> She'd stayed late at work, and she knew her family already had eaten dinner without her. The night was warm and breezy, with just a few high clouds drifting across the face of the nearly full moon.
>
> If she hurried, she could return an unwanted birthday gift, enjoy the weather and still get home in time to see her children before their 9 p.m. bedtime.
>
> But the men stalked toward her. Predators, young and aggressive.

While journalism of the facts has bothered me at times—"Kathy Sue Engle was seen being forced into her yellow Dodge Colt," "her body had decomposed"—the language is often bare, mechanical, technically authored by an individual but in reality belonging to no one. There's less manipulation, and the manipulation that does exist is for ease—chronological details, related facts placed closely together. But this journalist's writing was not about ease, and it wasn't about truth. Not when he writes that her body was "thin," a detail irrelevant to the story, save that it signals to the reader, "*This* is a body to care about." After all, "The death . . . of a beautiful woman is, unquestionably, the most poetical topic in the world," says Poe. And not just a beautiful woman but a good wife and a good mother. It's about sensationalism and mystery and the stories we love to consume—things were about to turn deadly for a white woman, on a night with a nearly full moon—and justified by what? "We're trying to get readers involved so more information will come forward" at best and "we're trying to sell more papers" at worst? On the one hand, yes, tell the story of my mother's death and other women's deaths but also of their lives. And do it without clichés and hyperbole and turning them into tropes.

It's the journalist's arrogance that pisses me off the most though. That he writes from *her* perspective. This man who knows nothing about Kathy Sue Engle, what she felt, what she thought, if she wanted to be home, if she wanted more work to do, if she wanted to go to a bar and flirt with other men, or if she did, in fact, want to kiss her children before their bedtime. He probably thought he was being clever, drawing the audience into "her" experience, without any consideration of the ethics involved, of the problem of representing what you do not know or will ever know.

I realize I imagine her too. But at least I confess I don't know her.

Maybe I'm angry because he never knew my mother and has no right trying to.

Or maybe it's because, in publishing this version of the story, he's claimed something I see as mine and mine alone.

If I had wanted a mother who is reduced to prey, I would have written her that way, or I would have let TV shows like *On the Case with*

Paula Zahn take her away from me when they called with an offer to broadcast their version of the murder.

When I have so little left, I cling to the power to preserve her, as if, as the daughter, I'm the only one who has that right.

I remember she used Vidal Sassoon shampoo and wore curlers with long metal pins, their tips red, yellow, and blue. Her favorite flower, the Shasta daisy. How she always lost her sunglasses and we were constantly driving back to stores. She wore a purple dress I loved, its pockets piped in turquoise and yellow. I remember we'd shop for unicorn stickers and plastic charms for my charm necklace, and then she'd forbid me to trade the good ones with friends. "*Never* trade the abacus," she said.

My aunt had called her a workaholic, though later she'd say, "Well that's just what Cindy told me. She worked with your mom and said she liked to work through lunch." A neighbor called her the Queen of Christmas. A former teacher called her a freethinker. When I asked what that meant, she just shrugged and said, "An ultra-liberal."

I remember she'd needlepoint every night, the yarn being pulled through the plastic canvases. I study those canvases now and marvel at the tautness of her stitches, how uniform they are. I remember how she made us hunt for pinecones and acorns, only ones with their cupules still attached, to make wreaths. How she used cinnamon sticks to look like tiny bundles of firewood for our homemade ornaments one year. How she wrestled Dad to see who could place their ornament, the Iowa State ball or the Oklahoma State one, higher on the tree. I remember how they argued over when to let me pierce my ears, Dad said twelve, Mom said eight, they split it down the middle at ten. If she had won, she would have picked out my first earrings. I remember she won me a collectible teddy bear named Bear Bryant, who's still sitting in my house with his houndstooth hat.

Dad said she flirted with the men in the store to "win" that teddy bear. The raffle was rigged. He told me she allowed him to have the garage and one corner of the family room as his own space. That she bought an expensive antique piano for no other reason than its looks, how he came home one day and found it in the living room. But she could do that, he said, because the money she earned from work was for play, his salary for the bills.

As an adult, I noticed all the empty decorative boxes in the house and on the piano, crystal boxes, wood boxes, boxes of stone. I asked him why none of them contained anything. "She just liked boxes for aesthetics," he said.

If this were a character description one of my students gave me, I might be able to draw conclusions, to say, "This is the type of woman Kathy was," but it doesn't matter if she was silly or spontaneous or fun, she liked arts and crafts, she loved chocolate you could find at any corner store. I don't want to know the *what* but the *why*. *Why* she loved an abacus enough to wear on her gold charm bracelet, to buy me a plastic one of my own.

Almost all our 8 mm home movies focus on Rolland and on me, the Engle children coming down the stairs on Christmas morning or being pulled on a zip sled. But one out of the eighty-four films gives me Mom, alone, looking right at the camera. We're camping, woods in the background, and she wears high-waisted jeans and a red T-shirt, its neck crooked from her clavicles and bony shoulders, her chin-length hair held back by combs. Dark circles age her eyes. She must not have slept well in the trailer.

I watched the films in our apartment in Houston, having paid for them to be converted to DVD.

A tiny fish, its striped tail noticeably dried out, dangles from her left pointer finger, its tip deep in the gills. Rotating the fish, she displays it for the camera and speaks words I cannot discern through the shaky and faded film.

Jerry walked by on the way to the kitchen, glancing at the TV. He stopped, eyebrows furrowed, stepped closer to the screen. "Is that you?" he said, trying to figure out how my thirty-year-old self could be present on a film from the 1980s.

"No, that's Mom," I said.

"It sure looks like you."

She turns her head to her right, listening to someone off camera, then presses her lips together. She extends her arm out straight to the camera, gritting her teeth and stretching in great effort to bring the fish closer to the camera while keeping her body back toward the woods.

"What's she doing?" he asked.

"She's trying to make the fish appear larger than it is," I said, chuckling.

I replayed it. Again and again. Twenty seconds of only my mother, silent, but moving, trying desperately to misrepresent the truth.

I saw her in the hallway of my middle school—an English teacher, but never mine. Her figure, in my memory, is like a photograph of a person in motion, fluid and smudged. She stood twenty feet from my locker, watching students pass. I tried to study her, the curves of her face, the curl at the bottom of her thick hair. She looked like my mother. Maybe the hair or face, teeth or smile. Not the body. Not bony enough. Not the hands.

With lockers slamming, bodies rushing between us, bells warning us to get to class, I couldn't linger long enough to figure out why.

It would be ten years before I'd see her again. After college. After graduate school in New York. After returning to Oklahoma and moving back into my childhood home and feeling that time had turned back.

I walked into the local Mail Mart, part of a strip mall that is like every other medium-scale suburban strip mall—tanning parlor, dance studio, random gift boutique that relies on the few wealthy old ladies willing to purchase cross-stitched dog purses—every couple of days to overnight my PhD applications.

She stood behind the counter with rolls of bubble wrap, her hair a duller brown but still thick.

"You're Ms. Johnston, right?" I said.

"You're Kristine Engle."

I wish I could put into words how familiar it felt, her voice like walking into a home decorated for Christmas. Every day that I went in with another batch of envelopes, I stayed a little longer.

"Hi, Ms. Johnston!" I'd say.

"I told you not to call me that."

"But calling you Chris seems weird since you were my teacher."

"I was never your teacher," she laughed.

We talked about New York, which I was still grieving for, and Long Island, where she had grown up. About how much we hated living in Oklahoma. About Aristophanes's *Lysistrata*, which she was reading to help her son with his college paper.

"Do you know it?" she asked.

"I've never read it," I said.

"It's interesting because the women withhold sex from their husbands in an effort to get them to end a war."

We laughed and guessed at what the world would be like if all women did this.

"You should use this strategy the next time Jerry won't let you buy another coat," she said.

I loved that she still had a trace of the northeast accent in her voice and that the skin just under her clavicles held beautiful deep wrinkles from summers on beaches.

I sat on a stool on one side of the counter, she on the other side.

"I used to study you in the hallways at school," I said.

"I watched you too," she said. "I'll never forget one particular moment, when you were walking down the stairs. You had a lot of makeup on, you looked right at me, and I just knew you were hurting."

"You look like my mother in some way."

"You know, even though I did not know your mother or your family then, I remember being personally affected when your mother died. I can't explain it."

Our Mail Mart conversations became lunches and ice cream trips and coffees, where I would notice how she wears only open-heeled shoes. We'd drink wine over dinners, Chris complaining about how her retired husband always has the TV blaring, me complaining about the trash Jerry leaves in the sink.

My father asked me, once, what this relationship was. "She has kids of her own," he had said.

I told him I couldn't define it, just that it feels familiar, and easy, and like we're each filling something that's missing.

"That's exactly what having a mother should feel like," he said.

Kenzie and I were playing dress-up at my childhood home. In my bedroom closet, she'd found a prom dress, a red halter with silver beads and sequins and a built-in bra with lots of padding, and had asked, while squirming out of her clothes, to try it on. I held it open, and she stepped into it, slipping the beaded neck over her head, turning to see herself in the mirror. The fabric pooled around her feet, and the only thing keeping the dress from falling to the floor was the halter around her neck. The pads sagged at her stomach, so she cupped them from underneath, lifted them up to her armpits, and said, "I've got *big* bustesses! Woo, woo, I'm a woman now!"

I didn't know how to explain to a four-year-old that being a woman is not only about the body. Or how to keep her from desiring the label of *woman*, to see girlhood as luminous, as something to hold on to.

I took a small fabric-covered box off my dresser. It contained my mother's jewelry, pieces I had never worn but would excavate at times, running my fingertips over the links of a bracelet, clutching a ring in my palm. She sat with me on the floor, Kenzie with her heels tucked behind her, her legs in the shape of a *W*. I couldn't understand how the body can pass down such an uncomfortable shape, when Kenzie has no memory of my mother.

I showed her the charm bracelet, Rolland's and my heads and the abacus, how you can slide its beads up and down. I showed her the KSE pin, explaining how the letters are the same as her initials, the same as mine too.

"Where you got it?" she asked.

"From my mommy," I said.

She slipped her wrist into the heavy gold bracelet, the first wrist it had touched since the wrist of my mother. "Do I get some when I'm bigger?"

"Yes," I said.

Kenzie picked up my purple phone, now faded into white and pink, placed the corded receiver against her cheek. "Oh, hi, Grandma," she said. "Just playing dress-up with Aunt Istine . . . Yes, yes, I'm the princess and the pauper Barbie . . . bye-bye, I love you."

I didn't know who Grandma was, since she calls no one by that name, but before I could ask, she handed me the receiver and said, "Your mommy's on the phone."

It shocked me, and I didn't know how to play this game.

I wanted to say, *Kenzie sits like you, Mom.* I wanted to ask, *As a grandmother, what name do you wish to be called? What jewelry should I pass down, and what should I keep?* But instead I stuttered, "Hi, Mommy," like I was eight. Kenzie was slipping her feet into my mother's black suede pumps and twirling and tripping in the shag carpet, unaware of the gift she gave: "We're playing dress-up," I said. "Having lots of fun. I miss you and love you, Mom."

When revising my dissertation and researching the old newspaper articles about my mother's death, I googled her name and came across her picture, posted in 2010 by someone with the username CSA FD, on his sub-board Victims, Young, Beautiful—Murdered.

CSA FD posted pictures of murdered women on his website, along with the details about their deaths, under message boards and sub-boards like Victims with the Same Name, Unsolved I-40 Murders, Murdered Pregnant Women, and Murdered or Missing Models. He said the board was dedicated to victims of violent crime and in memory of the murdered and the missing. And he included the quote "The Dead Cannot Cry Out For Justice. It Is A Duty Of The Living To Do So For Them."

Maybe he thought he needed to be their voices because women are marginalized and silenced and maybe his postings were meant to say, "Do not forget us." But there's something profoundly disturbing in the thousands of pictures of women he had posted, some of them in sexualized poses, and in the labels of his message boards, as if he got off first by a woman killed and then by deciding which folder to place her in, sometimes judging by her looks. It sickened me. It sickened me like the journalist who wrote the word *obliterated* for shock value.

I asked Rolland if legally we could have Mom's image and details removed, but he told me the photograph is part of the public domain. When I told him how creepy I find it that someone put Mom under the category Victims, Young, Beautiful—Murdered, Rolland said, "I don't know, I think it's great that someone thinks my mom is beautiful."

Maybe if he knew what it's like to walk with keys slipped between each finger like claws, he wouldn't feel pride like this.

I thought about contacting CSA FD and telling him to remove Mom's picture and that it is fucking sick how he relishes women's deaths, but I would have had to register on his website to contact him, and honestly I was afraid to say, "I'm Kathy Sue Engle's daughter" because I don't know what kind of man wants to research and upload thousands of stories of female victims.

So instead I'll say it here: Kathy Sue Engle is not just a face and a body and a victim but a person, even if I don't know exactly who she was, and she doesn't need you to cry out for her.

Imagine her inside an apartment or a house. Imagine her name is Kathleen. Or maybe Kath. Or maybe Kristine. Sometimes she uses the word *ding-a-lings*. Or she thinks *ding-a-lings* is a ridiculous word. She's jumped from relationship to relationship so she doesn't have to be alone. That man said, "You can't go to dinner with your friends." That one shoved her against the wall. Or maybe she just happened to be with someone else when she finally found a man to love, one who said, "I'll watch the kids while you're at the bar," or, "I'll follow you to any school you want." Sometimes she worries about life on her own. She'd have to kill the mouse in the tub. Or fix the router with a blinking light. She'd sit among her piles of paper, lines of words, lines of code, her needlepoint, her knitting in the basket by her feet. She'd have a glass of wine, a Riesling, or maybe a Malbec, pieces of cork floating on its surface because she's not as adept as he is with a corkscrew. Two children would be sleeping in the other room. She hadn't known how much she'd love them or how much she needed them to be gone. Or she never had children to begin with, having learned her freedom meant more. She'd open the app on her phone or flip the switch on the record player to play Air Supply. Imagine her walking to the mirror in the dining room, studying her face for her mother, her mother's mother, the entire motherline, wondering, *Where are they, if not inside me?*

Is it possible to construct her from fragments, like tiny pieces of code?

I'm here if you want me.

I'm sorry that I acted like a little girl this morning—I just hated to see you go.

I can't get to sleep without you there. You should see the deep indentations in the wall from me climbing the walls. (Oh, how humorous I am!). I'll be lucky if the walls are still standing by the time you get back.

You know I wouldn't mind coming east as long as it's not New York.

Did you know that Tran and Bill had a baby boy Thurs. night. They named it something odd—Scanlan I think. He didn't have any pictures—that's too establishment. Weird, weird, weird!

I'm glad you can't see me this week—the circles under my eyes have reached the middle of my cheeks.

I was bombed and went right to sleep. We started drinking wine. By the time Karen left at 1:00 we had finished 2½ bottles. I felt rather high.

I have some halfway bad and excited news for you.

Doss, please believe me. There's only you in my life now. Thomas is someone from the past—someone whom I loved very much in every way but now is only a friend whom I care about as a person. Please let me like him in this respect.

The house is so quiet and lonely without you. I've tried to think of a way to get the Army to send you home and I've finally thought of one. Tell them you're queer or better yet make a pass at someone.

Oh what a wino girlfriend you have.

I wore my outfit with the huge necktie. I didn't do too good a job making it look right. I need you to tie my ties. Also I've killed 2 bugs since you've been gone. It took real courage. I have not had enough courage however to pick them up & put them in the trash. They might still be there when you get home.

Oh, buy the way, I haven't started my period yet. Maybe (I hope) I'm pregnant.

My days are simply crappy without you (What a nasty mouth I have).

When I said I regretted what could have been, I do. In planning my life, I pictured myself married to one man and being happy and making him happy for the rest of my life. But things didn't work that way.

I find myself wanting to edit her, to fix the mistakes, tighten the wording, reduce the whine. She annoys me sometimes, how she uses the word *lonely* or a variation of it eleven different times in just a handful of letters, the way she's always apologizing, always begging. I'd keep the two and a half bottles of wine but make her want New York, as I did. I'd add that she felt ambivalent about having babies, rather than seeing it so simply. I want to rewrite her into the mother I want.

I don't do this with my father's letters though, never feeling the urge to delete his longing, instead finding it tender that he misses his girlfriend so much, even as he wraps his desire in formal language, singing the only erotic serenade he knows how: "Right now a very real sensation of my body aching for you is quite present."

I can't help but think it's because of how we judge women, and clearly I'm not immune. I'll remind myself of the letters I wrote Jerry when I was twenty, telling him "I cannot offer enough to complete you," of the scrapbook

I made him where I say, "I want to give you a son." I'll think, *Can't we just forgive ourselves for being young? For needing, even years into marriage, someone to kill the house centipede on the wall, its legs as long as its long body, or can't we start with acceptance, to see there's nothing wrong with asking a man, after I've decided to wear a shirt and tie to teach in, to help me tie a single knot?*

It's easy to be frustrated with the game of Memory, how one card is supposed to match another, how pairs should be removed from the pile, and in the end there's only a bare floor and a tidy stack of cards, but few of them ever actually match. The "better wife than a mother," the "workaholic," the PTA member, the homeroom mother, the passive, and the strong. The *I want a man who orders for me*, the *I'm gonna stick it to you with a puppy*. None of these women is my mother. And every one of them is. All interpretation, mere traces, none more valid than the rest or closer to the real. She is everywhere and nowhere simultaneously, and it vexes me.

But then I remember Hélène Cixous, how she argues the masculine is associated with mastery and the need to know, how we women should not appropriate men's instruments; "Leave that to the worriers," Cixous says, "to masculine anxiety and its obsessional relationship with the workings they must control—knowing 'how it runs' in order to 'make it run.'" I think of Carole Maso, who writes in her novel,

> Feminine can be read as the living, as something that continues to escape all boundaries, that cannot be pinned down, controlled or even conceptualized.
>
> Cannot be arrested, and which remains—
>
> Elusive.

The fragments aren't the game I thought I was playing, but it's a game I've come to appreciate: the contradictory, scattered cards and the gaps between them, this elaborate, illusory, tangled, illogical, and beautiful mess.

I remember she called our wired-hair terrier Retardo. How she used the word *tacky*. I can almost hear her say it. How we changed Jane to James in an Air Supply song, so we weren't singing about love for a girl. I remember she told me to shut up when I screamed rather than sang the lyrics. I can almost hear that too, that moment when a mother just can't take a loud kid any longer.

I remember her standing by the kitchen counter, looking down at me, scolding me never to call her Mother. "Only Mom or Mommy," she said.

How each April, I'd watch her pick up the phone on her birthday, listen for a few seconds, then hang up. I'd watch her watch the clock, then dial the number back, singing "Happy Birthday" to her twin. How Mom bought my cousin a Barbie because her twin had refused to; "The boobs are offensive," Barb had said, but Mom saw nothing wrong in Barbie's body.

I remember Mom livid, at Dad, for calling Barry Manilow "Barry Manhole" right before we left for the concert, how she almost left him at home. And the story of how, sleepless and enraged one night, she recorded a cassette of Dad's snoring, then played it at full volume while he was sleeping, to wake his ass up.

I remember she'd order Push-Ups from the ice cream truck, while I liked the Bomb Pops in red, white, and blue. How sometimes she'd give us chocolate pudding for breakfast, as long as we made a happy face in the pudding before we ate it, and every Christmas, she'd serve me chocolate pudding in a crystal champagne coupe. Even now, I'll do two twirls with a spoon for eyes and a long swoosh for a mouth. I remember she placed a bottle of Heinz ketchup in my stocking every year, something Jerry does now, and Rolland always got a jar of maraschino cherries. I remember she dressed up as the Easter Bunny and came to my first-grade class, carrying an Easter egg piñata that she had filled with Life Savers and fake spiders.

I remember two things the most: her blazer and her fingers. How that leather smelled, how her nails were cracked and chewed back, her cuticles dry and white. I don't know why these are the things I feel closest to. It could be because I saw them most often, that she wore the blazer with everything, though I don't know if this is true, that she'd gnaw on her fingers every chance she got. I could say they're what I touched the most, what most touched me, those mornings I'd hug her goodbye, the leather sticking to my cheek, her fingers separating my hair into doggy ears. Or maybe, even as a child, I was drawn to contradiction, to what is gnarled and what is smooth.

It seems like a lot, these fragments, but it's only when I list them that they feel this way. I'd trade the Vidal Sassoon and Easy Cheese just to be able to see her face or hear her voice or to have a memory longer than a blip, though, like the abacus, I won't give up *Her Majesty's Ship*, how she stuck large *H.M.S.* stickers on its side. Nor will I give away how she told me her dad died of brain cancer when she was twelve. She handed me a small figurine, a porcelain chair, meant only for display, that her father had given to her when she was a child. Even at a young age, I knew it was special, the chair itself and her passing it on to me. I can't remember what she said or how she looked when she held it out for my hands, but I can feel it still, the gravity and weight of the moment, a mother trusting her daughter to hold on to what she loves.

I read Cheryl Strayed's *Wild*, and when she writes of her mother's death and says, "One of the worst things about losing my mother at the age I did was how very much there was to regret," I consider the weight of that sentence, how it feels simultaneously distant and close. There wasn't enough time for me to walk away, to close the door, to not return a phone call, or to not visit when she needed me to. Not enough time for her to teach me the family cookie recipe and then watch me burn them for the holiday meal, or for someone to say I make them better than she does. Not enough time for me to say, "You're a slut for having an affair," or for her to tell me, "Your eyes could kill."

I never had to watch Mom hold her arms up and tap the skin on her triceps, the way she frowned because it swung like a sign in the wind, something her husband said she should watch out for. Or watch her pull the skin on her upper lip taught to erase the lines she thought of as cracked clay. Or watch her age spots grow.

Perhaps I witnessed the cosmetic transformations once, the hair being unwound from a hot curler, her body in a dress to her body in jeans, but I didn't have to see her body frail to below a hundred pounds, her voice go silent because talking with emphysema makes her unable to breathe, to see her fingers trembling because the weight of a needle and yarn became too heavy.

I'm learning this loss with my father, who wears compression socks and needs me to tie his shoes and who doesn't spend one day without pain. I've seen what he looks like on a ventilator, a fresh incision from his chest to his groin stapled and weeping. I've seen how his time, once spent reading history and consulting on software, has shifted to fixating on how often he does or does not go to the bathroom, on detailing to his children the consistency of his poop. "Today it was hard, the size of marbles."

I'm not happy I lost my mother young, just as I'm blessed to still have Dad, grateful that even with all the ways we hurt and will continue to hurt each other, we still sing, "I love you, a bushel and a peck," whenever we hug goodbye.

But I didn't have to watch Mom enter the kitchen and stare at the floor vent in its corner, her arms folded across her body, the sleeves of her red robe fraying, how she shivers and pulls the hood of her robe over her head, tucking her short gray hair into the folds of fabric. The skin of her neck and décolleté wrinkles like no other skin on her body does, creasing as deep as the life lines on her palms. She stands barefoot and remembers the linoleum that looked like inlaid bricks, regretting replacing it with this cold tile. Her toes curl, the varicose veins rising from her feet like the roots of a maple tree. She remembers the way she could once plop down by the vent, bend her knees back, and lean forward to read the paper, how the air warmed her body. But she knows she can't get to the ground anymore. Can't bend her legs back into the shape of a *W*. She shivers and sighs with the memory of Saturday mornings with Folgers and of the yellow ceramic ashtray's pinning the real estate section down and of holding a Salem in one hand, her chin in another, and she lets out a sob, quiet, but loud enough that her daughter can hear.

Mom is lying on her stomach, this time on the family room floor, her back arched, torso raised like a horse's neck.

This is my most vivid memory.

I'm sitting on the small of her back, my legs pressed against her ribs. I set the wicker basket behind her left arm, the hairbrush between her shoulder blades. Then I brush her dark brown hair, trying to be tender with her tangles. I reach into the basket, pulling out one barrette after another, snapping the plastic into her hair, pink flowers, yellow circles. I fill her hair with a hundred barrettes. When I finish, we turn to Dad, who sits amused in his chair.

"What do you think, Daddy?"

"She's beautiful," he says.

Even at seven years old, I hear the marvel in his voice as he looks at her.

I start taking the barrettes out, forgetting to snap them closed, as she taps the ash off her cigarette into a green glass ashtray, spherical and sliced on a forty-five-degree angle. When I think I have removed them all, I brush her hair again, making smooth what I had snarled.

She then asks me to scratch the dead skin off her scalp.

Such an odd and repulsive request, I think now, scraping someone else's dead skin off with your fingernails, even if it's your mother's scalp.

I must have learned sometime later that effacing is what you do alone, behind a closed door, with a fine-toothed comb.

I rise onto my knees and look down on her head and make rivers by separating her hair, white streams coursing through thickets. I examine them for scaly skin, and when I find the tiny dry patches, I scrape with my nails, flakes spreading throughout her hair. I think, *It looks like a party with a bunch of confetti.*

But then I accidentally press down too hard and break the skin. She doesn't notice or even seem to feel it, and the blood swells only to the size of pinheads, but it's blood and it's red and it's coming from my mom's body.

Sometimes I wonder if I'd remember twisting and snagging and brushing her hair and the barrettes like constellations if she hadn't told me to remove the dead skin from her scalp, or if the memory is vivid only because I harmed her, made her body bleed. Those red beads rising from her white scalp.

I dream I'm watching a home movie of my birth. Mom's in the hospital bed, on her back, me, tiny, in the cradle of her left arm. With her right hand, she grabs the placenta—it's like a giant thick piece of rolled-out dough—and pulls it over us, rolling her body toward me, wrapping us both in the cocoon. I think, *A placenta isn't thick like that or as big as a blanket, and besides, that's disgusting and unsanitary for her to do.* But the scene plays again and again, and I hear myself working it out, finding a way to reconcile—*She loved you that much, enough not to reject what her own body had made, enough to pull you both back in, to shelter you both, in a world for just the two of you.*

I was visiting Chris, whom Jerry and I started affectionately calling my pseudomom, at her home. I was sitting on a sofa with a floral print, my feet tucked under my legs, when I told her I liked the way her house had been updated, unlike my childhood home. I imagined what it would have been like to grow up there, to have cereal at that breakfast table before school, to garden with Chris during the summer afternoons.

We were drinking wine and arguing about baths. My baths last an hour or two, with bubbles and candles and jazz and staying so still in the water that when you breathe, you see the water breathe with you. Chris stays in ten minutes tops. I couldn't understand why she'd even bother with a bath.

In her backyard, a cocker spaniel played and then scratched at the door. "I love cockers," I said. "I had one growing up." And then I told her how we had gotten the puppy just a few months before my mother died:

Mom, Rolland, and I were going to Shepherd Mall while Dad went into work on a weekend. She had begged him to join us, but he refused. When just the three of us went into the pet store at the mall, we saw a black cocker spaniel puppy with fluffy, curly ears against the window, giving us the "saddest puppy dog eyes" Mom had ever seen. Rolland and I played with the puppy on the store floor, petting her belly and the thin white stripe of her chest, while Mom signed the papers. We decided to call her Sally. Then we walked through the mall, and I held Sally to my chest, deciding she was mine and no one else's. Mom stopped at a pay phone, one of several in a long row against a wall, and called my father. Knowing he'd be furious she'd bought a second dog, she said, "I told you, you should have come with us."

Chris threw her fist into the air and yelled, "Way to go, Kathy!" so loud it startled me.

She started laughing so hard tears came to her eyes.

"Way to go, Kathy!" she had said, as if my mother were in the room, drinking wine with her friend, telling the story herself.

I had told it so many times that I had stopped feeling it. Or maybe I had felt it but in a different way. Whenever I told it, the person listening was always saddened, as I was, because the story was about a mother who was not there. But Chris, in her exaltation and joy, with her fist raised in the air, transformed it.

She brought her back to me then, and I laughed too, at a woman named Kathy, who said, I'm going to work because I want to, I'm going to buy a piano without asking and for no other reason than to be a prop in a room, I'm going to want you on the weekend because I love you, and if you don't give me that, I'll give you the middle finger in the form of a puppy who will pee all over the goddamn house.

Now I see a bunny hunched in the corner of the stockade fence, a dog inching closer. She's flattened her body, chin touching the earth, her ears pulled back; she's as still and as hidden as she can possibly be.

But *this* rabbit knows it isn't about the dog's hunger; it's about the chase and squeal. There's power in this.

The dog inches closer and she sits up. She thumps her powerful hind legs, bares her teeth. She knows there's nowhere to go. But her heart doesn't quicken out of fear. It beats faster because she wills it to, because she hurries her own breath.

Before the dog can get close enough to bite, she bursts her own heart as a final *fuck you*.

Cleaving To

PART VI

✦

IN THE SUMMER OF 2008, A FEW MONTHS AFTER THE COLD case article that made Rolland decide to give up hope, I was doing laundry at the apartment in Houston when Dad called and said that I should sit down. I didn't sit down, thinking a joke would follow—"Well, Schnickelfritz, I have a date" or "I cleaned out the fridge!" Then he said he received a phone call from a retired homicide detective who now works for the cold case unit of the OCPD.

"They have a DNA match," he said. "His name is Kyle Richard Eckardt."

I quickly wrote his name on the refrigerator whiteboard.

"He's in prison at Stringtown for aggravated assault and battery of a Tulsa woman."

I wrote down "Stringtown" and "agg assault" and "Tulsa."

Years of planning for this moment, of building narratives in my head, and instead of screaming, fainting, or collapsing, I took notes.

Then I sat down on the couch in silence, shaking my head every few seconds, as I listened to Dad tell me how the detectives had been by the house to ask him about the Salems and the Marlboro Lights and the Colt, because the DNA match had originated from cigarette butts in the car. He told me Eckardt was twenty-one years old in 1986. A fucking kid. I had always imagined the men were in their forties, not boys like my students. It seems like this type of violence would take time to propagate and grow within a man.

I stared at the whiteboard on the fridge, Kyle Richard Eckardt now part of my home.

I kept staring at his name, written in messy blue marker.

Kyle Richard, of all names.

His initials, K. E.

Like mine. Like Mom's.

After we hung up, I called Jerry and told him we had a DNA match. He told me he'd be right home.

I didn't move from the couch. I just kept staring off, trying to imagine what our life was going to be like now, or looking at the pile of books I needed to read for my PhD exams in the fall and wondering if I could even pass them now, or reading the details on the fridge again.

I read, "White male, 21," and thought, *He's only forty-three now, I'm thirty, the same age difference as me and Lee.*

I kept wondering where Stringtown was and why it was called that. A town of strings. I kept wondering about the woman in Tulsa, what had happened to her, what she would say when the cops questioned her.

Thirty minutes passed before Jerry walked through the door, dropped his backpack on the floor, and hugged me.

I put my forehead against Jerry's chest, his shirt damp from the heat outside.

"What do we know so far?" he asked.

I pointed to the whiteboard and then repeated it all.

Jerry grabbed his backpack and pulled his laptop out.

It hadn't even occurred to me, as I sat on the couch and stared at his name on the fridge, to run Internet searches to find out more, as if the details in my notes were all that could be known.

"Rolland's already found a few links and emailed them to us," Jerry said.

I walked into the bedroom, where our desktop was. It seems odd to me, now, that we were in separate rooms, clicking links and reading. Shouldn't we have been holding each other, or at least our hands, as we learned who it was who may have killed her? But I guess sometimes, in tragedy, you choose convenience over comfort, or maybe it was the rooms each of us spent more time in that we needed the most in that moment, the objects familiar and soothing, like the bowl of tiny gemstones I'd run my fingers through.

In my inbox: links to the Department of Corrections, links to newspapers that covered his crime in Tulsa, links to his picture.

In one mug shot, he has a long beard, dark gray for the mustache, white on his chin, his hair growing white and in a mullet cut. His glasses are thick. In another, his head and face are shaved, the images so different except for the eyes and the bags under them, his black arching eyebrows. In one, he looks smug; in another, indifferent. He looked like he was in his sixties, much older than forty-three. Two years older than my mother when she died. He's big, six foot one, and almost twice mine in weight.

I felt a rush then, all the hate I've ever known coming into focus, narrowed to a man with a mullet. I wanted to put a stiletto to his throat or to cut him, a little at a time, over a period of days.

Then I noticed his birth date: April 10, 1965.

April 10. The same birthday as Mom.

I wondered how that was even possible and felt another thing taken from me. Now I wouldn't be able to honor her, through crying or visiting a garden or remembering the bracelets I gave her, without also thinking of his birth.

We learned that the Tulsa woman was dead. Her name was Terry Welch.

In January 2007, witnesses saw Eckardt beating her in front of her apartment before he dragged her inside. It wasn't until the next evening that people realized she was dead. She was found naked in her bathtub. She had two knocked-out teeth, severe tearing to her anus, bruises on her face and cheeks, cuts on her elbow and on her lips.

Her six-year-old son had been there the entire time.

Prosecutors didn't charge Eckardt with murder because the medical examiner never ruled her death as a homicide. She didn't have enough blood loss to explain her death. The autopsy showed severe intoxication, "near the lower end of the potentially lethal range." Because the bathtub may have contained water, they said she could have passed out and accidentally drowned. Or that she "drowned or suffocated at the hands of another."

They originally charged Eckardt with rape by instrumentation and aggravated assault, but he entered a plea agreement in February 2008, pleading no contest in exchange for dropping the charge of rape. We learned that he could be paroled in a year and a half, for time served and good behavior.

For days, Jerry and I studied Eckardt's photographs and read the articles over and over again. I thought about all the coincidences—is that what they were?—the initials, the names, the birth dates, the fact that he was forty-one when he was charged with assaulting Terry Welch, the same age Mom was when she died. I told Jerry to contact his statistics professor to ask what the chances were of a person randomly killing another person with the same first and last initials and with the same day of birth. It's over one in five billion. That's nearly the population of the world.

What meaning am I supposed to take, when it's violence that brings these details together?

More than that, though, I thought of Terry Welch. Of the medical examiner who didn't classify her death as a homicide, because her blood alcohol level was high. I didn't understand why he couldn't tell the difference between drowning and suffocation—wouldn't you have water in your lungs if you drowned?—or how murder is not the logical conclusion, when a woman has cuts and bruises and knocked-out teeth. After all, the coroner didn't know the cause of death in my mother's case, but they had ruled it a homicide. I couldn't stop thinking that, had Terry Welch not been previously seen in a liquor store with Eckardt, they would have treated her death differently.

Same with her neighbors who did nothing to stop it. He slapped and beat her, he dragged her inside, and they did nothing. Called no one.

Worse was her six-year-old son. He was there. The entire time. Alone. With his mom's body in the bathtub. A little boy tried to wake up his naked and bloody mother.

I swam laps at the apartment pool because there was nothing I could do but pull the water, transfer energy, swim until my body exhausted itself so as not to think. Pull again, again, for days. For as long as it takes for the police to charge him.

A little over a month after learning about Eckardt, I visit my father in Oklahoma. Sitting alone at the kitchen table of my childhood home, I listen to a recording of when the detectives stopped by and told Dad about the DNA match.

It begins with the detectives talking about developments in his wife's case over the weekend and that they have identified a suspect. Detective Bruce Liddell says, "He's not under arrest or anything, but we know where he is located." They tell him they don't have much information but they didn't want him to hear it first on the news, given the notoriety the case had back then.

"I appreciate that," my father says.

"Do you know an individual by the name Kyle Richard Eckardt?" they ask.

"No," he says.

It's clear they show him a picture.

What was Dad thinking then, seeing the image of Eckardt, his shaggy gray hair and beard, in front of him, on the kitchen table of our house? It'd been twenty-two years and here police were again, at the same spot where they took our fingerprints and hair. Did Dad move his stacks of newspapers off the table? Or the stack of Kleenexes that he blows his nose with, flattens back out to dry, and reuses? He must have. The detectives would need room for their notes. Papers or binders or notebooks, with quotes from my father from decades before.

Liddell has a quintessentially Oklahoman accent, not quite the Texas drawl but still with a slow cadence in his speech. He throws in a lot of *uh*s, he drags out his *all*s and the last word in each of his sentences, and he says, "I know it's kinda tough," when my father examines the picture.

Dad doesn't recognize the man in the photograph.

Liddell then speaks to Dad like he's a child: "He's a white male, and he was twenty-one years old at the time, okay, and so we're going to ask you questions now and want you to think about it, uh, everything that we talk about I will make a report on, but I want you, if there's something different, or if you say 'no' now and remember something later, you need to get a hold of us, okay?"

His *okay*s are soft. He lingers on them. I see a parent bending down to the level of his child, holding the child's hands in his, and saying, "Now remember, this is why you don't cross the street, okay?" I wonder if Liddell does this because Dad is aging, as if he can't understand, or because he sees the row of semitrucks that are about to barrel down that street.

They ask him questions about her car, who had been driving it, why it was in the shop a week before her abduction, who would have ridden in it and how often.

I can hear the frustration in Dad's voice when memory fails. He wants to be helpful. He wants to give them the answers they seek.

"This is what you said then," they tell him, as they read from a twenty-two-year-old report.

"I don't remember that," he says.

They ask him where the car ended up.

"I turned it over to the insurance company," he says and then describes how it was "totaled" because the FBI took out everything for evidence.

They ask him if he did much fishing, if he had any fishing equipment in the car.

"That I don't remember," he says.

I want to interject and say, *There'd be no reason for our fishing gear to be in Mom's car. We used the station wagon for the lake. And it definitely wouldn't be in the car in April.*

They ask him if he or my mom would have ever had a transient in the car.

"Certainly not," he says.

I'm listening to the recording and getting upset. I've known for over a month the details about Eckardt and Terry Welch. I've known the summary of this recording. But hearing the language is different. This language of interrogation, this language of the law.

"You were driving the Colt," they say. "You were driving it prior to that. When you smoked back then, did you ever put cigarette butts on the floor or put them in the ashtray?"

"Ashtray, yeah."

"You wouldn't throw cigarettes butts on the floor?"

"Nah."

"It wouldn't be common to have cigarette butts on the floor of your car?"

"No." My father pauses and then says, "I'm a little cleaner than that."

"Did you frequently clean the car?"

"Fairly. I mean, I probably vacked up above-average care of the car."

"At the time, do you remember how many packs of cigarettes you smoked a day?"

"Oh, I, I'm sure it was over one, uh, as far as Marlboro, my smoking. Kathy was probably over one, between one and two packs a day."

"So between the two of you, it would require cleaning the ashtray out pretty regularly?"

"Yeah, at least dumping it, yeah, yeah."

"Let me ask you, now this is just a question for me. If you were driving for five hours, how many cigarettes would you smoke in a five-hour period?"

"Wow. Probably one an hour."

They're questioning my father quickly, they're repeating their questions as if they don't believe his answers, like he's the criminal here. I'm listening to the recording and I know this isn't the case, that they are taking notes for a report, that this report can be used in court, that they simply want to verify the information so no doubts can be raised later, but I'm alone in the house and thinking, *Stop treating him this way. Stop the interrogation. Show some compassion for the man who has a photo of his wife's killer on the table.*

"Okay. All right. Well, thank you very much," Liddell says. "We hope to keep you advised about what's going on here."

"Gentlemen, I appreciate it," Dad says.

"No problem."

The legs of the chairs scrape against the tile floor as they stand to leave. I'm crying and shaking my head and thinking, *My God, this is what our life is going to be like now, endless and repeated questions about cigarette butts and clothing and Mom's habits and Dad's habits and who exactly was in the car and when.* They walk off talking. I can hear their footsteps get farther away, the front glass door open and close with its whine, then the wood door close, and Dad's shuffled footsteps getting closer. And just as I'm expecting to hear Dad's sitting back down at the table and the silencing of the recorder, just as I'm sobbing because I'm thinking about him sitting there, alone, with absolutely no one to console him after he's been thrown back into his beloved's murder, I hear peeing, a heavy and long stream into the toilet. "Jesus, Dad," I say aloud, listening to seconds and seconds of it, then the flushing. And now I'm laughing at the absurdity of it all. I never thought the sound of my father peeing, what is human and real, would be exactly what I needed to hear.

Nine months passed, as we waited for the detectives to do their work, with faith that charges would be filed, if only we were patient enough to wait. I somehow finished my PhD exams with high passes and continued to work on my dissertation, trying to write about Mom's death without having any distance from it. Jerry continued with his classes but was fired from his internship because there were days when he just didn't show up.

And then in April 2009, just before I graduated and tried to find a local teaching job, I found out that faith in justice isn't enough sometimes.

Detective Liddell had been back to Dad's house to have him identify items in the car: a loose-knit sweater in reddish gold yarn, a red sweater and skirt, a costume watch or a Swatch, a briefcase, a pair of heels, a package of Salems, a slice of black cheese. Dad told me over the phone, "Time has taken its toll."

I asked him if it upset him to see photographs of the evidence.

"Your mother's briefcase hurt, because I remember it so well, and her with it."

Liddell said the DA wasn't prepared to charge Eckardt because, while his DNA was found all over the car, they couldn't determine exactly when he was in it. A window of time exists between when the car was abandoned and the moment it was found, which means a defense attorney can easily argue Eckardt entered the car after the killers dumped it in Tucumcari. That allows for reasonable doubt, Liddell said. But why would a man, with a history of violence against women, enter a car with blood, with semen, with a sliced-off bra, a sweater with a slit and blood, with trash everywhere, and then sit and smoke cigarettes? I figured they could say he was homeless or drunk or cold, that an unlocked car, however dirty, was better than resting on concrete or grass, but with the details in the papers and affidavits, his guilt seemed more reasonable than his innocence.

I thought of the words Rolland said to a journalist years before, "It's almost like you're at the finish line, but you're just not there. You never get there," and how it seems we'll always be running, especially if we believe the world is just.

Liddell said Eckardt was scheduled for release in just a few months. Good behavior, where your life on the outside, your behavior then, is obsolete, significant only to your victims. I had always thought not knowing was the brutal part, the way any man, as long as he was older than I am, could be walking on the street, sitting in a restaurant, visiting a corner store, with the memory of how good it felt to hit her, the way we were always wondering if we'd get that call, if justice would be served, but having the DNA match and knowing he'd be released was far worse.

There'd be moments I could return to indifference, to where I was before, or perhaps not indifference but a feeling deep down, a shrug, an "I don't know," a giving in or giving up, a feeling that nothing has changed, just another "this is the man who did it but there isn't enough evidence to convict him," but then I'd think of Eckardt, walking out of prison, smiling as he stopped by a liquor store and eyed a woman with a child, and the rage and terror came flooding back.

I had told Jerry I didn't think I could do it, that I could play out Eckardt's death in third person, seeing a woman who resembles myself swing the bat for a smooth strike to the spine, but when I imagined it in first person, Eckardt's face in front of me, the kickback of a gun, the knife hitting bone, I couldn't continue the scenario.

But then I'd think of how Eckardt's mother once filed a protective order against her son because he hit her and knocked her against a refrigerator. And of how one of Eckardt's girlfriends had a cut on the back of her head that bled profusely; her eyes were black, her nose swollen, her lips cut. And I'd think of Terry Welch, with her knocked-out teeth, and of her six-year-old son, alone and terrified to go to the bathroom—and I didn't hesitate. I wanted to torture Eckardt. I wanted him to feel what his victims felt—the skin sliced open, deep black bruises, an animal's bite, fear. Yes, I wanted Eckardt to know fear, his six-feet-one-inch body brought down, incapacitated. Then I wanted every part of his body obliterated.

I'd think, *This isn't how it's supposed to be, a* known *murderer walking down the street.* But there are thousands of families who've been right where we were. How do they keep from hunting the killers down? What do you do when the system you've put faith in fails? Where does the rage go? What does it do to a person to keep calling that rage back, to no avail?

I sit outside at Inversion Coffee House in Houston. It's fifty-seven degrees—cold enough for a sweater and a scarf but warm enough to sit outside. I'm rereading the affidavits from Eckardt's arrests, and the people around me on their laptops have no idea that I'm thinking about cutting off a man's dick or paralyzing him from the neck down. With the passing cars near to me and loud, I turn up the volume on my iPod, thinking now of Mom's jewelry, bracelets and necklaces I keep as my own, how their origins are lost. And of the detectives, still at work on the case, wanting photographic evidence of her wedding ring and gold watch.

I've imagined Mom's ring as a souvenir the men kept. Or somewhere in the oil field at Sayre, the band pressed into the dirt by the sole of his shoe.

Or all this time in a pawn shop in Tucumcari, the bands unsoldered, placed on a velvet-wrapped finger.

I leave the café, traversing the cracked sidewalk, broken open by the roots of oak trees, toward a pawn shop up the road. I tell myself I'm an idiot. That I shouldn't seek to open another wound. But something unnamable is pulling me there.

This is the only time I've been inside a pawn shop; it's small and looks like a dirty garage with a concrete floor. There are two cases with women's engagement and wedding rings, so many small solitaires.

Perhaps 140 rings.

One hundred and forty stories, none of which we will ever know.

How many were pawned after being taken by force? If I place my ear to the glass, can I hear women scream?

A man asks if I need help.

"No, just looking," I say, pausing. "Well, I do have a question, a random one. If a man comes in to sell a piece of women's jewelry, do you think anything of it?"

"Do I think anything of it?"

"Yeah, do you ever wonder what the story is, or do you not really consider why he is selling it?"

"No, not really, don't think about it," he shrugs. "But everyone who comes in tells a story. 'My wife left me and left her jewelry behind.' 'I bought this for my girlfriend but . . .'"

It's clear he doesn't consider or even care about the women, how men slide their rings from bloody or bruised or dead fingers. So I interrupt him to ask how the pricing works.

"Seven to eleven dollars per gram," he says.

"Okay, thanks," I say, then leave.

Walking back to the coffeehouse, I think of the times I've imagined her killers confessing, telling me where they pawned her ring, how Dad and I would walk into a shop and find it among the others. But now that I've seen the rows of solitaires, small like my mother's, no different than thousands of others, her life no different, I know I'll never recover it.

I go home and weigh my own wedding ring on our kitchen scale. Four grams. Then it hits me. At seven to eleven dollars per gram, my mother's killers, like all the other men, sold the ring for enough to buy a couple of fast-food meals or a case or two of beer, when I would give almost anything and everything to get it back.

We would get a chance at justice though. In June 2009, just two months before Eckardt was scheduled to be released and right after I had graduated, we met with the Oklahoma City district attorney at his office to discuss the charges he planned to file. The OSBI lab had extracted additional DNA from evidence in my mother's car—this time a mixture sample of Eckardt's DNA and Mom's.

They'd finally crossed the timeline.

His DNA joined with hers. No longer could he say he entered the car after her body was dumped.

I wanted to feel nothing but joy for this moment we had all waited for, but by then I had learned not to trust it.

Rolland, Jerry, and I sat on one side of the table, two prosecutors and two detectives and my father on the other, the DA at the head. I studied Melissa Fisher, the lead prosecutor, as she sat down, her dark suit, her bleached blond hair, her many rings and bracelets, her acrylic nails. She seemed to strike a balance between feminine and masculine, and I wondered how many men in her office made remarks about her looks. Rolland had said she had a reputation as a win-at-all-costs lawyer, which made me like her immediately.

Detective Liddell talked about Terry Welch. I had only known him by voice, but now I could see he looked the part of a detective—suit, badge, thick hair with a receding hairline, a strong jaw that I imagined could intimidate a person he was interrogating. His speech, once flat and controlled, became more animated when he said he couldn't understand why the Tulsa coroner did not rule it a homicide. This crack in his measured demeanor, his clear frustration over a fuckup in a case, made me like him too. It made me think, *Finally, here's a man who values a woman's life.*

Rolland, Jerry, and I sat forward in our chairs, our forearms often on the table, and even though the chairs swiveled and were cushiony, we rarely moved or leaned back. Dad listened to the evidence with his palm on the arm of the chair, his elbow up, as if at any second he would push himself up and leave the room or as if he were bracing himself for a blow.

Liddell described the mixture sample, how it came from the interior of a beer-bottle cap that was found in the back seat of the Colt.

Melissa, who had worked a year on the case to prepare it for charges being filed, turned to him and asked, "I think one piece of forensic evidence is also we have a stain on the back seat that is a mixture, right?"

"Bloodstain?" Liddell asked.

"Well, I don't think that we can say it's blood. Don't we have a mixture on the back seat, an epithelial fraction of him and of, of her?"

"I don't think so," he said.

"Okay, we'll have to check on that," she told us.

They tried to keep moving forward, but Dad interrupted with questions about the processing of the car—who did it, when, what was left, was it a swath of the car seat that was collected or was the entire seat taken—a meticulous line of questioning, all leading up to what the four of us were thinking: *Why is there confusion about this evidence?*

Melissa was quick to respond: "Well, I may, may just be mistaken. Liddell knows the case far better than I do. He's lived with it for years. This is an enormous case. He has done a diagram of the car documenting exactly where in the car each item is because there is a ton of stuff in the car. There are twelve three-inch binders of police reports that I have not even read. He has read everything. I'm sorry. I should not have even brought that up while we were in here. That's my mistake."

But this was the stain we thought had brought us here, to the moment when charges were being filed, not the beer-bottle cap. We had figured the OSBI retested a mixture on the seat, the only mixture we remembered.

"If I may interject," I said. "Of course, memory is faulty, so it's difficult to remember accurately, but in *my* memory, when we had DNA testing done . . . there was a mixture, there was a sample of basically vaginal fluid and semen."

"I have the same recollection," Rolland said. "There was a semen stain from the back seat and the majority of that sample was used up somewhere closer to the commission of the crime in an attempt to blood type, pre-DNA, for the two suspects out of New Mexico."

Liddell then rambled for a while, about our memory accurately reflecting the reports and synopsis from the beginning of the case, about his not understanding all the intricacies and probabilities and statistics about DNA, about talking to the person who originally tested the evidence but who is now in Iraq, until he finally said, "To say that at this point that it's sperm, I would say no right now . . . We can put your wife and your mother in the car through epithelial fractions and blood—there was blood in the car. There is blood on the seat."

Rolland responded, "To follow up, and again, memories fade, but I'm pretty certain that we were told that *that* stain was semen. It was used up for blood typing and at the time that they did the first DNA in '99 they found one sperm cell left but could not get DNA from that one sperm cell. I am positive I was told that, whether or not that is in fact true, but I'm positive that's what we were told."

"I'll tell you this, if we had one sperm cell we would test it," Liddell said.

We all started laughing. Because of course they would.

But that didn't make us feel any better.

"You've got to understand," Liddell said. "You might look at something as an investigator and say, 'It's my opinion that's semen and blood in the mixture,' and as technology advances you learn that that's totally wrong but you've documented that ten years earlier . . . You can go through any case we have and there will be inconsistent statements, inconsistent interpretations of evidence."

Interpretations and *evidence*—two words that should be at odds with each other, especially when they've known what sperm looks like under a microscope for hundreds of years. How many families had been at this very same table, armed with memory and questions? How many times did they try to placate others with *interpretations* and *evidence?* I wondered, *What are we even doing here? If it's all interpretation, when nothing seems stable, why tell us anything? Ever? Now?*

Months later, in the middle of the preliminary hearing, the prosecutor will tell us, "We've just come across a note in the case file that says there are slides with semen on them, from an anal swab. We've sent people over to the freezer to look." And months after that, he'll tell us they didn't find any slides, and I'll want to say, *You should fucking trust us with our pain.*

Melissa looked at me from across the table and said, "I can tell you now, you can't tell vaginal fluid. It's not like you can test it. When you get a DNA profile from a vaginal swabbing it's an epithelial fraction of the victim . . . You can't say, 'This came from the mouth, this came from the vagina.' . . . It's skin cells or sperm cells. Period."

I said, "Oh okay," quickly, but I wanted to linger on yet another revision or interpretation or lie or protection, the detective, years ago, telling me the fluid from the beer bottle was saliva when I thought it could have been from Mom's vagina, when I had half hoped and half feared her body too had known the texture of glass.

Jerry reached over and placed his hand on my knee, knowing I was back in that room with Richard and his friend.

The DA then outlined more about the case and its challenges. He mentioned there'd been 250 suspects over the course of three decades. We had only ever been given the names of two, Travis McGuire and Ricky Martin. It made me think of how little we knew, of how much had been kept from us.

He said there was hardly any evidence that connected Eckardt to Mom. Just the beer cap really.

Beer cap. *Cap.*

I interrupted the DA: "Again, memory is kind of jumping back to me, but when we had the meeting to go over the first DNA testing that was done, we were told, and this one I *know* that my memory is not faulty—now the wording may have been faulty from the person that gave us the information—but we were told that there was a beer bottle, *not* a cap, but a bottle that had DNA on it."

Melissa and Liddell looked at one another and grinned, and I could see a shared experience, an inside joke, between them. If we hadn't been the ones asking the question, I imagine they would have laughed out loud.

Liddell leaned back in his chair, his face exasperated. He crossed his hands over his stomach, hands that looked much older than his face, and answered, "All of the reports we have say a beer bottle, and it's not a beer bottle, it's a beer cap, they wrote it down as a beer bottle . . . What we have is a beer cap, we have a car that smells like beer . . . We have no beer bottle, no pictures of beer bottles, so I don't know where this came from."

The other detective in the room hypothesized that someone originally wrote down "beer bottle cap" and that the "cap" was then dropped from the descriptions in every other report.

I felt her slipping from me again. I wanted to know a fraction of her pain, if only a sliver.

Then Melissa said, "There is a Pepsi bottle, not a beer bottle."

But that didn't have Mom's DNA on it.

But maybe it once did. Maybe it had deteriorated, along with some cop's attention to evidence.

I thought about how all of us, Melissa included, were trying to piece together details in the absence of transparency and honesty.

Then came the details about the legal proceedings—Eckardt would be charged with murder, we should expect at least two years' worth of legal proceedings—arraignments and preliminary conferences and preliminary hearings and trials. The DA described our case as a "really thin one," one that would never get stronger because DNA degrades, memories fade, witnesses die.

For a couple of hours, we had listened to the evidence and what our future may hold. I had listened to the attorneys and detectives say *epithelial* instead of *skin*, slow down their speech when they had to say *your mother* or *your wife*, describe how they just can't prove that Eckardt raped her because of all the damage to her body. We were tired, and it didn't feel like we were getting closer to justice or truth.

"I don't really have any other questions," Dad said, beginning to shift forward in his seat. "Except, uh, uh, Liddell . . ." His voice cracked and trembled and cut off, tears filling his eyes. It was a voice of a father I did not recognize. "Uh, I appreciate his efforts, he's uh . . ." He sat there, trying to regain composure, all of us silent. I couldn't reach out to hold him. I could do nothing but watch the beginning of twenty-three years of grief seep out of him, as he patted Liddell on the shoulder several times. "You've been very professional," he said. "I, uh, I appreciate that."

We left the meeting in bright sunlight, Rolland walking to his car, Jerry, Dad, and I walking to ours, Dad limping and slow, his hip stiff from hours of sitting. He wiped the sweat from his brow as I took off my trench in the Oklahoma heat.

Dad paused at the car's door and said, "Did I really just say, 'You've been professional'?"

"Yeah. What was that about?" I said.

"I don't know," he said, shaking his head again. "Strange."

We opened the car doors, slipped onto the scorching seats, and as Jerry started the car, I felt my head swarming with fatigue and heat and rage, with knowing that a blood sample or a sperm sample becomes something else completely; that a beer-bottle cap becomes a beer bottle with no photos or bagged evidence to back it up; that we were pitting binders and binders of evidence against memory, my memory, Rolland's memory, my journals; that we were trusting people who had combed objectively through the case for years against the moment I learned that there were sperm cells in the car; that there is no vaginal fluid or saliva, only skin cells or sperm; that I had remembered the Pepsi as a can and not as a bottle; that no one ever told me the mixture was vaginal fluid and sperm, I had just assumed it, so my own memory is faulty too; and that we would have two years or maybe more of this murky water, no, not water but oil, thick and black and covering us.

Dad snapped me out of the sludge and said, "I don't understand how your mother's DNA would end up on the *interior* of the cap."

"Maybe she twisted off the cap and it's her sweat or skin cells," I said.

"Maybe she was lying on the cap," Jerry added.

We slipped so easily into that detective's role, the one from ten years before, who told me it was Mom's saliva on the bottle.

I wanted to say, *I've already been there, Dad. I know the scenarios and know that dark leads to nowhere but dark. She picked up the cap with a sweaty finger, Dad.*

Or maybe it wasn't the detective's role we had slipped into but instead the father's, the one who had looked down at his eight-year-old daughter and said, "I hoped she died like a bunny rabbit would."

With the rustling of the maple trees, a thousand broad leaves rubbing against one another, the friction of vein upon vein, I'm in awe that the edges and narrowed five points of each leaf don't become broken or more frayed. I wrote a line of poetry once—"there is a *must* in the leaves, a returning rustling"—and I never fully understood it, until now, when I'm sitting here on the front porch of my childhood home, guarded by the holly in front of me, listening to the oncoming storm, the air thick with the smell of rain, a low, rolling thunder that belongs only to the plains.

The maple thrashes again. I recognize this thrashing. I understand it as a representation of myself, even as I know the storm is just a coincidence. I watch the top of the tree, dark leaves against a deep-gray sky, and say aloud, "I know," as leaves are ripped off the branches. I can feel it coming. I know I've lost the distance.

Just a few hours earlier, Jerry and I swam in his parents' above-ground pool, five family members and a robotic fish vying for space and taking turns near the heater. I listened to Jerry relay the information from the meeting with the district attorney. Charges being filed. Mixture sample. Blood.

I know the raw and the unfiltered is about to happen.

I know too that I can't stop it.

I listened to his parents ask questions. The beer-bottle cap. Terry Welch's son alone with his mom's body. I kept sinking below the water, swimming from wall to wall, back and forth, doing my best to avoid the legs of my family, because I was afraid to hear it again and to break down in the middle of the pool. Two short strokes, breath, *no death penalty*, two short strokes, breath, *Death Farm*, where they study how bodies decompose.

I should have said, *Stop. I just want to swim*, or, *I just want to watch Jerry and his brother try to dunk each other again.*

Jerry steps out onto the front porch and asks if I'm okay.

"Just watching the storm," I say.

"You sure you're okay?"

"I'm fine."

He reads the cues—no eye contact, shortness, eyes focused on the tree, knees curled to my chest.

"You just want to be alone?"

"For now."

"Okay," he says, a reluctance in his voice, though he knows it's pointless to stay, that it isn't time for me to speak. "Be careful," he says as he opens the glass door.

"I will," I say, knowing his *be careful* is a bit absurd, a conditioned response to "it's late at night and you're out here alone." But I can't argue with him, not when we'd been listening to details of Mom's abduction all day and had been reminded that nowhere is safe.

The maple thrashes again. Lee's maple next door moves in near unison, a dance, I think, until the wind really picks up. I shiver, my hair still damp from swimming. I look at my hands in the light of the porch lamp, remembering how earlier in the day, just after the meeting, the police rolled my fingertips and Jerry's in ink and then on paper, just as they had when we were kids. This time they said I could have my toeprints taken but remarked that the ink would stain my sandals. My fingertips are clean now, stripped with chlorine. I imagine my fingertips at eight years old, the arcs tiny, stained with black. A fingerprint card for show-and-tell.

And then animals.

Her body being dumped in the field.

Can't tell the difference in body fluid with DNA.

I want to run. Fast and hard. I want away from this goddamn house, this porch where the police once stood, waiting to tell my father that his wife had been abducted. I stand with my arms crossed tightly around my body and walk to the end of the driveway, steeply sloped and cracked. *Brutalized.* I need to flee, to burn off this energy, to somehow expel it through my pores, the nerves firing with muscles and then dying. Mom screaming. *But Jerry, what about Jerry, he won't forgive me, no he would, but he'd be terrified to find me missing. Don't do that to him. Don't make him scared like Dad once was.*

Trapped at the bottom of the driveway, I sit and bury my head in my knees and sob, and I don't know how long I've been here when it begins to rain in fat, sparse drops. I think maybe if I'm soaked through, maybe if the rain comes down hard enough and stings, it will feel better than this.

Jerry comes bolting out of the house because he couldn't see me hunched in front of the car. "Baby," he says, when he finds me. He tries to get me to stand, tries to pull me up by my wrists, but my body doesn't respond, resisting any position other than a ball.

So he picks me up. Quickly. Smoothly. As if I'm a box of feathers.

He carries me inside. And I'm aware, as he does this, of the rescue narrative, the man carrying the woman out of a storm, the stuff of bad fiction really, but, held by the support of his arms, I'm grateful. He sets me down on the living room floor, just inside the house. I'm sobbing, convulsing, in a way that is powerful and frightening. I feel like a child. A life ripped apart. The animals and the rape and the killing. I can't catch my breath. I can't stop shaking. My cries sound like someone else's, higher pitched, directionless.

Then a burst. The body says it can't keep it up. It calms itself just a little, my breathing becoming more even.

"What brought this on? Just today? The meeting?"

"I heard you saying it to your parents. Describing what happened. And it hit me. This happened to a human being. My God, Jerry. To a *human being.* And not just a human being but my *mom.* What she went through . . ." and then I lose it again, hyperventilating, my body clenched on the golden shag carpet.

"I'm so sorry, baby," he says, rubbing my back.

It isn't an empty sorry, and not one of sympathy but remorse.

"You don't need to apologize," I say, wiping my nose with my sleeve, lying beside my mother's beautiful and damaged piano. "You were just relaying the facts. I was too. I just didn't know that they would affect me like this. We didn't learn anything new today and yet it's different somehow." With our fingers in ink and police in the house and everyone trying to piece together how she died, it feels like 1986 all over again, but now I'm a woman who understands what I couldn't back then. "It's so close now," I say, my voice breaking, as I trace the tiger-stripe grain of her piano with my big toe.

A couple of months after the meeting with attorneys, Dad, Jerry, and I were eating at Lupe Tortillas in Houston. We loved their lime-marinated steak fajitas and fresh tortillas, as large as the plates. Dad was ignoring how Jerry and I tore the tortillas in half before constructing our fajitas, and instead he piled on the meat, the guacamole and salsa, the poblano and the cheese, an amount too heavy, too cumbersome, for the thin tortilla, so that when he folded it and wrapped it and picked up his creation, it bent and tore, the sauce leaking out, meat tumbling to the plate. "Havin' a hard time here," he said, his fingers plugging up the holes like a pipe.

I was already feeling my margarita, though I had only drunk a quarter of the glass, when we began discussing the upcoming press conference, where the DA would announce publicly that charges had been filed against Eckardt. Dad and Rolland had already agreed that I should write the statement, given my experience and degrees in creative writing, but we hadn't discussed who would read it.

"I can see an argument being made for each of us," I said to my father.

Jerry dipped his tortilla in the queso and took a sip of his Negra Modelo. He was probably hoping this would go smoothly.

"Part of me thinks you should read it," I said, "because obviously you're the head of the family, part of me thinks Rolland should because he's the one who fought all these years for this, and then I think I should read it because I'm the one who will write it and I know how it should be read aloud, the rhythms and pauses and such."

Dad piled more meat onto another tortilla, salsa beginning to dry on his shirt. It was clear he was concentrating, though I wasn't sure if he was calculating the weight ratios of beans to tortilla or the answer to my question.

"Well, we know Rolland won't be able read it," he said, referring to how Rolland cries when he tries to speak about Mom. Dad considered more cheese or more salsa. "I have to admit that out of a sense of patriarchy, I think either I or the DA should read it."

What the fuck? I thought.

I knew, even then, it was about the formality of the occasion, that the statement would be public, printed, played on televisions and browsers, and it therefore demanded an authority, and I understood his feeling that the parent should speak—I felt that too—but even without the word *patriarchy*, by his wanting to hand over *my words* and *my voice* to a DA with no attachment to Mom or to us, he told me my place as a woman is to be silent.

"That offends me," I said, an edge in my voice.

"I don't care," he replied, and he took another bite.

Jerry took a long drink from his beer. A group of servers sang "Feliz Cumpleaños" to a woman who donned a sparkling sombrero. I watched a server trying to vacuum up chips on the floor beside us, how the chips kept breaking into tiny pieces, embedding in the carpet. I thought, *It's fucking useless, how this mess transforms and never becomes clean.*

It may be the most hurtful thing he's ever done, not only because it showed that nothing I ever do will give me the right to speak—not losing Mom, not my own suffering or overcoming the struggles I faced, not attending top programs in the country and earning a PhD, not the years spent writing and teaching and presenting—but also because of his dismissal, that he didn't even care that he'd hurt me.

I ended up writing the statement, though I recognized that to do so was to participate in the history of silence. But it seemed worse not to have my voice represented at all, and, besides, I just didn't know how to persuade someone, especially my father, that patriarchy is not what I aim to uphold when I write and speak about my mother.

On the morning of the press conference, Dad sat in his robe at the kitchen table with my statement on top of his crossword puzzle. I ate my cereal, while Shasta whined from the family room because the cat rested by my feet.

"Are you nervous?" I asked him.

"No, not really."

"What I do is practice over and over, out loud, to the point where they are just words on the page."

"I've been reading it," he said. Then he covered my words with the crossword puzzle.

At the conference at the DA's office, we sat in a row of chairs while the DA stood at the podium. He said, "Yesterday afternoon, the Oklahoma County District Attorney's Office filed first-degree murder charges in the most recently solved cold case. Kyle Richard Eckardt is charged with the murder of Kathy Sue Engle."

Even though we'd known for a few months that charges would be filed, the emotion pierced me. For twenty-three years, we had waited for those words, and hearing the DA say them aloud made it official, palpable, real.

I felt the adrenaline in my chest, I was about to break down in tears, I reached over to hold Jerry's hand, needing the weight of his on top of mine, my hand sheltered under his palm. But journalists saw this and the cameras started clicking, a reminder we were being watched for moments like this. It snapped me back into performance mode.

After the DA finished his statement, Dad, Rolland, and I approached the podium. We were all in authoritative black suits, just like the lawyers in the room. Then Dad read my statement:

> Good morning, ladies and gentlemen. We would like to thank you for being here today and to thank the district attorney for allowing us to participate in this announcement, an announcement for which we have waited for many years.
>
> Over the last 23 years, as we have told the story of Kathy's murder to friends and acquaintances, to strangers we have just met, and to journalists, we have inevitably been asked if we have received closure, and, if not, if a conviction would provide it. The answer has always been and remains "No, we have not received closure," and "No, a conviction could not grant it," for nothing can erase the images in our heads of what Kathy endured. There will still be times when anger and a profound sense of not understanding resurface, and moments of grief will still arise.
>
> However, while closure is unattainable, the efforts of those who have worked diligently on Kathy's case are not in vain. What those efforts provide is the possibility for some peace—peace of mind in knowing that at least one of the men has been held accountable for Kathy's death and peace of mind in knowing that if Kyle Eckardt is convicted and if he does receive an appropriate punishment, then he will not have the opportunity to kill another woman, hurt another family, or leave another child without a mother. For these reasons, we

remain hopeful for the outcome of these developments and grateful for the work done by those at OCPD and the Cold Case Unit, by those at OSBI and the forensics lab, and by the district attorney and his staff.

It is impossible for us to thank each and every person who has offered us support over the years—time simply will not allow for that—so let us just say thank you to family members and friends, to members of the press, to members of law enforcement and the justice system, and to people who still tell us that they remember Kathy and her story. We are deeply appreciative of your support and acts of kindness.

At this time, I, my son Rolland, and my daughter Kristine are happy to answer any questions that you may have. We ask that, as the case proceeds, you respect Kathy's memory and our privacy as we go through what will be an emotionally difficult time. Thank you.

From the very beginning, his voice faltered. It was shaky, my words interspersed with *uh*s and stutters and tremolos, and when he reached the part about peace in knowing Eckardt can't kill another woman, my father lost his control. His voice went high. There were tears in his eyes. I reached over and placed my hand on his shoulder.

We then answered questions: "What did it feel like when you first found out?" "Do you want to say anything to Eckardt?" Rolland struggled to answer these. When he described when Dad called to say we had a DNA match, Rolland's bottom lip and chin quivered. He pressed his lips together in an attempt to contain the emotion, but everything about his face, his body, the tension around his eyes, the clenched jaw, the redness of his skin, his shaky voice like my father's, betrayed him. His body quaking under the weight of twenty-three years of silence, he said, "I was at work, uh, Dad called me, um, and I had given up of ever solving it. So it was a relief for me." I placed my arm around him.

When I answered, I was calm. Measured. I knew how to answer any questions they had. I'd answered them before. After readings. In the classroom, from students who were curious about my work. In my writing, where for years I had been imposing a form onto my experience in an effort to process, shape, reveal, control, and cope. I told the reporters I felt shock. That since being informed I had felt every emotion and that I thought this was normal. In the footage that later played on TV, you can see me using my hands, smiling, lifting my eyebrows, performing as if I'm giving a presentation. I looked the journalists in the eyes and described why I had no desire to speak to Eckardt—"I've thought about asking him why he killed my mother, but, in the end, it's pointless; I'll never be able to understand."

I would be lying if I said I didn't enjoy it when Dad broke down. Not that I wanted him to be in pain. I watch the video of the press conference now and tear up when I see him breaking, my father who cannot bear the resurgence of evidence and his murdered wife. But that doesn't change how vindicated I felt when his patriarchy crumbled and when I, a woman, kept steady, when it wasn't a picture of me wiping my tears that covered the front pages like Rolland's did, when instead I, holding Jerry's hand and looking nothing but solemn and composed, made page 8. How proud I felt when the journalist wrote, "The victim's husband struggled to retain his composure as he read a prepared statement. Beside him, his son fought back tears. Kristine Ervin tried to comfort both," how gratified when I didn't show them what they all wanted to see: the weeping woman. I want to say it's okay to cry—after all, trying to be stoic clearly hasn't helped Rolland and Dad, and of all the moments when tears were justified, this would have been it—but that acceptance only works if Dad can say, "These words are yours and you should speak them."

The Sound of Punishment

◆

FOR YEARS IT RESTED IN A SOFT GRAY BOX.

I remember how I sat on Mom's lap at the kitchen table, opening and closing the oval door of her locket, with nothing on its inside, just smooth gold that reflected my own face. I didn't notice the locket's intricacies, the edges that will later remind me of flying buttresses, nor did I care that it's etched with a flower. It was the door I was enamored with. To have a necklace with a moving mechanism. Click the clasp shut. Pry it open. Click it shut again. The locket slid across her sternum as she shifted her weight, reaching forward to ash her cigarette, then resettled as she leaned back against the chair, the locket resting against her body, rising and falling with her breath.

On the morning of the preliminary hearing, seven months after the charges were filed, I sat in my bedroom in my childhood home and held the locket in my hand, its chain so much longer than in my memory. The last chest it had touched was hers. I suspended it in the air, remembering how she offered it to me for my silence, to keep me occupied while she talked to a woman at the kitchen table. I then slid it over my head and into my silk blouse, its smooth back cool against my skin. I needed her, even if no one else could see and no one else would know. More than an unchanged memory, I needed an amulet between Eckardt and me.

In the courtroom, there was a clear separation of sides, with an aisle between the defense and prosecution. When I walked in, I thought, *I want no one to sit on the other side of the aisle; let us have more people present, so Eckardt knows he's outnumbered.* We all sat behind the bar.

The bench was hard, and as Dad slowly lowered himself down until he reached the moment that he must drop his weight with a thud on the seat, I worried about his pain. I thought maybe I should carry in a cushion for him the next day, but I also knew he'd rather suffer through a throbbing hip than let Eckardt see him needing a cushion.

The four lawyers, Melissa Fisher and Bobby Marten for the prosecution, the two for the public defense, unpacked their briefcases and folders and all talked to one another. You could tell by the way they laughed and leaned on one another's tables they had tried cases together before. It made sense, of course, but I didn't like it. I wanted to tell our prosecutors to stop fraternizing with the enemy. How quickly I claimed them as "ours," the *us* and the *them* immediately setting in.

Then Eckardt walked in.

My body tightened, becoming a fist.

I wore my four-inch stiletto boots, knee-high and suede. He wore sandals and socks and shuffled when he walked, his ankles shackled. As I watched him pass, just twenty feet in front of me, I thought my heel could make a good weapon, especially if I could strike it through his chest.

He sat down at the rectangular table across the bar and to our right; instead of sitting with his back to us, as I had imagined, his body was positioned adjacent to ours, where we could see each other easily. My mother's killer, so near and real to me. I wanted to slip off my boot, jump over the bar, jump over the chairs and table, and stab him, puncturing his lung or heart. I felt her then. I felt the locket on the bottom of my rib cage. I thought about the roses Chris had given me the day before—white roses, one for Mom, one for me, one for her, how connected the three of us are—and I breathed.

Eckardt then turned his head and looked right at me.

I wondered if he was imagining fucking me.

I wondered if he saw Mom behind my eyes.

I wanted my eyes to pierce.

I thought, *I will not break the eye contact first, I will not break, I will not . . .*

He looked away and I considered it a victory.

He had 8½" × 11" white paper rolled up and sticking out of the chest pocket of his orange prison uniform, but the pocket wasn't deep enough, so the fabric, thin and cheap and unable to bear the pressure, bent forward. I found myself wondering if something was written on the pages or if he'd brought blank papers to write notes on, as Rolland had, with his legal pad.

He wore glasses, thick like the bottoms of beer bottles, and his hair was dense, white and gray, cut in a mullet and spiked on top. I kept thinking how the gray aged him far beyond forty-four. He looked more like he was sixty. I kept putting Eckardt in the Colt and in the field as he looked at that moment, his body at 230 pounds, a Harley-Davidson tattoo on his chest, just under the prison uniform, forgetting that he was just twenty-one when he killed her, the same age as many of my students. He was probably lanky back then.

I kept thinking that a full beard hid the face she knew, though maybe he wasn't clean-shaven that night. I wondered if she'd recognize him, had she lived to sit in the courtroom, if his eyes were the same as the twenty-one-year-old's, his eyebrows just as thick, just as arched. I wanted to throw acid on that face and watch his skin sizzle and peel away like the film between the layers of an onion, obliterating any trait she might remember. I wanted to cut off the hands that had touched her.

I remembered Rolland once telling me how lawyers have to explain to the jury that the courtroom won't be like *Law & Order*. I knew not to expect quick resolutions or language that I understood entirely or evidence that was neat and tidy, but the stuttering and stammering surprised me, the way the lawyers talked in circles and said *uh* and *um* and *Your honor, I was trying to . . .* with their arms crossed like a child's. I had assumed there'd be more eloquence, that their speech patterns, perfected through years of practice, would be closer to dialogue in fiction. Instead, they sounded too human, too capable of mistakes.

One of the first people to testify was an eyewitness, a dentist who entered the mall with a friend not long before the men shoved my mother into the Colt and who kept describing the men sitting on the planter as "unkempt." She turned the composite sketches over and over in her lap, her head lowered, her face sullen. I did not know her but felt I understood what was going through her head as she studied the sketches from decades before and refused to look at Eckardt: *How lucky I am that it wasn't me that night.*

During the cross-examination, the public defender asked the dentist, "May I call you Doctor?" His hair was gelled perfectly in spikes, he was short, and he wore a handkerchief triangled in his breast pocket, as if he were going to dinner at Oak Tree Country Club. I doubted he'd ask a male dentist this question, and certainly not with that tone and grin, so from that moment on, I called him Weasel.

Through the testimonies, Eckardt seemed lost, childlike even, confused by the procedures and motions and objections and the law. I loved seeing him this way, his eyebrows furrowed, his head shifting as he looked from lawyer to lawyer. I thought, *I want him to be lost forever.* But he flinched and drove a hard stare into Detective Liddell, who testified that Eckardt is of normal intelligence—a term used to say he's capable of understanding the charges being filed against him and what his rights are. Eckardt's anger at this offense—to say his intelligence is normal and not high—showed us he's human after all. And how to get under his skin.

We looked at each other again, holding our stares for several seconds, but I broke it first. I smirked before looking away to let him know it was my choice, not a reflex from pain but instead a slow, calculated dismissal. I would not give him the pleasure of directing my body. I thought, *I can play this game all day long, and I will not be the one to lose.*

They called another eyewitness to the stand, this time a person who saw the abduction.

When I read, years ago in the newspaper articles, that there had been eyewitnesses, I had imagined small crowds standing on the curb outside the mall, how they held paper shopping bags, so heavy the handles creased their fingers. They were friends and family members who had eaten at El Chico together, shopped together, until this moment of parting in the parking lot. They laughed and were saying goodbye when they heard my mother scream, when they saw two men pulling on her, saw her kicking, fighting, biting, saw her fists trying to punch, her fingers to gouge. They were close enough to know she wore gold stud earrings. And the people did nothing but watch, perhaps too stunned to move. Too afraid to interfere. They simply stood there, their shopping bags weighed down as if by bricks, these people still as stone. And I hated them. Each and every one of them. For watching the scene for several long minutes.

I would have done something, I told myself. *I would have thrown myself onto the car as the men drove away. I would have punched through the glass if I had to.*

Instead of a crowd of people in their thirties, having aged not one day since I imagined them into being, I was confronted with Ron Hinther.

In my memory, though, he's Roy. Because the journalist who wrote from Mom's perspective wrote "Roy" instead of "Ron" in his cold case article, a mistake that ends up rewriting the real. Even though I know his name, I still see him as Roy with a heart-shaped face and small-framed glasses, a man with thinning hair who leaned forward on the witness stand, intent to answer questions.

He described how he and his roommate stopped by the mall and saw two men sitting on a planter at the entrance. The men "looked unkempt—unkept and sort of slouching, not having good posture," he said. He looked at Melissa as she asked her questions. He held his hands folded in front of his chest. "They seemed to just be sitting there and not do . . . and just watching."

"And as you were walking to your automobile, did you notice something unusual?"

"Yes," Hinther answered.

This was the moment my family and I had been warned about. "You're going to hear difficult eyewitness testimony now," the prosecutors told us just before they called Hinther to the stand.

This was the moment a person in the crowd would have to account for standing still.

"We heard a woman yelling help . . . I saw a woman and two men, and I believe about . . . what I see in my mind and I've always . . . since that time have seen in my mind, as I see the back door of the car open, a man at the trunk area, a man kind of holding the door on the back of the door and the woman somewhere in between the two of them at the trunk area of the car on the right . . . the left side of the car . . . It happened so quickly. I remember seeing a man hit the woman either in the neck or in the back, she lunges forward, and it kind of propels her into the back seat of the car."

He paused a lot as he described it. He kept closing his eyes. He lifted his hand to his temple, as if to unlock, in exact detail, the twenty-four-year-old memory.

"What I remember is the door was shut, a man gets in the front driver's side, a man goes around the back, gets in the other side of the front door of the car, and that car is backed out in just seconds."

"How about their height, their body build?" Melissa asked.

"Always being a small man myself, I know that they were larger than me, I felt like they . . . I used to sell men's clothing and I felt . . . as I'm thinking about it now, probably a 42, 44 jacket," he said. "It was just a simple thing of backing out of the . . . and I just remember the taillights. They just backed out into the driving area, and then there must have been a quick exit because I remember the hopeless feeling of standing there and watching those taillights go down Villa."

He closed his eyes again and shook his head at the memory, and I was right there with him, in the parking lot of the mall, watching the taillights disappear. When he opened his eyes, there were tears in them, and I no longer hated him for doing nothing. Instead I wanted to hold him, this man who knew my mother as I did, who described her as having "not black but brown wavy hair and a fairly pale complexion," who couldn't shake the memory, who couldn't save her, even after all these years.

"Could you see any movement inside the car or anybody inside the car at that point?"

"I remember thinking, *I hope I can see her head*, and I never saw her head rise above the window."

Melissa passed the witness, and in the time of transitioning between one person at the podium to another, from notes being jotted down, legal pads stacked, folders prepped and passed from hand to hand, Roy and I lingered on that image of the window, waiting for Mom to lift her bleeding head.

Weasel took the podium and asked him, "Would you say it was dark?"

"Well I . . . I kind of remember in my mind I see that Oklahoma glow in the . . . at the end . . . At the time I do remember the car looking out over those . . . the row of cars, and it seems like I remember that sunset, just a little bit of red in the . . . at the edge of the earth."

Weasel didn't pause to consider the backdrop, to wait in the moment of dusk and see the land, flat and dark, spreading out before him, the sky an indigo except at the horizon, where a spot glows red like an ember.

"So you're saying it's a four-door vehicle to the best of your recollection?"

"Correct."

After a few more questions, Hinther was passed back to Melissa, who showed him pictures of the Colt. "Do you think . . . it could have been a two-door car that she was forced inside of?"

"I remember that the door seemed big, and I guess that's why I was thinking there was a . . . that's how they got in so fast, okay . . ." Roy paused again, studying the pictures of the car, still frames of its taillights and doors. "Well, it makes sense to me that it was . . . it was difficult for her to get in because there was not a bench seat there, because I had often thought in my mind that she had landed on a bench seat, but she was . . . it was so hard for her . . . *that's* why it was hard for her to get down and get back there as I see it playing in my mind. And then all they had to do was shut . . . get in right behind her . . . To get in a car like that, I would have to put my foot in. And she got down so low, that's what I . . . I couldn't . . . I understand getting . . . you have to get down really low to get in those cars and that's what I saw, and that explains why she was crouching so much."

I watched Roy working it out, replaying it, the car in the photo now being rewritten in his mind. His testimony wasn't as disturbing as I thought it would be. I listened to Roy and kept thinking, *This is about memory, the slipperiness of it, the revisions and omissions, the mistakes.* I wanted to tell him, *We are not that different, you and I, each of us trying to reconcile what lies in front of us with the picture in the past.*

I watched Roy tearing up and thought about bearing witness, how lost in the common usage of that phrase is its meaning of burden and weight, of how his testimony was an attempt at atonement.

I thought, *There's such unexpected beauty here, his voice trying to recover what's been taken, the red at the edge of the earth.*

Before another witness was called to the stand, Bobby shuffled through the photographs of the crime scene, purposely keeping his body between us and the prints, before placing them in an opaque folder. How strange it was to have the pictures in the room, so close to me, when for years I thought that seeing them would help. I remembered the word *obliterated* and knew I didn't want to see her body.

But then Elmo, the oil field worker who found Mom's body, was called as a witness. His voice was bumbling and raspy, sometimes difficult to hear, and when Bobby, after all his careful preparation, handed the folder to Elmo on the stand, Elmo, his hands shaking in old age, dropped it, the photographs fluttering, face up, to the floor.

I told myself not to look but nanoseconds too late. Why is it that the eyes go looking, even when you don't want them to?

But the bar, a conference table, eight chairs, and two people stood between us and the photos. Still, Elmo used words like *odor* and *grisly* and *maggots* and *flies* and talked about how none of his coworkers believed him when he said they should call the police. So he took them to view her body.

I had thought the killers' leaving her facedown was the final insult, until I imagined Elmo and a group of men, their large and sweaty bodies circling around her on the ground, how they bent over for a closer look, even as they covered their noses from the stench, how they talked to each other about what was left, how my mother's body, even after death, was an object for men to gawk at.

When we adjourned on the first day, the guards took Eckardt out the far door of the courtroom, while Rolland leaned over the bar to ask questions to the lawyers. Jerry and I decided to go ahead and leave, and when Jerry opened the door nearest us, there stood Eckardt, just a few feet away, being led down the common hallway of the courthouse. Only Jerry stood between us. Both men were stunned, their bodies pulling back from the shock. In that pause, they stood motionless and looking at each other. Right there. So close. I felt grateful Jerry blocked me with his size, though later I'd wish I had been in front. That could have been *my* chance to strike him.

Later that night, as Jerry and I lay in bed, I asked him what it felt like in that moment.

He said, "I'm happy I have a few inches on him. And that he knows it."

On the second day of the hearing, Eckardt brought a Bible to court. I thought, *Fuck you, and if you really want to bring your Bible to court, then I'll bring my mom's Bible from her childhood and find a way to show off her penciled, cursive name to everyone with power in the room.*

All of it was a performance—if the first day hadn't convinced me enough, then this certainly did—Eckardt with his Bible, Weasel with his suit, even Roy Hinther's tears, which I'd found authentic and moving, until Melissa had said, "He'll make for a great witness for a jury."

I didn't like the laughter between the lawyers either, Melissa and Bobby, Weasel and the Other Guy, all convened at the bench to speak with the judge. They were whispering, shaking their heads, and interrupting one another as the judge looked back and forth at them like a parent. Then they all erupted into laughter, loud enough for everyone to hear. *Have some fucking respect for us,* I wanted to say. But then Bobby was asking a patrolman about Mom's car and he kept pronouncing Tucumcari as "Tucumary." "The car was located at a truck stop in Tucumary, right?" The officer shook his head no, the judge shook his head no, I shook my head no too. "I'm sorry, I mean Tucumcari." The fourth time he did it, Weasel wrote the name of the town on a piece of paper, underlined the second *c* three times, and lay it on the podium, and suddenly Dad, Jerry, Rolland, and I were all laughing, for this glorious moment, only a few seconds really, where the facades of the law cracked, letting what was ridiculous and authentic and human to emerge from the artifice.

A moment that passed all too quickly, as we listened to Bobby attempting to correct a mistake concerning the gas tank of the Colt, wanting to get on record whether the tank was empty or not. He tried six different ways of wording the question, but objection after objection was raised because he didn't correct the mistake under direct examination. He sounded like a boy throwing a tantrum because he took his finger off a game piece too early and watched it be captured by his opponent.

But this wasn't supposed to be a game. The prosecution had the police report; the defense and judge did too. They all could read what had been logged twenty-four years before.

I knew, if I asked Rolland, he'd tell me why the procedures are in place, and on another day, I might understand the logic, the reasoning, how it's meant to protect from something, but I couldn't accept it right then, not when her death could go unpunished because Bobby didn't ask a question at precisely the right time in precisely the right way.

The detectives and officers were much better at giving testimony than the dentist and Elmo and the eyewitness. The detectives were well-versed in the words to use and what roles to play, mastered from years of being on the stand. They used *Eckardt* when referring to the defendant; Weasel almost always said *Kyle*. They too knew the power of a name, how personal and intimate a first name can be, how it humanizes, turning the monster into the boy next door.

I thought about how my family and I use only *Eckardt*; even in my journal, that's what I write. I could use *Kyle Richard* to connect him to my neighbor who cinched a belt around my throat. It'd give me that connection with my mother I sought, but I can't bear to say it or even to write it. It could be for the same reason the prosecutors choose not to: maybe I want to deprive him, stripping away one of the few things he still has, but mostly I think it's an act of self-preservation: his name, unlike a bottle inside us, too common, too normal, too real.

They shifted other words too. Melissa used the word *infer* to argue there's enough evidence for probable cause; Weasel used *assume*. I found it enraging, this game of language, manipulated and shaped when there's so much at stake: a man's life, whether someone would pay for Mom's death, whether other women would be saved.

I thought, *If this is what it all comes down to, why not just call it what it is and play a fucking board game to settle it.*

For a year and a half, ever since we got the DNA match, all I had been focused on was Eckardt and Mom's death. I was consumed by what he did to her, by what he did to other women, by semen and blood and cuts and whether we'd ever have enough for a conviction. If I thought about Mom, it was only about her dying. But then, on the second day of the hearing, she came back to me in the form of a list:

What was item number 31?, Melissa asks a detective on the stand.

The officer answers, It's noted in my report as a fish fly.

And a fish fly, would that be like a fishing lure?

Yes, ma'am.

And then item number 32 is what?

A monofilament line that's approximately eight feet in length.

And is that, like, fishing line?

Yes, ma'am.

And then what is item 50?

It's a white bra that appeared to be cut between the cups.

Now, I want to, as quickly as possible, have you testify about what items were stored under that tag number, 96033.

The ashtray from the dash, item number 7.
Item 8, which is a blue sun visor.
Item 9, a computer printout paper.
> That paper, continuous and wide, with alternating green and
> white lines, holes on the sides for the spokes of the dot matrix
> printer. The paper of Mom.

Item 10, Kerr-McGee ink pen.
> I remember the logo, the *K*, the *M*.

Item 11, a plastic litter bucket.

Item 12, a black ink pen and a Goody hair pick.

> The same brand I own now.

Item 13, a Walmart sack with a paperback book.

> He's reading it slowly so it may be transcribed. It's a methodical battering.

Item 14, a plastic cup cover with the letters *AA*.

Item 15, the ashtray from the transmission console.

Item 16, a 16-ounce Pepsi glass bottle.

Item 17 was a brown Goody hairbrush.

> She carried a brush and a pick in her purse.

Item 18, a Birdie's breakfast label from McDonald's.

> Our breakfasts together before school. Cinnamon Danishes and pancakes on Styrofoam. We didn't go there every day, how special those Danishes and mornings with Mom were.

Item 19, two computer tape reels.

> She showed me machines at her office, how the reels spun so fast they almost looked still.

Item 20 was a red address book.

Item 21, a Budweiser beer-bottle cap.

Item 22, a Dr. Pepper–bottle cap, the pry type.

Item 23, a metro library card with the name K. S. Engle.

> I had forgotten our trips to the library in the afternoon.

Item 24, a County Seat shopping bag.

> The bookshelves, they were short.

Item 25, a chain necklace.

> And sunlight poured into the room where we sat on the floor reading together.

Item 26, a wood-handled ice scraper.

Item 27, a Kraft cheese wrapper.

> I bend forward, unable to breathe. Item after item. Mom and then Mom.

Item 28, plastic wrapper with cheese.

Item 29, one pair of sunglasses.

She'd always lose them.

Item 31 was the fish fly.

Item 32, the monofilament line.

Item 33, a 1984 map of Oklahoma.

Item 34, a gold earring.

Two days of testimony and this is what breaks me.

Item 35, another gold earring.

Not Elmo with his *odor* and *maggots*, not the eyewitnesses who describe the men as just waiting.

Item 36, one quarter, a dime, and one penny.

It's the specificity that wounds.

Item 37, a package of Triaminicin tablets.

I have my head down, my elbows on my knees.

Item 38, an advanced wristwatch, purple in color.

That watch may have been mine.

Item 39, two black ladies gloves, size seven.

I'm about to cry and I know it. I'm about to run out the courtroom's door. And Eckardt will see it.

Item 40, a child's book *Just Go to Bed.*

My book. My book with the little critter in his blue pajamas on the front.

Item 41, a computer-printout book.

Just Go to Bed. Please tell me she couldn't see this in the dark in her car. That she didn't think of the nights she read to me.

Item 42, a brown leather soft briefcase with miscellaneous papers.

Find the spider, she had said.

Item 44, a cigarette paper found on the floor mat.

I pull the locket from my shirt, grasp it in my palm.

Item 45, items from a handbag, consisting of an ink pen, Salem Light 100's cigarettes, scratch paper, two broken Salem cigarettes.

I close my eyes; the muscles around them are quivering.

Item 46, a pink cosmetic bag.

Jerry places his hand between my shoulder blades, but my

trembling doesn't stop; it's getting stronger, my entire body tense and quaking.

Item 47, a Sears credit card.

The locket in my palm, pressed so hard I imagine my skin embossed with an oval door.

Item 59, miscellaneous business papers.

Make it stop.

Item 60 was the rear-seat bottom section, and 61 was the rear-seat top section.

Please make it stop.

He ends the list.

I take a breath.

But I'm still shaking, remembering the life that was being lived before that night at the mall, feeling, for the first time in a long time, the mom who had been taken from me.

The wind was gusting as I leaned against the lighthouse at a lake, a reservoir in north Oklahoma City. I'd gone there alone because I needed to be by water, to listen to it after hearing so much testimony in court. But what I heard was the wind flapping my leather coat, even though I'd positioned myself where the lighthouse blocked the wind but not the sun, so that I could be warmed by the light on my black pants, black coat, black scarf. In the distance, parasurfers were gliding over water and in the air, their neoprened bodies in flight, lifting like music, their sails in the sky. My own body had grown tired and the water felt too far away still, so I walked to the end of the point, the heels of my boots puncturing the dirt, and climbed down a steep bank of rocks. There the whitecaps lapped the shore, the succession of waves quick, unlike the ocean with its slow undulations. And unlike the ocean, this water was red.

I felt relieved that the lake was small, its body contained, when the days in court felt anything but—endless waves of words like *olive green rope, odor, blood,* Weasel's claim that the prosecution's arguments were *dubious* at best. And Eckardt so near—just a man, one man, but the idea of him, the history of him, his presence taking up so much space. I thought of how everyone kept telling me I was strong, when all I wanted to hear was that it's okay to be weak. I felt like entering the water, submerging into the cold red of it, to be reminded of my body, erased by its mud.

I never considered how brutal the judicial process would be. After the preliminary hearing concluded and the judge said there was enough evidence to move toward a jury trial, my family and I ate at an art museum's café where lawyers like to lunch, where servers refold your napkins when you leave for the restroom and periodically scrape the crumbs from the table. We ordered french fries for the table, and they were served upright in a papered cone as I sipped an overpriced cappuccino.

Someone asked Rolland what he thought about the day, and he answered, "Well, a hole has been filled."

I was staring out the window onto a downtown street with little traffic, wanting to shake my head and say, *You have to fucking be kidding me. Did you not hear the testimonies, the evidence, as you sat there with your legal pad out, drawing diagrams of proofs and arguments? Did you not really listen? There's a hole for what her scream sounded like and the taillights fading away. A hole for* brutalized. *One for the anal swab with sperm. Another for the odor of her body. A hole for the clarity of Eckardt's face, now so much clearer than Mom's. A pit for exhaustion.*

I didn't say this. I told myself for Rolland a hole may have been filled but for me many more had been dug, so many there was no place left for solid footing.

I'll be dreaming of Eckardt again and Jerry's arm will hit my pillow, a movement that jostles my head and works its way into the dream. *Blunt force trauma* transforms my husband's restless body into Eckardt's hitting me from behind. I'll shoot up out of bed and touch the back of my skull. All day I'll reach my hands back to cradle it, as if a heavy bruise is swelling there, as if the body can map its dreams.

Or I'll be getting dressed in the morning, sliding the straps of my bra over my shoulders and hear the detective say, "white bra sliced between the cups." I'll hook the clasps, feel the cold blade between my own breasts, and see her on her back, Eckardt above her. It probably happened quickly, but my mind plays it in slow motion, the knife nearly static against her skin, my skin, that long moment of suspension that Rolland will never understand.

Or I'll be walking the dog in the morning, just before dawn, on poorly lit sidewalks around the apartment complex, where I'll see two men talking beside a car, one of them leaning across the hood, his back to me. *It's morning, Kristine*, I'll say to myself, *not the light of dusk. They're probably the nicest, most innocent of men. And Shasta will protect you.* But as I pass them, their bodies behind me, I'll think *blunt force trauma to the back of the head* again, Mom's body being shoved into the back seat of a car. My skull just above my neck will ache. I won't see it coming. Right there, the crack to the bone. I'll begin jogging, faster and faster, until I'm running as quickly as I can, cutting corners, rushing to reach the next gate in.

Or I'll be in a bookstore trying to write and instead I'll seek out *Just Go to Bed*, my Little Critter book that was bagged as evidence from her car. I'll pick it up and read, "I'm a cowboy, a space cadet, a race car driver, a ship captain," the little critter's playing each role and the parents' yelling, "Just go to bed," and I'll think, *How do you rape and kill a woman with a children's book beside you?*

Or I'll be brushing my teeth at night before bed, and the image of Eckardt shoving a beer bottle, cap on, deep inside her, will spark in my mind. I'll tell myself no. I'll tell myself the imagination can do no good, but the images still fire like a gun. My insides cringe.

Or Jerry will touch me as he slides into bed, just his hand on my side, and I'll wince. I won't even want his fingers, my *husband's* fingers, to course through my hair as he drifts off to sleep. I'll get out of bed and go to the couch because touch is just too painful now.

I thought of the Danaides in Greek mythology, women condemned to trying to fill a vessel with water when the vessel has holes, how heavy their pitchers become as they pour the water endlessly, but instead of a vessel, I have a field and not enough dirt. I wanted to tell Rolland, *There will always be holes. Ones that can never be filled.*

Just a few weeks after Eckardt was arraigned, as I sat at the kitchen table with nearly 250 essay folders surrounding me, seemingly propagating in multicolored stacks, fortressing me in, and as Shasta kept trying to tear one of the folders apart because my student's bearded dragon had crawled on it, Dad called and said, again, "Are you sitting down?"

I no longer cared.

"They have a possible match on the second man."

"Sure. Okay. Why not," I said.

"His name is Steven Boerner. He's from Michigan. The crime lab sent the fingerprint to the FBI two years ago and it just came back with a match. I didn't ask why just two years ago. They don't know yet why he was incarcerated. He was born in November 1958."

I did the math: he was twenty-eight when he killed Mom.

The fingerprint was sent twenty-two years late.

"There's good news and bad news," he said. "He's dead."

"That's good."

"He died in a trucking accident in 1992."

"Good."

Jerry walked into the room and noticed my face as I listened to Dad and took notes. "What's going on?" he whispered.

I mouthed, "They have a second match."

His jaw dropped.

I rolled my eyes.

He looked over my shoulder at my notes on the backside of my rubric.

"At some point in the past, OSBI received a tip that Boerner was involved in the murder of an Oklahoma woman," Dad said. "But the tip wasn't very specific, so there wasn't anything to be investigated. That's all I know for now."

I had rolled my eyes.

"How are you feeling?" I asked.

"Well, I'd like for him to have to face the music."

I think now of the origin of that phrase, how disgraced soldiers were removed from the military barracks to the sound of drums, that beating a public humiliation.

"How'd Rolland react?" I asked.

"Like you. Relieved that he's dead. Actually, he was more upbeat than I've heard him be in a long time."

"That's good, I guess."

"Well, I'm sure we'll learn a lot more soon, and I'll let you know anything new, of course."

"Okay, love you."

"Love you too, darlin'."

Twenty-four years of wondering who killed my mother, and my reaction was to roll my eyes. Not joy. Not relief. Not anger even. Just disbelief. And annoyance. *Of course now*, I thought, *after we just suffered through the hearing, right when we're in the middle of the trial process for Eckardt. Of course now, when I have 250 essays to grade.*

I had rolled my eyes, and I had said, "Why not." Not even as a question.

And the quick "That's good" when Dad told me he was dead. With no hesitation. An answer of self-preservation. I couldn't take another trial, more details about her death, another face in my dreams. If only Eckardt were dead too.

And what a fucking waste of time, years spent wanting to find a man who died just six years after she did. I thought about how I was only fourteen then, skating at the rink, imagining the police coming to my school to tell me the men had been found, of how I was just beginning to shoplift and to feel boys' hands on me, of how I was still years away from learning the details of the case, of how Terry Welch's son was still years from being born.

Boerner became just a name in the newspaper or at meetings with lawyers, a name with a few facts tagged to it. He was a truck driver. He died in an accident. Unlike with Eckardt, I didn't have affidavits or articles or narratives to read that provided glimpses into his life. And only one image of him appeared—a fuzzy black-and-white mug shot from 1981. His hair is dark, a few inches long, and sticks straight out. He wears a dark shirt. His eyes, one much smaller than the other, look not at the camera but to his left. He manages to appear both angry and scolded like a child.

Years later, Rolland and Dad won't even remember his name.

With Eckardt, the idea of the men materialized, one step at a time: first just his name and the stories; then the mug shot, with color and clarity, just a few years old; then the video of his arriving at Oklahoma County Jail, a body moving and human. I felt much more vulnerable then, and he showed up in my dreams not as a blurred person but as a man with a mullet, standing behind me with a club in his hands. And then came the moment when he walked through the courtroom's door.

But Boerner is dead. There will be no shift from the imagined to the real. And there's something about the image itself, the graininess of it, that seems to place eras between us.

The distance is comforting, really. Maybe it would have troubled me if we didn't have Eckardt, if the police had come to us, decades after her death, with photos of two dead men, who lived and died without being held accountable. I probably would have researched them, seeking out their family members, their origins, their stories, trying to trace them to the parking lot of Shepherd Mall, while feeling safe, knowing they couldn't hurt me and I couldn't hurt them. Eckardt gave me a human to hate, but I was coming to see how excruciating that embodiment could be, so I felt grateful Boerner was dead, even while I hoped he'd been trapped in his truck, fire inching up his body, searing his skin a little at a time.

Nearly a month after we learned about Boerner, the DA wanted to meet to discuss the new developments. Because I had begun teaching a summer class, I couldn't be there and instead listened, along with Jerry, on a conference call with the attorneys and detectives and Rolland and Dad.

I sat at our kitchen table with my notepad while Jerry sat on the floor in the nearby spare room. I hated that I wasn't in Oklahoma, to read the faces of the lawyers, to be there for my father, to go to lunch afterward and talk it over as a family.

We had assumed the discussion would focus on Boerner, which it did, but the DA shocked us when he said the death penalty was now on the table for Eckardt.

He told us Boerner's fingerprints were on the steering wheel and the outside driver's side of the Colt. He said that in 2007, a man who had once been a cellmate of Boerner's called the OSBI and said Boerner had described how he and another guy had kidnapped a woman from a store in Oklahoma.

I was writing down notes as quickly as I could, fragments about phone records and Boerner's history and which family members of his were still alive, but then the DA said Boerner admitted to his cellmate how Mom died:

Boerner was the driver.

Mom was in the back seat, and Eckardt was raping her.

They took her to the field.

Eckardt slit her throat with a knife from behind.

I started shaking and gagging but the DA kept talking.

I had to keep it together, I had to keep on listening, I couldn't think of her throat, not when the DA wasn't pausing. *You must keep moving,* I told myself. On the notepaper, I wrote, "keep writing," and then repeated the word *writing* thirty-one times. You can see my tremoring through my cursive, where every letter looks like it's vibrating; not until I'm about halfway through does my handwriting become recognizable and smooth, that repetition a mantra for control.

Then he said a traditional autopsy could never be performed on Mom's body after it was found. People were always shocked about its condition, but the slit throat would explain why it decomposed as fast as it did.

"She suffered significant trauma to her body," he said. "That's what's changed. We can now show what Eckardt did to your mother is 'heinous, atrocious, and cruel.'"

I looked at the word *suffered* in my notes and wrote *writing* seven more times.

He said he was giving us one week to decide whether or not we wanted to file for the death penalty. "It's a gamble," he said, and it would likely mean fifteen years of appeals if we got a conviction.

I wrote, "I didn't want to know, I wish I didn't know," and then right after, "Rolland says, You don't understand how big of a relief it is to be here."

As we were saying goodbye on the phone, I stood up from the table. I clicked the receiver off and suddenly Jerry was there, catching me before I hit the floor, my body collapsing, finally unable to bear the brunt of it. I was crying violently; that's the only word to use. Think seizing, think someone pounding with a mallet deep inside your body, how from its depths you hear a wail, so low you think it can't be human.

In all my years of thinking about her dying, I rarely imagined a method of killing. Maybe she died from bleeding in the brain from all the hits to her head. Maybe from a gun fired into her chest and a coyote had consumed the bullet. Maybe dehydration and blood loss, her body spent. Those were the only scenarios I remember. I typically focused on the before and after: being grabbed in the parking lot, her wrists being bound, the rape in the car or in the field, her body lying facedown, then the animals biting. It was horrific enough.

But this. This was so much worse. I kept seeing her standing in the field, her breasts and vulva exposed to the air around her, Eckardt standing behind her, his chest pressed against her back, his arms holding her against his body, and then he reaches around and slices her throat. It's an intimate kind of killing, unlike standing at a distance and shooting a gun. I couldn't stop imagining her eyes clenched, her legs shaking so much he was helping to hold her up, and the blade, cold before it slices.

I too was shaking and gasping, on the floor beside our table, with Jerry doing everything he could to contain me, but there was nothing that could be done to stop that outpouring, nothing to be done until my own body was spent. Only later would I be grateful for being there in Houston, away from that conference room with Rolland and Dad and the attorneys. I don't know how Rolland or Dad made it out of the room and to their cars. I don't think I could have held it all in. Though maybe that's what everyone should have seen, a daughter severing.

I canceled my classes for one day. When I returned the day after, on just the third day of summer session, I explained to my students why I was absent. I began crying and they weren't prepared for it. They stared at me with scared looks on their faces and I couldn't stop it, I couldn't pretend I was all right, I couldn't play the role of the levelheaded professor. For days, I barely slept or ate. I walked Shasta alone in a field by the bayou, thinking air and an easy walk in a space we loved would help, but instead I looked around at the empty field, may as well have been the oil field in Sayre, and began running full speed, trying to outrun him, to outrun her, to outrun the slit throat. I tripped and fell and saw her body falling facedown and I wanted to scream, but there simply isn't a sound for pain like that.

Each day, we came up with new ways to hurt him. Jerry wanted to place Eckardt in a room with a clock in view, position a noose around his neck, and then, every day, at exactly the same time, stretch the rope just one inch. I preferred the torture in *Taken*, stabbing metal rods into Eckardt's legs, sending an electric current through his body, and walking away while he's still alive and screaming. It was louder and likely quicker, though I don't really know how long a body can be electrified before it dies.

Each fantasy became more violent, as if learning Eckardt's brutality created a near-equal and opposite reaction, not just in what we wanted to do to him but also inside of us. I felt horrified by wanting to get a hundred knives and stake them through his body, but I also didn't know how to stop the wanting.

I didn't know the origin of revenge may lie in wanting to make sure the person doesn't hurt you or the group again. At the societal level this makes sense: hurting Eckardt may teach him not to harm another woman. It's the group's way of saying, *Don't you dare try this again or you'll be ostracized.* But I wanted him in pain, wanted him alive and staked down in a field so nature could do its work, and then I wanted him dead; I wasn't interested in his learning not to hurt someone again, as if he could go on living among us.

I didn't know how studies show those who get revenge actually feel worse than those who never do; instead of purging aggression from their bodies, revenge increases it, the punishers ruminating on the offense rather than letting it go. I never considered how his suffering may not be enough.

If I had known then that successful revenge is not about payback but about delivering a message—that the only way for vengeance to feel worth it is if the offender shows he understands it's because of his own actions—then instead of letting it go, I would have had Eckardt say, "I know you're doing this because I killed her," before I flipped the switch on.

Jerry and I lie in the bed, me tucked into a ball, him stretched out with one arm curved around my body.

"What are you thinking?" he asks.

"I feel like a rag doll," I say. "Punched to a pulp."

"I want to make him a victim."

"All I see are throats."

"Beat him to within an inch of his life, let him heal, then beat him again."

"I don't think I can take anymore."

I curl tightly beside him. I want to cry, but I don't have enough in me to shed a tear—to shed, like peeling skin, as if crying were passive and easy.

He wraps both arms around me, and I begin to stretch out, body unfurling like a hand. I hold my lips against his neck, my forehead to his cheek. He squeezes my shoulders.

Then we're kissing, tremulous at first, as if we are both asking permission to remember our bodies. He presses his lips harder against mine; I press back. His skin, my skin, hungry to forget the bodies that don't feel like ours. I roll onto my back, open my hips. I want him inside me, my husband, my beloved, who is right here with me, wanting to kill the very thing that is causing me pain. He enters me like easing into cold water. The slow rhythm of two people who haven't touched in months. I love that pensive wave, the tender rising and falling of our bodies.

But then he breathes harder, faster, he clamps a hand on my ass, he pounds, then pounds, then pounds, and pulls my hair so my throat is exposed.

This is how we used to have sex, back in the early days of our relationship, when I liked it rough, or thought I liked it rough, but I don't know that I'll ever want to be in that body again.

I don't tell Jerry to stop when he pulls my hair harder. Instead, I moan. Because I know, with no way of getting Eckardt alone in a room, Jerry needs something to slam against, a way to momentarily forget, and I want to offer him that, even though I know I don't want to be this body now, not when I'm holding back tears and I feel limp, thinking of how much blood would have spilled in the grass, how Jerry wants to hear bones crack. I feel like I'm sinking in violence all around me and I can't fight for a breath, much less the voice to say, *I need you to be gentle and slow.*

Afterward, I cry in the shower, my head under the water in a way so many women have done. Because it's the first time I can think of where Jerry couldn't see beyond his own pain and his own body and couldn't hear me when I had said, "I don't think I have anything left in me." The water courses down my back, and every part of me feels weakened and exhausted and raw. I know Jerry and I will come together again, I know he'll be able to hear what even my silence means, but right now, with the water so hot my skin is red, I feel alone, and I'm wishing for my mother to be here with me, washing my hair with the fingers I love, telling me to cover my eyes as she rinses it. I want someone here to shield me from hurting.

I couldn't believe the DA had left the decision to us and that he'd given us only a week to decide. I wondered if he gave every family this power or if he handed it to us because the case was high-profile in Oklahoma. If he went against our wishes, either by seeking the death penalty or not, and we criticized him to the press, it could be, in Rolland's words, political suicide for a person in an elected position. Maybe it was selfish, a way for the DA to let go of the responsibility of a death penalty case— the burden of proof is higher, but that's the choice the family made. Or maybe, when so many victims are silenced and excluded from the process, he saw this agency as a gift—*I can't bring your mother back, but I can let you decide the punishment you want and the risks you're willing to take.*

Rolland and Dad were quick to answer yes. I envied them sometimes. How clean and simple they made it seem. Jerry said he'd answer yes too, if the decision were his, though he thought death by lethal injection was too easy.

I thought of Eckardt in an execution room, a glass wall between us;

he'd be lying on a table with IVs in his arm. Even if it were painless—which, given the problems Oklahoma has had in obtaining the appropriate lethal-injection drugs, cannot be guaranteed, especially when inmates have described the burning and the pain that come from botched executions—I don't think I could watch a person die, a human with a past and experiences I'll never know. Maybe he had known his own kind of pain; maybe death wasn't justified.

But then I thought about Mom in her car. Bleeding. Terrified. A terror I can never fully fathom, no matter how much I learn or know. Torture that lasted not minutes but hours. I thought of the words used for her body: *brutalized, raped, obliterated*. Words used for Terry Welch. For his girlfriends. Words for the women we'll never know.

Wasn't pain what I'd always wanted for him, even from the beginning? Here the DA was saying, *You'll get your dungeon and the chance to kick him where it hurts.*

But I kept thinking of the hamster I had in my twenties, how she became sick and bloated and got stuck in the tube of her house. When I got her out, I cupped her in my palms and sobbed and heaved, not because I loved her that much but because a living thing was gasping for air, and there was nothing I could do to stop it.

I thought of Eckardt strapped down on a table, incapacitated like I'd wanted. What would I feel? Vengeance? Relief? Like we finally kept a promise to Mom that we didn't know if she even wanted? If he were to turn his head and grin at me, the way he grinned at Terry Welch's family when they were in court, I'd ask for the mixture of drugs that causes the burning. If he were to say to me, "I'm sorry," I think I'd beg for them to stop, my hands and my head against the glass.

Rolland had told me the IVs go from a prisoner's arm to a hole in the wall, behind which the executioners stand, none of them knowing which drug they are administering and if they are the one to do the actual killing. I could see how the responsibility would be shared—the prosecutors who argue the case well, the defense who doesn't, the jury who says death is appropriate, the judge who agrees, the person who stands behind a wall and unknowingly stops a heart from beating—steps that diffuse the decision to kill a human being.

But I was aware that it all began with us, that we could spare a person's life by saying no.

I thought about the victims in other cases who'd told the DA, "Do not kill for our family." I didn't know how to say, *Yes, kill for me,* or even, *Kill for my mother.* I didn't want to own a death. But this death would mean he'd never hurt another person again.

Then I thought about Eckardt's sister, how it was clear, in court, she loved him. I didn't want her to watch her brother die. She didn't deserve to sit in a room for a couple hours while they strapped him down and hooked him up, to see the curtain pulled open and then the eyes of the boy she remembered, to wait seven long minutes for his heartbeat to stop, to listen for his final breath. I wanted to spare her further pain.

I kept thinking how Jerry had said, "You have a good heart," while I rocked back and forth with the dead hamster in my hands.

But then I imagined Eckardt pulling Mom naked from her car, how far he may have made her walk with her arms bound behind her back, how she might have looked up to the stars in a plea.

I kept thinking that a week wasn't long enough to decide, not when we'd just learned how Mom had died and all I could think about was her throat, wondering how much force it takes for a knife to enter skin, if it's as easy as pushing a syringe. I grappled for days and felt like I couldn't talk with Rolland or with Dad, that they wouldn't understand. I thought I might always be wavering, but I also didn't want to miss my chance, in case I really did want him dead.

When Rolland said the DA needed an answer, I told him, "I guess so."

I told myself my decision didn't matter, it was two against one after all, but I knew this was a cop-out, a way to cover up what I didn't want to admit—that I was afraid to go up against Rolland and Dad, afraid to feel alone, that more than I wanted to spare a human's life I needed to feel close to them, like I did the morning after she'd been taken, when we sat on my bed and held on to one another.

I washed our Mazda at the car wash on Montrose, Houston sun beating down, my quarters stacked on the edge of the coin-op machine. Because Jerry and I didn't have much money, I had brought a bucket and my own soap, using my quarters only for the water. I had just finished scrubbing, the entire car covered in suds, and was wringing out the sponge at the back of the car, when a man approached the front of it.

His hair was short, his face clean-shaven, his denim shorts smudged with mud.

"Excuse me," he said. "I don't usually do this. I'm not a bad man. Just down on my luck. And I'm sick. I was wondering if I could have three or four dollars for the bus?"

"I'm sorry, sir, but I don't carry cash with me," I said, shrugging my shoulders as I looked at his eyes, nearly level with mine. He looked just as sweaty as I was, his forehead glistening as he stood in the sun. I was just about to tell him he could have the rest of my quarters after I rinsed the soap from the car when he started shouting at me.

"You know I don't ask dumb questions that I know the answer to! That's the problem with our capitalist society. But you have them quarters over there. And this right here"—he pointed to the car, his voice cutting through the sounds of the street—"is just a material thing, *not* a necessity. And you're spending your money washing it!"

I surged toward the front of the car, sponge in my hand, my body not quite mine. "You really want to judge me? You? Who's wearing a chain like that? That's not a necessity!"

"What, this?" He held out the thick metal necklace. "This ain't nothing! My nephew gave me this!"

"My father gave me this!" I yelled, full voiced, my arms outstretched to signify the car, though technically Dad had loaned me the money for it.

"Man, you wouldn't throw a brick at a dog, would you?"

I walked straight toward him, my shoulders squared. "I'd throw a brick at a dog that's snarling at me."

"I'm not snarling!"

"That's *exactly* what you're doing," I said, pointing my finger, no, my arm, my whole arm at him. "When you stand there passing judgment on me and yelling at me. *That* is snarling."

He turned and walked away, stopping every so often to yell back at me, though I couldn't make out the words. I walked to the bucket. I could have swung it at him. I could have turned the water on and hosed him down with the high-pressure wax. My hands were shaking, my heart pumping fast and hard, and I knew, immediately knew, that my reaction was more about Eckardt than this man in need, more about Mom's slit throat and the upcoming trial and the prosecutor's latest email that said, "This is the one of the most heinous crimes I have ever been involved in prosecuting." Normally I would have shriveled and apologized, feeling the anger later, in the safety of my home, but my surging was instantaneous. My voice so steady and sharp. And I knew it was about being approached during the simple, everyday task of washing a car. Like stopping by the mall after work. That it was about the car itself. That I would use a weapon, any weapon—the bucket, the sponge, my arm, the water hose—to fight an unknown man standing beside my vehicle.

I felt simultaneously afraid and proud of myself.

Later, Jerry would tell me I needed to be more careful. But I wouldn't let him take this from me. This moment when I didn't step back for my quarters and instead rushed forward, no longer waiting for a strike to the head. No longer being the woman everyone expects.

In September 2011, just over three years after the original DNA match and a year and a half after the preliminary hearing, we were preparing for the trial, set for November. But then Rolland and Dad called on a speaker phone.

"The defense is offering a plea agreement," Rolland said. "It's an Alford plea, which means Eckardt doesn't admit guilt but does have to acknowledge that there's enough evidence to convict him, in exchange for life without parole and waiving all of his rights to appeal."

In front of me, Jerry lay on the living room floor, Shasta trying over and over to get him to wrestle by picking up his wrist in her mouth and stepping on his bicep with her hind leg.

"They're offering a plea," I told him. He muted the TV, sat up, and studied my reactions as I listened to Rolland explain that the Alford plea would allow Eckardt to save face, especially to other prisoners, because he could say he was innocent and got screwed by the system.

"Now I know how I personally feel," Rolland said, "but I don't want to influence your thinking or Dad's."

I just wanted to be quiet for a moment to let the news sink in, to really penetrate. Even though we had known from the beginning that a plea was a possibility.

But the silence felt intrusive too, so I asked, "What else has been going on?"

We spent several minutes talking about rugs and shop vacs and having to go to the dentist to get a tooth pulled, what is new, what is broken, as I tried to adapt.

I knew how I felt. I could sense it in my body, a seething.

I said, "I guess I'd like to hear what you two think," even as I was aware that I was allowing the men to talk first and that they wouldn't change how I felt. I just wasn't ready to speak.

Dad said, "I don't like that Eckardt doesn't have to admit guilt. That just doesn't sit right with me."

"I look at it as a prosecutor and a judge," Rolland said. "I look at the end result. It means Eckardt won't be able to come after you or Kenzie or Leanne, which is my greatest fear. And by the way, we don't have to reach a consensus. I won't be upset if you feel different."

I thought about how I'd never known Rolland was afraid like this, that while I spent years imagining the men showing up at my door or dragging me screaming into a car, he was terrified of the very same thing for me.

I thought too of Rolland's getting his identity wrong, not really responding as a judge but as a brother, a father, a husband. But I didn't tell him this. Instead I asked, "But as the son of a murdered woman, do you feel the same way?"

"I do."

He made it sound so simple.

"What I am losing or giving up," he said, "is the moment the jury comes back and announces he's guilty."

Exactly. We'd miss the climax, the crescendo, that moment when twenty-five years and especially the last three burst in our chests in one fantastic crash.

But that wouldn't be all we'd lose.

"Look, I get it," I said. "It's safer. It's more logical. It's a result I'd want from a jury trial. It keeps other women safe. But Mom didn't get to choose how her life ended, so I don't want Eckardt to get to choose how his life ends. I don't want him to have that power."

"All of that is valid," Rolland said.

After rehashing the same points multiple times, we said we'd be in touch and we hung up. Then Jerry and I mulled over the pros, the cons, the possible unknowns, what would be gained, what would be lost. He stayed on the floor, his back to the TV. I knew he wanted to hold me, but after years of marriage he knows when I'm not ready to be held.

"It feels empty, Jerry. It feels flat. All this buildup, this anticipation and anxiety these last three years and then this 'package,' as Dad called it. And goddamn it, I don't want him to have control over his life."

I sat on our new geometric rug, tracing the large arcs of a circle with my fingers, thinking of Terry Welch, of the detectives' telling us that a man like Eckardt doesn't commit a murder like Mom's once, of Eckardt on a table, of the moment a jury says, "We find the defendant guilty," of Eckardt's saving face in prison, telling others, "No, man, I didn't do it," of Mom facedown, of Mom had she survived.

I buried my head in my knees and said, "I really just want Mom to speak to me right now, to tell me what she wants."

"You should call Chris," Jerry said. "Maybe she'll be able to tell you." He slid the phone across the rug to my feet.

I dialed her number. I heard her say hello. I said, "Chris, I need you to channel Mom for me."

She thought I was joking.

I told her the news and that I didn't have an answer. I told her I needed to know what Mom would think.

"You know I can't do that, Kristine."

She stayed quiet as I repeated every point and ranted, "I want him to suffer just as Mom suffered, I want him to be afraid, I want him to have no control, but no matter what outcome we get, even if it's the death penalty, the punishment won't equal her suffering because he does not love, because he wouldn't know what it's like to worry for your children."

"I *know*, absolutely know, your mother told him she had children."

I imagined Mom on her stomach in the car, her hands being bound with fishing line behind her, pleading not just for her own life but her children's. To wrap her arms around us again. To spare us from suffering a life without her.

I lowered my head into my hand, squeezing my temples with my fingers. "I just don't know what to do, Chris."

"I don't know either," she said. "But as a mother, not your mother, Kristine, I can't speak for her, but as a mother, I would not want my children to suffer through a trial. That preliminary hearing was bad enough, it was so painful, and I would never want my children to go through that. You've already been through too much."

I began crying, feeling like she had said exactly what I needed to hear. What Mom would have wanted me to know.

A day later though, I was all frenetic energy again. I swam at the Y, but it was loud with two people per lane and splashing and music, so I drove to a nearby lake, searching for a place that was quiet. There were just a few people there and a breeze to ripple the water. I sat with my back against a tree, several feet from the shore, filled with trash and algae and duck poop. The wind was at my back, so I could smell the minerals, the dirt, the water, the smell of home, instead of the rot from the lake. A white wood cross stood out in the water. A marker for some-one who had drowned. Its crossbeam crooked, its paint battered off. I thought of Mom's grave in Winthrop, so far away, of how my aunt Mary updated us every Memorial Day on its condition. I sat in the grass, tying blade after blade into tiny knots, remembering how I once sat barefoot in the grass on her grave because I wanted to feel closer to her, of how I ran my fingers through the blades as if they were her hair.

A few hours later, Jerry drove home from work and joined me. When I saw him walking toward me in the lime-green polo shirt I loved, I smiled.

"How was work?"

"Fine," he said. "Whatcha been thinkin' these last hours?"

I told him it *did* make a difference to have a jury declare him *guilty*, but it couldn't be worth the risk of *not guilty* or a short sentence or fifteen years of appeals, where the case could be overturned or returned to another trial. "That'd be forty years of this shit," I said.

Jerry stood with the lake and the sun to his back, rowers in sculls gliding by, their rhythm so consistent and certain, each oar entering the water like a breath.

"The plea agreement means none of that," I said. "It means I can come closer to forgetting."

But then I thought of those times I'd wanted him dead, so in thirty years I wouldn't be sipping on an Earl Grey at a sidewalk café on the East Coast and think of him, about his prison life, about how easy or difficult it had been on him, about whether he'd been institutionalized or not, and, if so, about how they should release him into a world that had no place for him. I knew if he lived, there'd be no forgetting.

I thought about the women who'd be saved if he lived the rest of his life behind bars. That's something I had wanted. To spare another son from finding his mom's body in a bathtub. Another daughter who'd spend her life searching. But saving them didn't feel real. I stared at the cross in the water and felt no closure, no resolution, no release.

"Was all this worth it when I feel nothing?"

"Maybe it's about learning," Jerry said. "You learned with the cause of death that you don't want to know everything, and a trial would mean you'd know most all of it."

"Yeah, maybe," I said. "Maybe it's best to take the plea."

But then Rolland called to say the DA wouldn't accept the plea unless we all agreed to it, and he used the words *quick* and *dry* and *not much to it really* to describe what a plea hearing is like, and I felt enraged all over again. Flat, hollow, dull, and void. Twenty-five years for ten minutes in court.

Shouldn't punishment have sound—for us and for Eckardt? Shouldn't we feel its weight?

Everything suddenly sped up. We agreed to the plea after just a few days of deliberating, and a week later we'd be at the hearing, watching a judge sentence Eckardt to life in prison.

I swam at the Y's indoor pool and then did gentle yoga. At the end of the seniors' lap swim, the pool was quiet, the swimmers slower, no arms slapping the surface of the water. I chose the lane beside a man who used a snorkel and barely moved. I lowered myself in and stood on tiptoes because somehow that one inch of skin, dry above the cold water, makes you feel warmer. The man with his bathing suit trunks stuck to his bony legs floated beside me, as if he were studying the pool's floor for sea life and it were a soft current, not his own legs, that eased him forward. I placed my goggles on, submerged into the cold, chlorined blue, and gently kicked off from the wall. It occurred to me then, in the slowness of it all, in the welcomed silence under the surface, that I was moving at a senior's pace.

Gentle yoga was filled with women who told me about their bone densities and how hard it is to get out of the bathtub. They asked me not to laugh when they tried to stand up from the floor. Their bodies were breaking. And there I was, thirty-three years old, my body more or less healthy, but I was broken too, just not in a way they could recognize. I took my time getting off the floor. I felt fractured inside. The fissures wouldn't heal if they were jolted.

I wondered if they'd let me swim during the fifty-five-plus lap hour. I'd say, *I promise I won't surpass your speed. I promise I'll be quiet. My body has not earned the quiet like yours, but my insides have. Please let me be with you. I don't belong with people my own age. That man there—speeding his way to get through by the end of lunch hour and slapping the water so loud— he is not me. That woman with proper form, swimming miles and miles in training—she is not me either. I am the one sinking in the deep end, trying to stay still and find a way not to return for breath.*

"I still don't like that Eckardt isn't taking responsibility for Kathy's death," Dad says, when I ask him over the phone if he's still okay with the plea-bargain agreement. "I agreed just to make it easy. I want it over with."

I don't know why he used *Kathy*, as if he were talking to someone other than me. I think of the time Mom scolded me for calling her *Mother*. Of the time, years after her death, when the three of us were on the boat, Dad unwinding the rope, Rolland pulling my ski from the well, and I asked, "Will you hand me Mother's life jacket, please?"

"What?" Rolland said, sharp and quick.

"Um, I mean, will you please hand me Mom's life jacket?"

Rolland couldn't see that *mother* was easier.

Maybe *Kathy* gives Dad some distance.

Or maybe he needs the intimacy of her name right now, to feel close to her here at the end.

"Do you think you will give a victim's impact statement?" I ask him.

"Why would I do that?"

"The victim's advocate told Rolland we have an opportunity to address Eckardt, the only opportunity we'll ever have. She's afraid we'll regret not taking the chance to speak."

"I could see making a statement to address the judge to influence the sentencing," Dad says. "But not addressing Eckardt. To me, we're not the victims. Not me, not you, not . . ."

"Mom is."

"Right, Mom is," his voice cracks.

My heart breaks a little then.

"She's the victim, and I would want to talk about that. And just like right now, when the emotions are getting to me, I don't want that to happen in front of Eckardt. I won't let that happen. I won't let him know he's gotten under my skin. He would relish it. I've known too many guys like him. They're bullies."

"Yeah, we were affected, but our suffering is nothing compared to hers," I say. "And besides, what good could it do to describe her suffering to a man who enjoys violence against women?"

"Right. I could speak all day in front of a judge. But not to him," he says.

It makes me wonder what he would say, if he talked about how she's the victim. Could he come close to describing what she must have felt, the absolute horror of it? How much has he imagined the parking lot, the monofilament line cutting into her wrists, the agony of anal tears? Can he ever know the terror of a bra being sliced off, and not even in the back but between the cups?

I think there's no way he can tell it, no way his experiences with bullies can approximate her story. My own history can lead me closer but still not close enough.

For days leading up to the plea hearing, I walk around the apartment, unpacking boxes while Jerry's at his new job. IBM paid for the packing and the move, so no boxes are organized as I want them; the books aren't boxed by genre and in alphabetical order, the kitchen utensils, even the plastic ones, are wrapped in layers and layers of paper and boxed with shoes. Nothing is where it needs to be, paper is all around me, and I keep thinking, *I want Mom to speak through me. What would she want to say to him? What's the story she would tell?*

I call my mother-in-law and ask her to tell me. She's a victim of domestic abuse, from her first husband many years ago, she's a mother, so she must know, but as she tells me what she would say, I'm arguing with her in my head. *No, that's not right, those aren't the words.*

I know then what I want to say.

After I write the statement, I send the prosecutors a draft and hear back from Melissa, who says I cannot call Eckardt any names in my statement. Something about decorum in the courtroom. "You're kidding me," I say, because the violence of my words can never match the violence that Eckardt has done and because this is the moment I should get to say whatever the fuck I need to. But I have no choice, really. I revise it and shift the nouns over to adjectives or adverbs. She then asks me if I need her to read it in court because Rolland has requested that the prosecutors read his. I tell her I want to try to get through mine and that if I can't, I want her to be the one to read it and not the other, male, prosecutor. I say, "It's important to have a woman's voice speak my words."

Jerry and I had just arrived at my father's new house, single-story, easier on his hips, after several hours of driving from Texas. The plea hearing was just two days away. It was a Wednesday.

I was sitting on the floor in his open-floor-plan house, a style I do not like, his kitchen, the breakfast table, his couches and TV all part of the same room with nothing but tile and carpet differentiating them. I thought, *I miss separate rooms and divisions, miss entering a family room and feeling like I'm home.*

I was sitting with my back against the kitchen island, and Dad was sitting at the table, the same table where Mom ashed her cigarettes into the green glass sphere, where I, as a child, licked the cheese off Doritos and put the moistened chips back into the bag for someone else to eat—I had done this openly and no one seemed to stop me—but the table, its wood grain stained from years of newspaper print pressed against it, seemed like a different table now. The light was wrong.

We'd been going over the plan for the next couple of days—when Mom's sister Mary would arrive in town, who was meeting at the courthouse, who was driving, when the press conference would be—when Dad said to me, "I have something to tell you. You may want to sit down."

"I am sitting down," I said.

"I mean at the table."

I thought maybe it had to do with the hearing, that there'd been another change in the plea. I thought, *There's no way I can take anymore, not when we're this close.*

"I'm okay on the floor," I said, thinking the floor was the safest place to be.

"Lee," he said, and hesitated, "is dead."

"What? How?" Already I was thinking car wreck, drunk driving, maybe he was on his Harley, or maybe in his truck, distracted by his dog, and then I remembered how he had a black lab, a puppy still, in the bed of his truck once, and Lee was driving, and the dog leapt out; I remembered how Lee cried in the middle of the street, traffic all around him, limp dog at his feet.

How fast the mind skips in only a second between a question and an answer, how much it can cycle through in a tick of the mantel's clock.

"Suicide."

I asked, "What?" as if I were surprised, but I wasn't really. Lee with his drinking, his thinning face, his plans to flip houses and move to a home with acres of land, plans that never seemed to happen.

"A man from up the street called me this morning, after he saw the ambulance."

"How?"

"You know that thing Lee built in the backyard?"

I remembered. We never knew what it was supposed to be. He had built it after we broke up. A giant trellis, for lack of a better word, built from four-by-fours, it held nothing but a hammock, tiny under its towering boards. Like so many of his plans, it didn't turn out like he wanted.

"He hung himself from it. A neighbor girl, on the other side from us, saw him through the fence."

"When's the funeral?" I asked.

Jerry was looking back at me from over the top of the love seat. At his height, it was easy for him to study how I was reacting. I was surprised that I felt nothing. Instead, I kept thinking of Lee's mother, who had lost one of her husbands when he was working on a construction site, a wall falling and smothering him. I thought about how, as a teenager, I had wanted her to be my mom; she tanned in a tanning bed, she had spiky short hair, she had spunk. I thought of the women she had worked with at a shelter, how she coped with loss by helping women who lose.

"I don't know yet," my father answered.

"Will you go?" I asked.

"I don't know. Depends on when it is and how the next few days go."

I didn't want to get off the floor. I felt heavy, Lee hanging from a trellis, his mom identifying another body, me about to speak to a killer in court. Maybe the chair at the table would have been better, or maybe the weight would have caused its oak legs to break.

A few hours later, I lay in bed with Jerry and searched online for an obituary or details about a funeral. Instead I found Lee's Facebook page.

Five days before, he posted a picture with the caption "Selling 2k of motorcross gear for $300," and under it, he told someone who wanted to know if there was a bike for sale too, "Sorry, the bike was sold. Dammit I must be getting old."

He posted a selfie a day before he died, gray in his goatee, a closed-mouth smile. His eyes looked so weary. He took the photo in his backyard, and though you can't see the structure in it—you can only see his house and the towering maple above it—I knew he was standing under its wood.

He wrote on his last night, "I have many theist friends. Good for u. Let's debate!!!?" and then he commented on that post, "Too late tonight. I'm ready."

Then "Forever is a long time . . . Especially towards the end."

Then he wrote, for the last time, "Later!"

I didn't sleep well during the night, kept thinking of Eckardt, of Lee, his mother, the comments women were writing on his Facebook page, saying "Lee was always so nice to me," the plea hearing, the question of the funeral on my mind, the chance Richard would be there. I thought of Lee wanting the body that didn't hesitate to jump thirty feet into water, his dog following right after. I thought of him wanting his hands not to hurt, his back not to hurt, his body to work as it did when he had the seventeen-year-old next door.

The next day, I drove to my childhood home. Even though Dad had moved into a new house, there was still so much to go through and remove, things of my mother's, things of my youth.

There were vehicles at Lee's house when I pulled up. I walked over, hoping his mom would be there. Lee's sister answered the door, the one my father had once busted through. I stepped into the entryway, where the framed collage of Lee's girlfriends once hung, me in the middle, hair wet from a hotel shower, Lee pulling me into a kiss. I stepped on the carpet where we first fucked. That's where his mother hugged me. I had to bend down a little.

"I'm so sorry," I whispered, my arms around her shoulders.

"You know, Lee always loved you," she said.

I wanted to say that *that* wasn't love, but he was dead and she was hurting. Her body was so small in my arms, I could feel her spine through her shirt. When I pulled away, I saw her eyes behind her glasses, the pain in them; I wished I could soothe her somehow.

I asked her what happened, and she told me she blames the dosage of antidepressants he'd been prescribed. She said she'd woken up in the morning, as usual, but didn't know where the dog had gone. She found Lee in the backyard, hanging, his toes touching the ground.

"Lee, that isn't funny," she had said.

I was covering my mouth; I was shaking my head. Only later would I think of my father, laughing at the police on our porch. Why is it we believe in bad humor first and not the plain truth laid out before us?

"Murphy was there with him," she said. "He kept dropping his ball at Lee's feet."

This is when I broke down crying. Not when Dad told me as I sat on the floor, not when I studied Lee's eyes in his picture, not when his mother hugged me so hard, like I always wanted her to hug me. But at his dog, wild and big and dopey, trying to get Lee to play.

"I'm so sorry," I said again.

"Lee always loved you," his mom repeated.

I thought of how hard it might have been, having a girlfriend who said yes to everything and then turned away. I thought of that motorcycle ride, how he reached back to stroke my thigh and said, "I miss you," so tender, his voice soft and sad.

"We always teased him about robbing the cradle," his sister said, laughing.

"I *was* really young," I said, hoping it would be enough to convey that I didn't think a cradle should ever be robbed.

"'Robbing that cradle, aren't ya?' I'd say when I saw him."

"Has the funeral been set?" I asked.

They told me it was scheduled for two days later.

I told his mom I didn't know if Dad and I could make it. "The plea hearing's tomorrow," I said. "And I don't know how much I'll have left in me."

"I understand," she said. "You can go see him now if you want to. He's at the funeral home. He looks good, they did a good job, he looks like himself."

I couldn't imagine seeing him in a casket, his hands folded on his chest, resting in a way he never rested. He liked to sleep on his side, his body curved, hips and shoulders dipping low in his waterbed.

Only later would I know I made the right choice. There was no way I could look at his neck, how they would have tried to conceal the wound, and not see my mother's throat or her bound hands. Only later would I think of Jerry, of how he wanted to place a noose around Eckardt's neck, raising it an inch at the exact same time every day, making Eckardt dread the clock and the tightening knot. Only later would I think I'd want to tell Lee how wrong he was to fuck me at seventeen. Or I'd say, *How could you do this to your mom, to make her find you that way?* Or perhaps I would have nothing to say at all, his life and death punishment enough.

Sometimes there's isn't enough time to cycle through the reasons.

Which was why my immediate response was, "I can't do it. I want to remember him as skiing behind his boat, he was so beautiful when he skied, the way he could cut across the wake."

They nodded their heads, remembering Lee skiing with only his bare feet.

The morning of the plea hearing, I sit on the floor in the guest room of my father's house, trying to decide which boots I should wear with my black suit. The stilettos? Or the platform ones with a chunkier heel? I decide on the platforms, thinking the heels feel tougher, less able to buckle or break.

I slide on a blazer over my silk blouse, blue like the ocean and rippling. Then mother-of-pearl earrings, a gift from a friend who also knows what it's like to be raped. Then a watch from Jerry, a bracelet from Chris, and Dad's wedding ring. I hold Mom's locket in the palm of my hand, opening and closing its gold oval door, then slip it over my head. But I don't tuck it into my blouse this time. No, I want it on display today.

I open my journal and read what I wrote the night before: "Tomorrow is the day you can finally confront Mom's killer. Savor it. And know that it is okay if your voice cracks, your hands shake, or your lip quivers. You speak for you and no one else. Tomorrow you reclaim your power to say what you have wanted to say for 25 years. And you'll be surrounded by people who love you."

I pack my journal and slip the photograph of Mom and us at the zoo, the one with "Save mommy" written on its back, between the pages.

Piece by piece, I am armored with water and metal and paper and stone, my body layered in stories, layered in love.

Jerry, Dad, and I are in the car on the way to the hearing, the potholes on I-40 knocking us around. It's gray and cool and rainy outside, which makes me want to sit in a café with a good latte. Jerry keeps Dad occupied with discussions about usability studies for software development, while I sit in the back seat, earbuds in, listening to Chuck Mangione's "Bellavia," again. It gives me a quiet strength, with its slow tempo picking up speed, but it isn't what I need right now. I need movement. Something loud. Something with a charge. So I switch to Garbage to hear a female voice raging.

In a conference room in the courthouse, I pace while everyone else sits. It's quiet in the room, everyone speaking in whispers. I take a sip of Dad's black coffee. Someone asks me if I want a cup. I tell them, "No, thank you." I want enough caffeine to jolt me but not enough to make me shake.

Melissa, her blond hair pulled halfway back, her suit still a little ill-fitting, pulls me aside, telling me I will be the last person to read. "I said we're going chronologically by age, with the statements from your mother's older sister, then her twin, then your brother, and then you, but really it's about you having the final word," she says. She winks at me and walks away.

Someone tries to hug me but I pull away. I'm afraid I am like a turret made not from stone but from sand and that I will crumble if I'm touched.

A friend of Rolland's from childhood sees Chris walking down the hallway and says to Jerry, "She looks like Kathy." I think of the times I stared at Chris in the hallways of my middle school, thinking the same thing, but now Chris is just Chris, the pseudomom I love. She wears the necklace I've given her, a lariat where a ring holds together two chains, a symbol for Mom bringing us together.

It's time to go to the courtroom; everything suddenly feels more serious, like we're proceeding down the aisle at a funeral. And in a way, we are. We're headed to give eulogies for Mom, for the children we were before her murder. And we're sending a man to a type of death.

We walk down the hallway, attorneys in front, then Dad, then Rolland and his wife, hand in hand, then Jerry and me, hand in hand, then family and friends behind us. I start laughing as we walk.

"What are you thinking?" Jerry asks, squeezing my two fingers.

"The ants go marching two by two, hurrah, hurrah," I sing quietly.

In the courtroom, the attorneys tell us to sit in the jury box facing Eckardt. Chris tries to sit in the audience, but I grab her. "I need you here with me," I say.

In the jury box, I'm trying to decide where to sit, whom I will need to comfort, whom I will want to comfort me. I sandwich myself between Dad and Jerry in the swivel chairs, thinking Rolland has his wife there for support. The box is elevated, with two rows of theater seating, so that we, the victims and loved ones as jury, sit higher on the floor to face Mom's killer.

At first, I don't even notice Eckardt sitting at a table across from us, shackled and looking at forms. His hair is short, spiked up in the front, his beard is short, he wears the same socks and sandals that look like shower shoes. But his glasses are different, less thick, his eyes more clearly in view.

The attorneys for both the prosecution and the defense stand at a conference table with our statements in front of them. They're reading one, then shaking their heads, then arguing with one another.

"Shit," I whisper.

"What?" Jerry asks.

"They're going to make me change my statement again. They're going to make me cut parts even though I revised it."

The male prosecutor walks over and says to me, "The defense attorneys take issue with the word *rot* here and would like to see it changed to *die*."

"Fine," I say. "May I see your pen?"

I scratch out *rot* and write above it *die* in the lawyer's black ink.

The lawyers and Eckardt move to the bench, the judge reading paperwork aloud, asking Eckardt, "Do you understand?" He answers, "Yes, ma'am," with his head bowed, his shoulders hunched in his orange uniform. When he signs his name on a form, his handcuffs clicking against each other, he shakes his head no, as if in disbelief of something.

He looks beaten.

I love that he looks beaten.

Every minute or so, he turns his head slowly, just his head and his shoulders, a pivoting of his upper body, to look at me. Not at Dad. Not at Rolland. Not at my mother's sister. Always at me. He stares for a few seconds, returns to his forms, then turns back again.

I don't see rage in his eyes through his new glasses. Or guilt. Or sympathy. Or an apology. Or fear. He looks at me with curiosity. It's as if he doesn't quite know what to make of this presence in the room.

A déjà vu.

A recalling of a dream.

Eyes so familiar.

I wonder if he has a clear picture of what Mom looked like, if a mind can build a memory of a face when it's being beaten with a fist.

It's clear he sees Kathy Sue Engle but sees her changed, her hair a little lighter, a little straighter, her shoulders not as small, and not with a look of fear but contempt.

He's baffled by a Kathy Sue Engle silent and out of reach.

Everyone goes back to their respective tables, and when my aunt reads her statement, I look over at Dad. He's staring across the room at no one. I've never seen him look so cold and still.

Rolland has a handkerchief in his lap. It's dry and folded into a tidy white square.

Bobby walks to the podium to read Rolland's words:

> For me, this ordeal began the April morning after Mom was abducted. I was asleep by the time Dad was notified by the police. Dad let my sister and me sleep.
>
> When I woke up, I found several of our neighbors in our house; and from that moment to today, there are so many things that I do not understand or comprehend.
>
> The first thing that my dad told my sister and me was that Mom had been abducted. I had no idea what that word "abducted" meant. Dad explained that it was a kidnapping.
>
> Now I understood that word, but why would someone kidnap my mom? Was it for money or for a car? I could not comprehend why someone would do that.
>
> I wish I was still that innocent. Being 13 years old at the time, I did not think about nor contemplate all of the vile, vicious, and heinous acts my mom would endure.

Rolland's staring at his handkerchief, turning it over and over and over on his thigh.

It's as if his body is about to rupture, pain as oil packed under the earth. So much effort to keep it contained, Rolland, my brother, splitting open and open and open.

> Over the years, I will come to learn the facts of my mom's death, but knowledge doesn't always equate to understanding. Why would a person be so cruel?
>
> Today I know there is no answer to that question. The defendant might offer any number of excuses or

explanations. None of them will ever be sufficient. His acts make him less of a man, less of a human. His choices have forfeited his right to live in a free society. He deserves to live out his years in a cell. He deserves to have all of his choices taken away from him. When he dies in prison, his name will be lost and he will be forgotten.

I also know that there is far more love and compassion in this world than this defendant's brand of evil.

From that April morning in 1986 to today, I have been surrounded by an army of family and friends. It would be possible to spend weeks recounting all of the acts of kindness my family has received.

For 13 years of my life, I received my mother's love.

Rolland's shoulders are shaking; he's turning the square over and over.

I can't reach him, with Jerry between us, and I don't know if I should even try. I don't want to distract from his words being spoken.

Rolland with his head bowed. Rolland whose body holds caverns of pain, deep and dark and quaking.

His wife turns away.

Jerry lifts his hand to comfort him but hesitates. I know he's afraid to jolt Rolland with a touch from another man.

So Jerry's mother reaches forward from the row behind us. She lays her hand on Rolland's right shoulder in such a gentle way and keeps it there until he takes a deep breath, until his sobs begin to soften.

When she takes her hand away, it's as if she's pulling some of that pain back with her, a siphoning through touch.

For all of my life, I have received my father's love. Both of them taught me what a loving family is.

Today I have a wonderful wife that I know my mom would adore. I hope that I'm a loving and attentive husband, and I hope that our marriage emulates Mom and Dad's.

Finally, I know that my mother still lives. She lives in me; she lives in my sister; and she lives in my daughter. Her presence was taken from us, but her love and her spirit cannot die and it cannot be taken from us. Our family will persevere and we will flourish.

Bobby walks away from the podium, with the word *persevere* reverberating in the room.

Then it's my turn. My heart is pounding. I don't want to trip, I don't want to cry, I don't want to forget my words, I don't want the microphone to screech, I don't want to be too quiet or too loud, I don't want to rush, I don't want to stammer.

I don't want him to see me as weak.

I need you, Mom.

I set my journal down on the floor, "Save mommy" tucked between its pages, and say to myself again, *It's okay. Savor this.*

I stand and Dad swivels his knees to let me by, his first movement of the hearing. I walk to the podium, my shoulders squared, my head high, my heels sturdy. The locket taps my breastbone with each step.

I rest my elbows on the podium, forearms up its slope, clasping my hands on top of my statement. I know now that I won't need it.

He's to my left. Eight feet from me. Nothing but this podium and a table between us.

Will my words be enough to cut him?

I look to the judge, who looks at me. Dryly. No encouragement in her eyes. No smile to say, *You're okay.*

I take a deep breath.

It is really my mother's words that need to be heard. It is her voice that matters.

My voice trembles and breaches and breaks.

It doesn't matter how many times I have practiced this; I cannot fight feeling the most truthful sentences I have ever said aloud.

> But because it is impossible to hear her or to know what she would want to say, I have decided to speak a few words.
>
> For over 20 years, I have thought about the men who killed my mother. I imagined them and dreamed them. They were always young, strong, able to hurt others. In my imagination, they were all-powerful, and, in that way, they became a myth.

I've steadied my voice. It sounds like my own.

I look at the court reporter, the bailiff, the judge.

> But now, 25 years after my mother was murdered . . .

I turn to him.

> . . . I stand in front of you—an old man, a weak man, a man whose actions show just how afraid he really is, how cowardly.
>
> It is cowardly to hurt women.
>
> It is cowardly the way that you killed my mother. You couldn't even face her.
>
> It is cowardly to take this plea agreement.
>
> In doing so, you have given up all of your power.
>
> Life without parole.
>
> No appeals.
>
> This means that you will no longer be a presence in my life.
>
> You're gone.

You will die behind bars and barbed wire, every bit
as fearful as you were 25 years ago, while I, I will be
living a life absent of you.

He looks right at me. Until I turn to him and call him an old man.
He lowers his head then. And when I say, "the way that you killed my
mother," I crack him. I crack him. After he has listened to statement
after statement with his head bowed, so calm and still, I crack him. An
emotion rises up, escapes as a quick, strong grunt, as if I've jabbed him
from the inside. As if the truth is expelled in the form of a huff. He
shakes his head no. I read guilt. I read memory. I crack him. I crack that
goddamn body of his. Me. My words.

I have never felt this strong.

I feel so tall.

As if I am hovering just above him, my body laid out as if in flight.
My body, my words, the words that are my body looming heavy and
large, unreachable, unavoidable. He has nowhere to go. He cannot
touch me in this moment, and he cannot touch her either. I could stay
here forever, in this space above him, with nothing but my power between us.

I walk back to the jury box and Rolland grabs me, hugs me, and
says, "I love you, Goof," while the judge is looking at me and saying, "I
am truly, truly sorry for your loss and thank you for your courage to be
here. Thank you. Court is adjourned," and Eckardt is being whisked
off in shackles. I'm confused by this. I don't understand why she hasn't
declared him guilty or said that he is sentenced to life. Jerry tells me
she did this before our statements began, I just hadn't heard it, and
as I catch a glimpse of Eckardt's orange jumpsuit leaving the room, I
realize I really did have the last word.

I find Chris and hold on to her. We are sobbing and in such a tight
embrace I can feel our stomachs heaving against each other. "You were
perfect," she says.

Then I'm holding on to Jerry, my face buried in his chest. When I ask him if Mom would be proud, he says, "Yes, baby," and he kisses me softly on the forehead.

Random people from the audience are tugging on my arm and telling me, "Eckardt really watched you. You look like your mom. I think that's why."

Then Jerry's mom is hugging me and telling me, "Those were your mother's words, not yours, she would be so proud."

And then my father. Who is silent.

I put my arms around his neck; his body is stiff.

"Did I do okay?"

"Yep."

I pull back and take his hands.

"I didn't embarrass you, did I?"

"Oh, no, that's never a concern."

He's looking not at my face but to something far off in the room.

"I still acted with dignity, didn't I?"

"Yep."

And then he lets go and walks away.

I watch his shoulders in his dark suit squeeze through spaces in the crowd. I want him to stay with me.

I remember the time when I was thirteen and expelled from school for months. I spoke in front of the school board to say how sorry I was, and, though they didn't reinstate me, Dad hugged me after the hearing and told me how proud he was of me for speaking. I want that now. I want him to see the significance, to see his daughter standing up to her mother's killer, to see me as grown-up and strong, so different than the eight-year-old who could only imagine her revenge. I want him to see this as Mom standing up too. I want to hear him say, *I admire you for fighting in a way I could not do.*

A few days after the plea hearing, Jerry and I needed to leave for Texas, to return to work and our lives there. We loaded the car with items

from my childhood home—Mom's clothing that I wanted to keep, photographs that had been buried in a closet, a box containing her baby
shoes and three inches of her baby hair, tied with a tiny rubber band. I
couldn't run my fingers through the hair yet or even look at it for more
than a few seconds. Not when her death still felt so close.

Even though the house was a mess—boxes everywhere, piles to sell,
piles for trash, Mom's piano tall and sturdy and waiting for me to claim
as my own—I still took a deep breath when I entered it, feeling like I
was home.

Right after Mom died, Dad was told by a psychologist friend that
adults need change during trauma—new job, new city, new home—but
children need stability. "Keep everything else the same," he had said,
"everything but her absence." So we stayed in our house, Mom's needlepoints still hung on the walls, her Hershey's Chocolate World coffee
mug stayed in the cupboard, the piano stayed untuned. Dad gave up
promotions that would move us to other cities, gave up a relationship
with a woman he loved because she wouldn't move into our home.

I grew up feeling held by our house. Though a few rooms would
change—alphabet wallpaper to Pepto Bismol pink, a guest room to an
office, antiques to chrome—the house grounded me when everything
else felt slippery and charged. I knew it was ridiculous to hold on to it,
especially when the stairs were too difficult for Dad and its chimney was
separating from the rest of the bricks, its foundation cracked, my beloved
silver maples choking its sewer lines, but I didn't want to let it go.

Rolland and I were sitting on the stairs, like we did when we were kids;
Dad was standing at the bottom, leaning on the banister. A couple weeks
before, Rolland and Dad had been to the house, and Rolland had taken
the needlepoints he wanted. I wasn't happy about it. All of us are attached
to Mom's needlepoints; they're what she made, they're what she loved.

"Before I go, I'd like to talk to y'all about something," I said. "While
you didn't take any of the needlepoints I want, I hope in the future, if
we're in a situation like this again, we can talk it over as a family before
we take what we want."

Then Rolland was erupting and throwing his hands in the air and yelling, "Fine, you can have them, I don't want to fight," and Dad was trying to calm him down, to tell him to listen to me, and I was shaking my head at how we'd all been thrust back twenty-five years into a moment when two children were squabbling over something that mattered and a father was caught between them.

But at least it was grief that was finally recognizable. How often do we read in books or see on the screens a story of a family fighting over a dead person's things; or of an older sibling who says the younger one got everything—fewer rules, more gifts, more affection; or of a son who is denied what gets passed on to the daughter, like the jewelry or the brown leather blazer; or of how no family member really knows the others' histories or pain.

It was strangely comforting, Mom's death becoming common and cliché.

Then Jerry and I were standing in the entryway, the front window stripped of the brass mobile she once hung and the rocking horse that played "Toyland." We were saying goodbye to my father, who'd been mostly silent in the days after the plea hearing.

"Goodbye, Daddy," I said.

He hugged me, hard and tight. He wouldn't let go.

"It was a big week for our family," he said, his voice breaking like a wave. He kissed me on the cheek, then pressed his cheek to mine. He held it there, for a long time. I could feel his breath catching in his chest, but I wasn't ready for him to cry, having absorbed the coldness he needed to get through the plea. For the last few days, I had said nothing about Rolland's speech or mine, nothing about how strong I felt, floating above Eckardt in the room, nothing about how I did my best to reclaim her.

So instead of asking if he was all right, I said, "Are you going to get my ear?" a game we played in my childhood, where he was a monster trying to eat my earlobe off.

"Thinking about it," he said. "I probably should."

He kissed my cheek again. And again. Holding on so tightly. I knew I couldn't stay, but I didn't want to leave, not when he was coming back to me, and not when he had no one to go home to.

Even a few years removed from the plea hearing, even as Jerry and I are living in a state over a thousand miles away from Oklahoma and I'm teaching at a university and focusing on doing well enough to get tenure, I find myself thinking of what it'd be like to visit Eckardt in prison, to sit just feet from him with nothing but plexiglass between us.

I imagine him sitting neither stiff nor leaning back with his arms folded nor leaning forward. My God, what would I do if he actually leaned forward?

No, I see him in a slouch, hands plopped into his lap, muscles lax.

Would it feel like a betrayal if I saw him? I'd be moving toward something, someone Mom had wanted to escape. I'd be speaking to him as if he were a person on the other side of the glass.

The scenes in movies show corded telephones. This seems too intimate and familiar though, one voice connected to another's voice, both hands close to the face, one body mirroring the other.

No, I'm leaning back. So is he. A plate of glass with air holes separating us.

And what would I say? Sometimes I imagine I say nothing. Just indeterminable quiet between us. Sometimes I imagine asking why. And maybe he would know the context already, would recognize me as the daughter of the Shepherd Mall woman, whose name he never knew. Or maybe he doesn't know my face as well as I do his, and he ends up asking, "Why what?"

Would I say, "Why did you kill my mother?" or "Why did you kill Kathy Sue Engle?" Would I see the words *my mother* as a vulnerability or a strength, showing him how I can say them without flinching?

Maybe he'd look down then. Maybe he'd sigh, tired from a few years in prison. Or grimace, as if a pain deep down just stabbed him from within. Or maybe he'd just sit there, shoulders relaxed, hands in lap, and blankly stare.

"I didn't do it," he could say, and I would wait it out, for as long as it takes. Or he could say, "Because it felt good. Because I wanted to." Or, "I don't know," with a voice that shows he's as baffled as I am, our shoulders in a shrug. Or, "Because Steve wanted to and I didn't know how to stop him." Or, "Because I had just turned twenty-one and this was my way to celebrate." Or, "Because my own mother beat me and I couldn't find a way to kill her instead." Or, "Because your mom was just so small and pretty."

None of them good enough. None I can understand.

And there's the chance he could actually hurt me again, through his answer, a detail I couldn't foresee and don't want to know. He could take me right back to the field where he slit her throat.

We all want to know, to trace the anger back to its root, but I decide that's the work for someone else to do.

So I return to the why in the imagination. There'd be no anger in my voice when I ask him. No desperation. No wavering. No hesitation. No shrug to suggest mere curiosity. No shaking of my head. Just a why of conviction. Of a woman who has arrived at this why as a conclusion, after twenty-eight years.

Maybe that why is all that needs to be said. Maybe the question is the answer. Maybe the question is enough.

In Rolland's victim's impact statement, he says, "When he dies in prison, his name will be lost and he will be forgotten." In mine, I said, "I will be living a life absent of you." Neither of which is true.

We won't forget Eckardt's name, even when he dies, and his name is written into history, in newspaper articles and videos online and even in my writing; we have, in some ways, immortalized him. And Rolland and I aren't living a life where he doesn't exist. Though we won't see him in court anymore, he creeps around, resurfacing at times, and he's even tried to get out of the plea, though the motions have been denied every time.

Years after the plea, Rolland tells me about how he purchased fishing magazines and took them home because he planned to cut out pictures of people happily fishing and then to mail them to Eckardt in prison. Because Eckardt had loved to fish.

See this man who's your age and holding a twenty-pound catfish? That will never be you, Rolland wants to say.

I tell Rolland I've thought about mailing him pictures of the mental institution he went to as a kid.

It makes me think of a line from Foucault: "Since it is no longer the body, it must be the soul. The expiation that once rained down upon the body must be replaced by a punishment that acts in depth on the heart, the thoughts, the will, the inclinations."

I think about how some prisoners get to wear their own clothes. Some prisoners get to watch TV. Some get to take classes in prison. Even creative writing. Some prisoners get to have dogs or to care for horses or to participate in rodeos.

I get pissed each time I hear of something like this.

A few seconds later, I'm ashamed and disturbed.

Because I know I've translated every prisoner into Eckardt, regardless of the crime, without questioning their guilt or claims of innocence. I used to think my reaction was about not seeing an inmate as human, what I imagined killers do with their victims, but then I read that's not how cruelty works—we wish to belittle, humiliate, ostracize, punish, and kill precisely because we recognize the other as fully human. I don't care to deny a beast or a rat the ability to learn, and Rolland doesn't want to make a monster grieve for the fishing rod in his hands, for gentle waves rocking a small boat on a lake; no, our desires are far more troubling and dangerous than dehumanizing Eckardt: we have wanted to exert power over, and strip everything away from, another human being.

This isn't the person I want to be though.

I remember a dream where Eckardt was standing in front of me. Tall and heavy. Shaved head. Eyes with dark circles. He was silent and still. I felt the rage begin. The skin on my face tightening. A tension in my lips. A tension in my temples. My entire body stiffened. A pulling back. A revving up. A surge. I punched him just below the rib cage. Centered. Direct. Knuckles in the gut.

But I was the one who doubled over.

A loss of breath.

An explosion on the underside of muscle. He still stood there, as if I'd never even hit him. I looked up at him and thought, *This is the differ-ence between you and me. I can feel the pain of others.*

In my waking hours, there's a residue, like a phantom limb or a scar that aches in cold weather. I remember the dream and feel the urge to double over. It hurts still. Three inches above my belly button, the dia-phragm tenses, ready for another blow to myself.

When they were preparing for the trial, the prosecutors had planned to get a 1981 Dodge Colt, her Colt if possible, and to place all of the evi-dence back in it to stage the crime scene for the jury. They'd mark every spot that Eckardt or his bodily fluids had touched. Because they knew the power of a tangible object.

I imagined the car in a warehouse or a garage we'd have to walk to, well-lit, with plenty of space to walk around it. I'd walk to it, shocked by how small it is, smaller than a modern Mini Cooper. I know I'd stand there, trying to figure it out, through the size of my body, the size of Eckardt's body, the size of the back seat, which positions they were in and how, logistically, he could rape my mother in such a tiny space.

I'd peer inside, at all the evidence back in it—the library card; the McDonald's breakfast wrapper; the sunglasses she'd lose in wallpaper stores; the beer and Pepsi bottles that make it seem like her death was their entertainment, like how my neighbor Richard and his friend drank longneck beers while telling me to touch myself. Her sweater, her skirt, her bra, her blood. The leather gloves that are the size I wear now. My Little Critter book with our spider, next to a marker for his DNA.

I know the twelve jury members would place their faces to the glass like voyeurs, not understanding how these are the details of a death and a life lived in the shadow of it.

And I know I'd never get the six-year-old back, the one who played pranks on her mother:

While Mom shopped for groceries in Safeway, Rolland and I would wait in her car, one of us hunching on the floorboard behind the seats to pretend to be missing. I remember curling myself into a ball, small enough to easily fit on the floor, and trying not to breathe loudly or laugh when she came back and loaded the paper bags into the hatchback.

"What happened to Kristine?" she'd ask, after she opened the car door and sat down in the seat.

"She ran away," Rolland would say.

"That's really too bad. I guess she won't get any ice cream at Braum's." I'd jump up from the floorboard, so happy I fooled her.

One time, though, Rolland and I both hid on the floorboard.

I don't know when she saw the empty seats, from how far away. I don't know if she dropped the sack of groceries, if she ran to the car, if she looked through the glass or just opened the door, her hands shaking with terror. I can't even remember what she said. Only the feeling that we had scared her and I didn't understand why.

I've already lost the girl who didn't understand that fear; I didn't want to lose the girl who'd jump for ice cream and make her mother laugh.

A trial, with the Dodge Colt and the autopsy photos and the pictures of her in the field, makes me think of the hot wall in torture. I'm grateful I didn't have to move an inch closer.

I think back to the *Daily Oklahoman* article in 1999, where Rolland had told the journalist that getting a DNA match or clearing the original suspects would be closure for us either way; how naive we were then, believing in resolutions.

I think of the email Rolland wrote to our family, after we learned the cause of death:

> At this point, I'm going to stop reciting facts to give you a choice. The anonymous tip indicated how the woman was killed. We were told this information. All three of us struggled with it. Dad told us a long time ago that Mom died from being so scared. That was easier for me to accept because it didn't involve suffering at the time of her death. I knew that Mom suffered greatly throughout her ordeal. Learning the likely cause of her death was like hearing she was dead all over again for me. If you don't want to know, I completely understand. But, if you would like to know, you can send me an email and I will explain further.

We weren't given a choice, as I listened on the phone to the DA give details about Boerner and the slit throat. I would have said, *Yes, I want to know.* But I should have said no.

I think of Dad, who says to me, thirty years after her death and after being put on oxygen for his COPD and using a CPAP machine to help him sleep, "I'm dreaming again, and I don't like it. I keep having dreams where something's happened to your mother or to you, and I can't reach her in time, and I can't do anything to protect you. I want to go back to when I didn't dream."

And of me and Jerry, as we were cooking a special dinner for just the two of us, years after the plea. We were in prep mode, before the main dish and side dishes were all ready at once, before the kitchen was a mess and grease had splattered on the floor. We were dancing and singing to "Save the Last Dance for Me," chopping onions and celery and rosemary and garlic, when Jerry tapped my bicep with the flat side of his chef's knife and grinned—a way to tease me about never learning to be comfortable using knives. Before the cause of death, I would have said,

"Heeyyy, that's not nice," and I would have laughed and punched his arm or sprinkled him with water from my glass, but now I just recoiled my arm and body, turned away, and walked up the stairs.

"Where you goin'?" he said.

"Just have to go to the bathroom. Be right back."

There I cried on the toilet with my head in my hands, thinking, *It'll never end, I'll never be able to watch a scene in a movie—and there are so many—where someone has a knife to a throat without having to close my eyes like a child, I'll never be able to see someone draw their fingers across their neck in an exaggeration or joke, I'll never be able to laugh again if Jerry touches a blade to my skin, without thinking of Mom, of how she must have felt in the field. There are just too many knives around us.*

I think back to our summers at Lake Eufaula, its bright-red water, dirty and difficult. Whitecaps. Waves compounded by waves. But as evening would fall on a Sunday, the weekenders having left, the wind would die down, the water becoming like glass, smooth for miles and silent. I used to think that's what knowing would be like. Unrippled. Pristine. All versions becoming one. But I know now the surface and silence are an illusion. There, by the dock, water spiders skip along the top of the water, the tap-dancing of their feet creating tiny ripple upon ripple, and below the surface the large fish of my memory—the one wearing my lavender T-shirt and my plastic yellow visor, two beloved objects snatched from our boat by wind—moves heavily and slowly, pushing water to and fro, while the river still flows in its channel, shifting the red earth below. I know now there's no such thing as stillness.

Cleaving To

PART VII

✦

THERE'S A STORY I DON'T KNOW HOW TO TELL.

My friend says, "Grief keeps you reaching back." She tells me to look for the pieces. "Cluster them."

We never knew the body contained language. The alphabet imprinted in the lines on a thumb.

Long before humans wrote the symbols, our language was rooted first in the body.

Some stories are unsayable. I've tried to write this again and again, but the language fails me each time. I tell myself to write around it. To cluster those pieces. But they are simply too beautiful to touch.

Let me begin here:

I don't know Lesley Katzilierakis.

But the story sounded true.

My mother had been abducted from Shepherd Mall. We had gotten DNA from evidence in the car. We had been frustrated by the back-log. In fact, way back in 1999, in an article in *The Daily Oklahoman*, a woman from the OSBI described the backlog of 150 cases, just waiting to be entered into the federal database. But they weren't only cases that were waiting; hundreds of victims and families were too. Rolland had told the journalist: "We were pretty patient, and we are just starting to run out of patience."

The truth rests in the body. In language. The alphabet.
　　CODIS. Combined DNA Index System.

But I don't know Lesley Katzilierakis.

In February 2009, six months after the original DNA match, when things weren't going well with the case and they didn't yet have the mixture sample from the beer-bottle cap, I received an email from a man named L., who worked at the OSBI.
　　He said:

> Mrs. Ervin,
>
> My name is L. I am the supervisor of a previous acquaintance of yours, Lesley Katzilierakis. I have a very unusual request that I would like to ask of you.
>
> 　　A little history here first. A few years ago, Lesley was at a social gathering in Dallas Texas. Lesley tells me that a girl named Kristine was also at the gathering and struck up a conversation with her. Kristine began to tell the story of how her mother had been tragically killed when she was a girl. Kristine went on to say that there was DNA evidence in the case that had not matched to anyone yet, but since the DNA was in a CODIS database, hopefully one day there would be a match. If I am correct, the Kristine she is referring to is you. According to Lesley, it was this conversation that convinced her to go into forensics, which eventually brought her to the OSBI working in the CODIS database unit.

Lesley is receiving a recognition for 4 years of service at the OSBI. She is the person who processes ~95% of all CODIS DNA database samples, and has a passion for the work she does. Whether you knew it or not, your conversation sparked a passion in Lesley that has benefitted the lives of many. For that I thank you.

Here is my request. Instead of me presenting Lesley's award, I would like to have you do it instead. I know this would mean a lot to Lesley, and I know she would enjoy seeing you again. If this is something you may be interested in, can you please let me know.

Thank you for your time.

L.

I don't know Lesley Katzilierakis.

But the story sounded true.

That's what I told L. when I replied to his email. I don't remember a social gathering in Texas where I met a girl named Lesley. "I'll need more information," I said. "A picture perhaps. But even if I'm not the person she's thinking of, I'd be honored to present her with the award, so that I, on behalf of victims' families, can say, 'Thank you. Your work matters. Your work offers hope.'"

The power is in the alphabet. A body of text. The text that is a body.

He responded, "Even if you do not remember the meeting with her, you should know that your conversation changed her life." He told me her name had not changed. He attached her employee picture, where she stands in front of an American flag and wears a black suit. Her hair is red and shoulder-length, its ends flipped out. He said he'd been snooping around and discovered the social gathering had been a bachelorette party. Then he wrote, "If you are able to make it to town, I would also like to give you and your family a tour of our forensic laboratory. We have a picture of your mother in our hallway as a reminder of why we are here."

My mother is in a hallway. She watches them as they pass.

The language fails me every time.

I remembered a bachelorette party in Dallas, for a friend of mine named Sara. We had dinner at the Cheesecake Factory, where she opened boxes of lingerie. We sucked on penis-shaped lollipops in the hotel room before heading to a piano bar. I remembered everyone at the party. No one named Lesley. I searched through the photographs. No one who looked like her was there.

But the story sounded true.

I wanted to say, *I admire you for the work that you do.*

L. and I made plans for the presentation, which would take place during the summer when I was out of school. Right before Jerry and I traveled to Oklahoma to present the award, we were told the OSBI lab had extracted the mixture sample on the bottle cap and finally crossed the timeline.

Something still keeps me searching for meaning, in the chance that a man randomly kills a woman with the same initials and birthday.

But I did not know Lesley Katzilierakis.

L. emailed the speech he had prepared. In it, he talked about the conversation I had with Lesley, how it impacted her life, and about all the work she had done since joining the lab. "Since 2007," he wrote, "Lesley has performed DNA analysis on over 12,000 offender database samples" and "she has eliminated the backlog of the offender samples at the OSBI three different times, enabling the unit to process samples as they come in the door . . . Years later, one of the routine offender database samples Lesley was processing hit to an unsolved case. Investigators now have DNA evidence that links an individual to the murder of Kathy Sue Engle. The conversation Lesley had with Kristine nearly 8 years ago has come full circle."

I read his speech and thought, *The story cannot possibly be true.*

In March 2008, Eckardt's DNA was collected when he was convicted for assaulting Terry Welch.

A year and a half later, Eckardt was set to be released from prison for good behavior.

The backlog was two years long.

Without Lesley Katzilierakis's clearing the backlog, he would have been released months before his DNA matched to my mother's murder.

And it was Lesley Katzilierakis who got the hit.

There is no language that can reach this.

"Cluster the pieces," she says.

The morning of the presentation, as Jerry, Dad, and I headed to the OSBI, I sat in the back seat of the car and listened to Mangione's "Bellavia," the flügelhorn starting so mellow and soft and then rising to a wail—that sound the transformation of grief into hope.

I stared at the flat Oklahoma horizon and the flat brick homes and hoped the story was true. What if Lesley Katzilierakis looked at me, then at L., then back at me, confused? "Who the hell is this?" she would say.

It isn't just the alphabet they have found in the lines on thumbs. A dog print. A smiley face. A snowman. The symbols in our bodies.

The OSBI building was new, with pristine flags and landscaped trees with thin trunks outside of it. Rolland met us in the parking lot, and we all walked into a grand atrium of off-white stone. So much light in that space. Like a cathedral.

L. greeted us with handshakes before he whisked us away to a conference room. Dad hobbled and tried to keep up, knowing the whole point was to keep us a secret.

"I've already thrown up in the bathroom," L. said, as we all sat down at the table. "And I doubt I'll get through my speech because I'm a crier."

"I understand what you mean," Rolland said.

L. left the room to attend the ceremony.

Then the four of us stood in a hallway and listened to a woman's voice give L.'s speech. Because the story was too beautiful for him to speak.

But I didn't know Lesley Katzilierakis.

When we heard the woman say, "Lesley, the work you do every day is valuable, it is necessary, and has an impact on the lives of others in ways that can best be described by people like Kristine," we walked into a deep room with long tables on two sides of an aisle, a person in every chair, the floor inclining up toward the back, where a crowd stood against the wall. I was overwhelmed by the number of people, and there, at the front with L., stood Lesley Katzilierakis, who turned to me and said, "Oh my God," before she broke down in tears. She hugged me then, her head just under my chin, her hair a dark brown, not the red of her picture.

I still didn't recognize her.

She seemed familiar, something about her mouth and her freckles, but I couldn't picture her at the piano bar or around the circular table while we all ate cheesecake and tried to figure out a clasp on a bustier. But she clearly knew me, as she stood, shaking, beside me, a piece of paper fluttering in her hands.

What is it that I said?

I know I began by confessing that when L. first emailed me, I didn't recognize the name or the story but that I still wanted to present the award. I said I wasn't there to take credit for a story but to say thank you. To Lesley for clearing the backlog and giving me my mother's murderer—we were now one step closer to justice because of her. And to every person in that room, working each day to give hope to victims and their families, I said, "I admire you for the work that you do."

I have never felt so honored to speak.

L. asked my father if he wanted to say anything.

Dad kept his hands tucked behind him as he leaned against a wall. "There's no way I can follow that up," he said, his voice breaking.

Then Rolland, through sputtering sobs, said, "For so many years, I felt it was my responsibility, and I had given up." He turned to Lesley, his face contorted and red, his voice barely above a whisper as he pointed to her and said, "But you never did, you never did."

The room clapped when she hugged me again. I hugged her back, this woman in a pantsuit who came up to my chin.

She pulled back and laughed and said, "You remember me now, right?"

"Of course," I said.

She must have been at the piano bar that night, where we stood watching Sara dance on the stage, her candy necklace half-eaten and tight around her neck. It's the only time I was in Dallas for a bachelorette party.

We walked the building together, L., Lesley, and my family, and there, in one long hallway with a glass wall, hung the framed photograph of Mom, the one from our family portrait, where she wears a light gray-blue shirt dress, her hair curled under with a large curling iron, her lips a rose pink. But she was surrounded by text—an argument for obtaining DNA upon arrest, even for misdemeanors—and a timeline marking each of Eckardt's prior arrests.

See how Terry Welch could have been saved, if only his DNA had been taken earlier, it said.

The picture of Mom wasn't the only one there. Next to her was another high-profile victim, then another, then another, a long line of victims and stories and agendas on the wall. It made me think of all the stories that aren't being told, the names that never make the news. I knew if we had been poor or Black or Mom had been walking out of a bar that night, her picture would not be in this hallway. The statistics on missing Indigenous women are enough to show us who is valued. Even with Terry Welch, the OSBI had reduced her to only a name, on this photograph of Mom, a murdered middle-aged white suburbia wife.

"We hand a copy of this out to legislators," L. told us, as he pointed to Mom's photograph and the reasons why DNA should be registered like fingerprints.

I couldn't argue with his point, not with knowing that Terry Welch and her six-year-old son could be living their lives, whatever lives they may be, had Eckardt's DNA been taken when he was arrested for marijuana or for domestic abuse.

But I didn't like Mom's death attached to an agenda. *Her death is ours*, I wanted to say.

But the day was about Lesley Katzilierakis, so I said nothing as we walked the sterile white labs with computers and tubes and microscopes and swabs, listening to L. explain to us junk DNA and why we didn't need to fear Big Brother. Then he explained epithelial cells and how DNA technology traces only the maternal line.

I thought about the power of this.

Of violence being coded and passed down through mothers.

As if violence has its own markers.

We stood in a small lab of swabs and storage tubes, me wondering if my eight-year-old self's fingerprints were stored in one of the rooms, L. showing Jerry the reference points used for CODIS, when Rolland asked Lesley Katzilierakis, "So how do you and Kristine know each other?"

"We were both in Amy's wedding," she said.

And then it came flooding back—yes, Amy's wedding, Lesley was a bridesmaid with me, she had such a beautiful singing voice, and yes, she had told me I didn't have to take communion but I should still kneel as I moved across the altar, and yes, we had danced for hours at the reception, laughing and drinking champagne, and yes, we had eaten at IHOP after the reception, still in our full-length satin dresses, and yes, at the bachelorette party in Dallas, we went bowling and drank beer, and yes, I met Lesley first at someone's house, before bowling, and we stood in the kitchen, sunlight streaming in from a patio door, finger food on the counter, and, yes I told her about Mom and DNA and the hopes of finding her killer one day. How could I have forgotten that? I had marveled at Lesley's laugh, so genuine and loud, as we stood in that kitchen of light.

"She has the most amazing voice," I told Rolland, as if to say, *I remember.*

The story was true.

I did know Lesley.

I had told her Mom's story. My story.

She had gone to graduate school for forensics, then to work for the OSBI, and then she cleared the backlog and got the hit.

It's too perfect to believe. Too perfect to be told.

We walked more hallways, more labs, until we stopped at posters on a wall that showed many different thumbprints, gathered from the latent print unit and submitted to the databases. The prints were magnified, each one with a different shape in its core—a number, a Santa Claus, anything but a typical arc or whorl. One person's thumbprint contains a *J.* Another a face. At the top of the poster, it spelled out *OSBI* in thumbs.

My family held our thumbs to the light.

I wanted a *K* to be there.

"Cluster the pieces," she says.

I stood there, Lesley with her singing voice, explaining the most common shapes in thumbprints, and I thought, *I don't know what to do with this—this stuff of make-believe.* Rolland, with his years of keeping in contact with detectives, needing to find Mom's killers, using the tools he knew to get the DNA testing done. And then me, coping with the loss through the only tools I have ever known—letters, symbols, stories— which led Lesley to forensics and to the match.

It's too beautiful—the fingerprints with the alphabet in their cores, text and body and text, Rolland fighting through the law, me fighting through my words, my mother's killer found through the power of language and grief.

The Sleeping Place

✦

I'VE COME TO ANDROS, GREECE, THE ISLAND OF WINDS, TO swim in water the color of ink, and it's here, among goats and stones and the little lips of foam that ride cresting waves—"little sheep," they call them—that women tell me of their ritual of digging up a body, three years after it's been buried, and of cleansing the bones with wine, before they are transferred to a box and stored in an ossuary or a corner of a grave.

It makes me think of exhuming you, of pulling you from the brown earth of Iowa. I imagine your casket, dented from the pressure of the dirt, placed before me in a room lit by candles.

I wonder what it would be like to open it, if the gaskets would still be sealed, if I could hear an exhale of a breath held for thirty years.

I imagine your bones laid out as if you were on your back, your arms to your sides, your body's frame whole and undisturbed and intact, though I know this would not be true, that even in coffins our bones will not settle.

Sometimes I imagine a rabbit's bones, tiny and huddled in the corner, tucked into folds of white satin.

I want to hold you.

I want to trace your pelvic bone, rounded and smooth, as if worn by water, and to think of how I once rested there. My fingers will remember your womb.

I want to dip the linen in wine and clean the bones of your cheek. Tenderly. As if you were crying and this cloth of your blood, my blood, the blood that is the history of woman, can calm you.

I want to cradle your skull in the palm of my hand, as if I were laying you down to sleep.

It will be like crossing wires of memory.

I'll save your hands for bathing last, hands that once pulled me into you, those mornings in the kitchen, when you were curled in the corner and kept warm by the vent and your red robe. You were turning the pages of the paper, Salem smoke rising in ribbons from your chewed fingers, until you saw me and moved the paper aside. You held me then, my back against your chest, your arms a swathe around me.

In memory I suspend us there, me nestled in the burrow of your body, until you whisper, "Try to get away."

This was my favorite game we played.

You'd loosen your arms just enough for me to escape, but when I'd lurch forward, you'd catch me, pulling me back to your body.

"Try to get away," you'd say again.

I'd try a slow way out. I'd push your arms to your sides, plant my feet on the linoleum floor, and then inch away, as if I were a Band-Aid slowly being lifted from a wound, but you'd capture me again, your fingers, your hands, your arms, so quick and strong, clutching a body that didn't really want to be let go of.

It was your fingers that once stitched needlepoints you loved, that brought what you craved to your lips.

That washed my hair in our morning showers, then weaved it into braids or doggy ears.

Fingers that linked your body to my body with touch.

I want to shift your bones so you are sleeping on your side, like you did on the living room couch. I want to crawl into the casket and curl behind you, wrap my arms around your rib cage, so small it seems like a child's.

I want to close my eyes and finally rest, with my hand on top of your hand, my fingers between your fingers. To whisper "I love you" in the language of knuckle and bone.

Acknowledgments

FOR LESLEY, WITHOUT WHOM I WOULD STILL BE SEARCHING, without whom more women would be hurt. Never forget how your work saves others.

For the detectives, forensic specialists at the OSBI, and the district attorneys, the names I do not know and the ones I will never forget—Chance, Burke, Prater, Harmon, Lindstrom, Eastridge. I am more at peace because of your diligence.

To Terry Welch's family: The resolution to our case came at too brutal a cost. I wish you comfort and strength in those moments when it still hurts.

For the English Department and the College of Arts and Humanities at West Chester University, for the support through grants and development funds. For Inprint Houston, for the fellowships and support.

For all the people who have made me feel seen and supported and safe while working on this story. For Tamara, Melissa, Ann, Lynn, Eirini, Ashley, Adrianne, Joj, Tom, and Kitsi.

For my aunt Connie, who encouraged me with books and travel and kinship and museums, lessons I have not forgotten.

For Cramer, who, after I told her I wasn't going to take another creative writing class, said, *You'll be back*, and who stayed during lunch to draw the female reproductive anatomy on the whiteboard for me.

For Lisa, who demonstrated such patience while trying to show me the necessity and beauty and power of feminism, who waited for me to be less terrified of it.

For Sharon, for the boundaries you keep and the boundaries you break. Your words will always resonate within me.

For Rubén, who said, *Go to the texts*, and allowed me to see my experience as part of a broader conversation. For landscapes and unexpected graces.

For Mark, who said the story needs the expansiveness of prose, who handed me scissors to fragment and braid.

For Mary Krienke, who saw the memoir more clearly than I could see it myself, who believed in it when I had my doubts. For your earrings and berry bowls.

For Harry Kirchner, for that first phone call where you made my comfort the priority, for how you shaped my mother's story and mine with empathy and grace. You make the literary world more inclusive through advocating for women's stories.

For Jacqueline, for being the version of me that I wish I could be, for your guidance and the coffees that got me through. Tag, you're it.

For the Aegean Arts Circle and the women who embraced me there. For Diana and Amalia, for floating in a sea of stories.

For Keya, for your half-eaten gifts of candy and chocolate, for always inspiring me to persevere. For showing me that out of trauma, exquisite and profound kindnesses can emerge.

For Robert, the only person who would ever dare to spar over who had the worst 1986 or to give me Slap Ya Mama spices. Who shows with every action and every word that it is possible to outgrow your pain, to be loving toward others, even when you aren't loved in a way you deserve.

For Amanda, for rushing into the ocean with me to reach dolphins, for rushing through the sky. For the talks we've had on paddleboards and piers. You keep me adventurous and hopeful and young.

For Jess, for the trust and the stories we give each other, for the lack of judgment. When I think of the reader I want for my memoir, it's you.

For Connie, for the nights of wine and laughing so hard we cry.

For supporting my relationships with your daughters. It's the closest I'll ever come to being a mother.

For Dana, for nearly forty years of your mother's touch, for raising your sons to be respectful and open and tender.

For Chris. There is a reason my mother brought you and no one else. She knew you would tuck me into a fluffy white comforter rather than letting me be alone while I'm hurting. She knew you would bring her back to me.

For Angie, the keeper of feathers and bones, for that first cup of tea and reading to me by the sea. For how your voice has held me. For our connection and how it ripples beyond language.

For Dawson, for giving me goals to strive for and achieve, for being the one who knows how much it means to swim in the red water of Eufaula, how it contains our laughter, our joy.

For Dad, for loving her so deeply, for giving me permission to love and grieve deeply too. Thank you for never letting go. No matter all the ways I move away, I'll always need you.

For Jerry, for asking the questions that make me go deeper, for the promise you didn't know you were making when you stapled flyers along I-40, for keeping that promise. For giving me a reason to return to the shore.

Notes

p. 58   "eat like acid" from Frank Bidart's "Curse." *Star Dust*. New York: Farrar, Straus, and Giroux, 2005.

p. 68   "Another girl says she wants to know what happened . . ." from *Sarah Perry's After the Eclipse: A Memoir*, Boston: Mariner Books, 2018.

p. 146   "Motherline" from *Motherless Daughters: The Legacy of Loss*. Reading, MA: Addison-Wesley, 1994.

p. 206–56 All courtroom testimony is copied from the court transcript for Sate of Oklahoma v. Kyle Richard Eckardt, CF-2000-4563, Kim Fowler, (Okla. District. 2010).

Sources

Air Supply. "All Out of Love." *Greatest Hits*. Arista, 1983.

———. "Here I Am." *Greatest Hits*. Arista, 1983.

———. "The One That You Love." *Greatest Hits*. Arista, 1983.

———. "When the Time Is Right." *Air Supply*. Arista, 1985.

Associated Press. "1979 Texas Tornado Led to Safety Changes." *USA Today*, April 9, 2004. usatoday30.usatoday.com/weather/resources /safety/2004-04-09-wichita-falls-tornado_x.htm.

Bidart, Frank. "Curse," in *Star Dust*. New York: Farrar, Straus and Giroux, 2005.

Bloom, Paul. "The Root of All Cruelty?" *New Yorker*, November 20, 2017. www.newyorker.com/magazine/2017/11/27/the-root-of-all-cruelty.

Boland, Eavan. "Anorexic." Famouspoetsandpoems.com. Accessed June 11, 2019. famouspoetsandpoems.com/poets/eavan_boland/poems/1195.

Braun, Bill. "Lack of Info Scuttles Murder Case." *Tulsa World*, April 6, 2007.

———. "Man Faces Trial in Rape, Assault." *Tulsa World*, May 2, 2007.

———. "Tulsan Handed 10-Year Term in Woman's Assault." *Tulsa World*, February 21, 2008.

Chandra, Vikram. *Geek Sublime: The Beauty of Code, the Code of Beauty*. Minneapolis, MN: Graywolf, 2014.

Chicago. "Remember the Feeling." *Chicago 17*. Rhino/Wea, 2006.

Cixous, Hélène, and Catherine Clément. *The Newly Born Woman*. Translated by Betsy Wing. Minneapolis: University of Minnesota Press, 2001.

Clark, Jennifer, and Majella Franzmann. "Authority from Grief, Presence and Place in the Making of Roadside Memorials." *Death Studies* 30 (2006): 579–99.

Clay, Nolan. "In a 1986 Oklahoma City Cold Case, Former Drifter Sentenced to Life in Prison without the Possibility of Parole." *Oklahoman*, September 16, 2011. oklahoman.com/article/3604697/in-a-1986-oklahoma-city-cold-case-former-drifter-sentenced-to-life-in-prison-without-the-possibility-of-parole.

———. "Shepherd Mall Settles Suit in 1985 Death." *Oklahoman*, October 2, 1989. oklahoman.com/article/2283181/shepherd-mall-settles-suit-in-1985-death.

CSAFD. "In Memory of the Murdered and Missing." Accessed June 11, 2019. csafd.proboards.com (site discontinued).

Doty, Mark. *Heaven's Coast: A Memoir*. New York: HarperCollins, 1996.

Edelman, Hope. *Motherless Daughters: The Legacy of Loss*. Reading, MA: Addison-Wesley, 1994.

Ellroy, James. *My Dark Places*. New York: Vintage, 1997.

"Emotional Message in a Bottle Thrown off California Pier by Woman Battling Cancer Three Years Ago Washes up 6,200 Miles Away in Guam." *Daily Mail*, October 7, 2013. www.dailymail.co.uk/news/article-2447726/Message-bottle-thrown-California-pier-years-ago-ends-6-200-miles-away-Guam.html.

Foucault, Michel. *Discipline & Punish: The Birth of the Prison*. Translated by Alan Sheridan. New York: Vintage, 1995.

Haney, C. Allen, Christina Leimer, and Juliann Lowery. "Spontaneous Memorialization: Violent Death and Emerging Mourning Ritual." *Omega: Journal of Death and Dying* 35, no. 2 (1997): 159–71.

Horner, James, composer. "Somewhere Out There." *An American Tail*. Amblin Entertainment, 1986.

Jaffe, Eric. "The Complicated Psychology of Revenge." *APS Observer*, October 4, 2011. www.psychologicalscience.org/observer/the-complicated-psychology-of-revenge.

Jensen. "Discover Dark Tourist Destination: Topeka State Hospital." Visit Topeka (website), October 25, 2018. www.visittopeka.com/blog/post/discover-dark-tourist-deistination-topeka-state-hospital-in-topeka-kansas (page discontinued).

Kalfopoulou, Adrianne. "Poem in Pieces, a log." *Duende*. Accessed June 11, 2019. www.duendeliterary.org/adrianne-kalfopoulou.

Mandel, Lois. "The Computer Girls." *Cosmopolitan*, April 1967.

Maso, Carole. *AVA: A Novel*. Norman, IL: Dalkey Archive, 1993.

McCoy, Kathy, and Charles Wibbelsman. *The New Teenage Body Book*. New York: Perigee, 1992.

McCullough, Michael E. "The Forgiveness Instinct." *Greater Good Magazine*, March 1, 2008. greatergood.berkeley.edu/article/item/forgive ness_instinct.

McKeon, Gina. "Message in a Bottle: 10 Famous Floating Note Discoveries." *ABC News*, April 9, 2014. www.abc.net.au/news/2014-04-09/ten-most-famous-message-in-a-bottle-discoveries/5376040.

Meston, Cindy M., and Lucia F. O'Sullivan. "Such a Tease: Intentional Sexual Provocation within Heterosexual Interactions." *Archives of Sexual Behavior* 36 (2007): 531–42.

Morel, Pierre, dir. *Taken*. 20th Century Fox, 2008.

Mosbergen, Dominique. "This Is the Oldest Message in a Bottle Ever Found." *Huffpost*, April 20, 2016. www.huffpost.com/entry/oldest-message-in-a-bottle_n_57170ce9e4b0018f9cbb9a43.

Noonan, David. "Meet the Two Scientists Who Implanted a False Memory into a Mouse." *Smithsonian Magazine*, November 2014. www.smithsonianmag.com/innovation/meet-two-scientists-who-implanted-false-memory-mouse-180953045/.

Oklahoma Legislature. "Oklahoma Statues and Constitution." Accessed April 24, 2009. www.lsb.state.ok.us/osstatuestitle.html.

Perry, Sarah. *After the Eclipse: A Memoir*. Boston: Mariner Books, 2018.

Poe, Edgar Allan. "The Philosophy of Composition." *Graham's American Monthly Magazine*, April 1846.

Pollack, Sydney, dir. *The Interpreter*. Universal Pictures, 2005.

Rankine, Claudia. *Don't Let Me Be Lonely: An American Lyric*. Minneapolis, MN: Graywolf, 2004.

Raymond, Ken. "'I Didn't Think Daddies Were Supposed to Cry.'" *Oklahoman*, March 16, 2008.

——. "Suspect Match Brings Hope in 1986 Oklahoma City Kill-ing." *Oklahoman*, August 5, 2009. oklahoman.com/article/3390535 /suspect-match-brings-hope-in-1986-oklahoma-city-killing.

Schumacher, Leel, dir. *A Time to Kill*. Warner Bros., 1996.

Shell, Paul. "Body Identified as City Woman." *Oklahoman*, May 5, 1986.

——. "Engle's Kidnappers Had 4 1/2-Hour Head Start on Patrol." *Oklahoman*, June 21, 1986.

——. "Kidnapped Woman's Car Located in New Mexico." *Oklahoman*, April 26, 1986.

——. "Missing Woman's Car Spotted." *Oklahoman*, June 28, 1986.

——. "Woman Abducted at Shopping Mall." *Oklahoman*, April 25, 1986.

Simon, Paul, songwriter. "Bridge over Troubled Water." *Simon and Garfunkel's Greatest Hits*. Sony, 1990.

Stallone, Sylvester, dir. *Rocky IV*. MGM/UA, 1985.

State of Oklahoma v. Kyle Richard Eckardt, CF-2009-4536, Kim Fowler, (Okla. District. 2010).

Strayed, Cheryl. *Wild: From Lost to Found on the Pacific Coast Trail*. New York: Vintage, 2018.

Thornton, Anthony. "Mall Security Not to Blame, Policemen Say." *Oklahoman*, May 12, 1986.

——. "Police Officer Says Walking, Jogging Alone Can Invite Attack." *Oklahoman*, May 12, 1986.

——. "Woman's Body Found; May Be City Kidnap Victim." *Oklahoman*, May 1, 1986.

Wright, James. "On the Skeleton of a Hound." In *Above the River: The Complete Poems*, 13–14. New York: Farrar, Straus and Giroux, 1992.

KRISTINE S. ERVIN grew up in a small suburb of Oklahoma City and now teaches creative writing at West Chester University, outside Philadelphia. She holds an MFA in poetry from New York University and a PhD in creative writing and literature, with a focus in nonfiction, from the University of Houston. Find out more at kristineservin.com.